The Famous Case

of

Myra Clark Gaines

DANIEL CLARK

FROM AN ENGRAVED PORTRAIT BY FAVRET DE SAINT
MEMIN IN THE CORCORAN GALLERY OF ART SIMPLY
LABELED "CLARKE," BELIEVED TO BE DANIEL CLARK,
WHEN REPRESENTATIVE OF THE TERRITORY OF
ORLEANS.

The Famous Case
OF
Myra Clark Gaines

❧✦❧

NOLAN B. HARMON, JR.

Louisiana State University Press

Baton Rouge, Louisiana

1946

Copyright, 1946, by
LOUISIANA STATE UNIVERSITY PRESS

To

Nolan and Lamar

Author's Acknowledgment

THANKS are due to many who assisted the author in assembling the material for this story of the colorful father and indomitable daughter whose lives make what the Supreme Court officially termed our country's "most remarkable case." Librarians and their assistants in many cities—in the Enoch Pratt and Peabody Institute libraries of Baltimore, in the Howard-Tilton Memorial Library of New Orleans, in the public libraries of Wilmington, Delaware, Richmond, Virginia, and Nashville, Tennessee; those in charge of the room of American history in the New York Public Library; above all, the staff of the Law Library of the Library of Congress—all these and many others have been as helpful as they must here be anonymous.

Special thanks are due to the author's father, the Reverend Nolan B. Harmon, of Mississippi, who first told him the story of Myra Clark Gaines and recounted his boyhood recollections of her. Were it possible, the author should like to express again his gratitude to his father-in-law, the late George Holt Lamar, of the District of

Columbia and Maryland bar, whose able legal mind assisted greatly in working through the implications of many moves in the case. Last but not least, the author is deeply grateful to his wife, Rebecca Lamar Harmon, who acted as typist, critic, and general collaborator in the work.

N. B. H., Jr.

Contents

CONTENTS   xi

Illustrations

Book 1

Daniel Clark

Daniel Clark

ON A short December day in the year 1786, upon that vast flood of tawny water where the Mississippi flows into the Gulf, a stately sailing vessel was slowly beating its way in across the bars. Voyages as made in ancient sailing packets and ships of that time usually proved to be interminable affairs, survived rather than enjoyed, and even the inhospitable reaches of the lower delta, fringed by the distant coast of the marshes, seemed far brighter to an Irish youth on that ship than the waste of water over which he had come. Certainly the river held a promise of journey's end, for his destination was New Orleans.[1]

Not yet twenty-one years of age, the young voyager, both in face and bearing, showed the unmistakable stamp of the gentleman. Even in an age rampant with personal force and individualism, a casual glance was enough to tell that Daniel Clark was a striking character.

He had been born in Sligo in Ireland and was one of two sons in a family of six children. The Clarks, whatever their circumstances at a later date, had at one time enjoyed considerable prestige. Daniel Clark in later life took pride in tracing his lineage back to the old kings of that half-mythical, half-historic but wholly captivating period of Ireland's history.[2] But at the time he was born, the fortunes of the house of Clark were on the downgrade, perhaps, as was claimed long after, because the Clarks chose to give up their holdings and influence rather than their religious beliefs. Of this there is no certainty, but it is sure that in spite of the dwindling resources of the Clark family, they managed to send their son over to Eton for his schooling. Upon the completion of that, Daniel Clark's parents moved to America and established themselves at Germantown, just outside Philadelphia. There they continued to reside for the rest of their lives.

Another member of the family, Colonel Daniel Clark, had for some years been a resident of the little city of New Orleans in faraway Louisiana, and from him in due time there came an offer to the nephew who bore his name to come to that place and join him.[3] Thus it came about that on the ship then breasting the roily mass of slowly moving water was this young and vigorous product of Eton and Ireland.

To the modern American who looks at a map of his country, New Orleans is near the mouth of the Mississippi River, but the ascent of the tortuous mass of water from the Gulf to the city itself in a cumbersome sailing ship then meant fully one hundred miles of tiresome beating upstream, and hours of additional weariness in cramped quarters.

One may picture the thoughts of this youth who for the first time found himself on the yellow flood of the great river, little dreaming that this same current was to bring vast fortune to him and one day to open an empire for his race. But from the Balize Pass of 1786, as one looked over the turgid water, the prospect was anything but pleasing. Even today a forbidding view is presented to one who first sees America at the entrance to the Mississippi, and 1786 was long before Eads came along and put river and ocean each in its own place.

But the longest voyage must end, and at length Daniel Clark saw his boat tied up at the levee and for the first time set foot in New Orleans, a subject of his Excellency, Governor Miro, and of his Catholic Majesty, Carlos III.

II

New Orleans then was not the New Orleans of today, though there still clings to it that timeless flavor of the old world which renders it distinct among our nation's cities. The casual visitor comments on and delights in this today, but when Daniel Clark landed there late in the eighteenth century, the character of the French-built, Spanish-ruled town was truly unique.[4] Basically the city was French, and perhaps in soul New Orleans will always be so. But the town which Bienville had laid out and French governors had ruled, with the whole province of Louisiana, had a scant score of years before this been turned over to Spain by treaty. The Creoles had been very bitter at first against the Spanish governor—who happened to be another Irishman —but after "Bloody" O'Reilly had actually taken possession, the Spanish power was found not unbearable to the easygoing Louisianians, as succeeding governors came and ruled the province in the stiff, detached way of the soldierly Dons.

Not only was southern Louisiana Spanish; so was everything else around and about it in the new world. From St. Mary's River on the Atlantic, the whole curve of the Gulf, with the Floridas east and west, in fact, everything south of a more or less indefinite line somewhere around Natchez and north of Baton Rouge—all was Spain's. Across the Mississippi, everything. There was no parallel south of the Canadian border which the Spanish authorities would have admitted as limiting his Catholic Majesty's empire, while Cuba and half of South America were under the same sway. Over all this territory, the *Nova Recopilacion,* or Spanish provincial law, held control, while viceroys and intendants, alcaldes and *gobernadores,* set their seals to official documents in the name of Spain. Outwardly something of the glory of the reign of Charles V or Philip II was being perpetuated; but inwardly the empire was as weak as the dotard king who then sat upon the throne in Madrid.

Meanwhile the star of another power was beginning to rise. To the north of New Orleans, somewhere about the Walnut Hills in Mississippi and in the Natchez country, were appearing the outposts of another race. The term *race* and not *nation* is used advisedly, for in the year 1786 under the Articles of Confederation, the American states were scarcely more than a collection of separate commonwealths, somewhat jealous of each other, but proud of their mutual triumph in securing freedom from the British crown. But no matter how weak their political coherence might be, the racial force of this people, true source of their strength, was even then fermenting with the leaven of a fast-growing power. The nation-soon-to-be was putting forth its tendrils through the lush valleys of Kentucky and Tennessee in the shape of wagon trains and individual families "on the move." These regions were being settled rapidly and were already state-conscious. Farther south other settlers were working their way across or down the deep rivers of the Alabama country, while following the great river itself a few hardy families had come into the Mississippi Territory. Where the boundary line between their own and Spanish lands lay was rather indefinite, something to be quarreled over. Even more troublesome was the fact that Spain was absolutely refusing to let any shipment from the American settlers go down the Mississippi. No treaty had yet been concluded between the United States and Spain and it was strongly intimated that one never would be signed in Madrid unless the United States should cease to demand trading privileges on the Mississippi. Meanwhile Spanish galiots were patrolling the waters as far north as the Ohio River. Not a single American flatboat could get past them.

III

Knowing little and caring less about northern settlers or international complications, the young Irishman who had been transplanted into the new world immediately went into his uncle's employ and began at the bottom of the commercial ladder. He was at first given but a minor clerkship in the firm of Clark, yet by the vigor of his personality and a certain Irish *sang-froid* and magnetism, the new arrival made friends immediately. Before long he was given another post, one in the office of the Spanish government itself.[5] He wished to learn Spanish, and the Dons, for their part, were glad to employ a young man who could handle the niceties of both French and English. So it came about that under the personal supervision of Governor Miro, Daniel Clark spent some weeks at work upon lengthy official documents, observing keenly all the while he made translations. Personal contacts here and in other places were made, and, though the new arrival was but a subordinate in a commercial house, he was soon recognized as an addition to the social life of the city, a social life that in a fashion all its own was superior to that of other provincial cities of the new world. Coming as the nephew of an influential citizen, having youth, education, buoyancy, and a personality of extraordinary force, it is not strange that when young Clark threw himself wholeheartedly into the business, social, and political activities of the town, he should find himself accepted as an equal of the young Pierres and Jules, and the older Beauregards, Marignys, and Boulignys of the Creole city. Days were spent in his uncle's counting house but the nights were kept free for more interesting matters. There were the coffee shops, or perhaps the hall of some *maître d'armes* where the young men about town held rendezvous every evening and from which they could sally forth into the more riotous gaiety of smaller parties. Occasionally came a ceremonious affair of Creole society hedged about with an elaborate punctiliousness. It was a luxurious life and a gay one.

One day about a year after Daniel Clark had come to New Orleans and while he was working in the offices of the Spanish government, he looked up to see entering a rubicund, soldierly individual who radiated vast assurance and good humor on all sides. The visitor was received with instant respect by the Spanish officials present. He turned out to be General James Wilkinson of Kentucky, formerly of the Continental army, who had come to New Orleans to see what he could do about obtaining some special personal trading privileges from the Spaniards.[6] Young Clark took to him at once and was interested to find that the visitor apparently had business in the city with his uncle. So the event proved.

Exactly what Wilkinson came to New Orleans to do no one to this day fully knows. It is said that he had first borrowed some money from his Kentucky friends, fitted up a vessel with supplies and sent it downstream, taking care to send with it a pair of blooded horses as a present to the commandant at Natchez. Be that as it may, the General and his cargo both arrived intact at New Orleans, and there he mysteriously entered into some sort of "arrangement" with the intendant. Certainly he entered into a definite and public partnership with the elder Daniel Clark, an agreement which was to prove extremely profitable to both parties. This had to do with trading privileges and the tobacco fields of Kentucky. When the General left New Orleans he had $3,000 of Colonel Clark's money with which he was to begin their upriver trade.[7] He had also won the admiration of the Colonel's nephew, young Daniel Clark.

Business soon began in earnest. But the launching of flatboats consigned to the house of Clark in New Orleans seems subsequently to have occupied very little of the General's time. He was more interested in an enterprise of a different sort and was soon involved in the intricacies of

Kentucky's famous "Spanish Conspiracy," an attempt to break the western settlers away from the United States and have them declare themselves an independent government under the protection of Spain.

But someone attended to the business of storing tobacco in the flatboats and pushing them off from river landings in Kentucky, for cargoes soon began to drift unmolested past the Spanish forts. "The King of Spain ordered more tobacco than Louisiana produced," explained Daniel Clark at a later date, "and paid for it about 9½ per cwt. In Kentucky it cost but two, and the profit was immense." [8]

No doubt because of the liaison with Wilkinson and his understanding with the Spaniards, the Clarks were in position to garner their share of this immense profit. Furthermore, Wilkinson got the Spanish governor to allow certain American families to settle near the river—a particularly large group about Natchez, where tobacco was also the principal commodity produced. These settlers at first either had to use the New Orleans firm's boats or work through Wilkinson in order to get their produce floated down and sold without risk of seizure. The Clark mercantile house acted as a convenient agent and reshipped supplies actively. Trade grew apace. But one who knows the force of Anglo-Saxon might will foresee that the young, expanding nation would not long brook such a situation on its western frontier. New England, of course, was not interested, nor was the seaboard, but the settlers of the western lands, daily increasing in number and strength, began a murmur which was soon to grow into a roar from Loftus Heights in Mississippi to the Kanawha country.

IV

A year after the visit of Wilkinson—and the second of Daniel Clark's residence in New Orleans—what the old chronicles call "the great fire" occurred. It was Good Friday, 1788, and in five hours of blazing pandemonium, over eight hundred buildings were reduced to ashes.[9] The whole conglomeration of wooden structures which had stood since Bienville were swept away and all but three commercial buildings were destroyed.

Out of the ashes Daniel Clark saw arise the Creole city which took the place of the former ramshackle wooden town. Building went on rapidly, and there were wrought into the lines of the rising city the arched doorways, the fan windows, the peculiar ironwork, the small patios with their low arches sheltering inside stairs—the whole of that curious Creole architecture which has lasted to the present and which creates an atmosphere utterly unique among American cities. The lines of the older city, now enveloped by twentieth-century buildings, show about them even today the unmistakable marks of the Spanish occupancy.

The first dotting of American names was noted about this time, chiefly of merchants and tradesmen. Among these, coming as the representative of a Philadelphia concern, was a rather sobersided young man by the name of Daniel Coxe, who soon became a close friend of Daniel Clark.

By this time Clark himself had passed out of the class of clerkly subordinates and was becoming a factor in the life of the city. His uncle spent much time on his plantation to

the north, and as the months passed Colonel Clark made it
clear that he preferred to leave the running of the business
more and more to "Dan." The Colonel saw with immense
satisfaction that he had made no mistake in bringing his
namesake to New Orleans, and, while he never considered
"Dan" more than a "fair" trader, the old officer realized
that his nephew was an asset to the firm in ways other than
haggling over the price of tobacco or collecting the rents
of a plantation.

The connection between General Wilkinson and Colonel Clark was dissolved in 1789 by the death of Isaac B.
Dunn of Kentucky, a third partner, but cordial relations
continued to exist between the Clarks and the General.
The proper "channels of influence" were now open to them
and perhaps to a few other favored merchants. Trade
within Louisiana and with the Florida and Mexican provinces was also proving remunerative, and the future looked
extremely promising to the merchants of the city. In view
of this beckoning prosperity, an agreement was entered
into by Daniel Clark and his young friend, Daniel Coxe
of Philadelphia, that they should form a partnership and
in the future operate under the name of "Daniel Clark" as
one firm. Their partnership was destined to last.

Coxe was about the age of Clark and, like him, proud,
intelligent, and ambitious. He was colder than Clark and
much more regular in personal life, but he and the young
merchant of New Orleans were drawn together from the
first. A voluminous correspondence began and was kept
up from the time they signed articles. Letters were exchanged between the young merchant in Philadelphia and
the young merchant in New Orleans in which business

and personal matters were discussed with perfect freedom. The firm of Daniel Clark began to prosper.

V

In the meanwhile General Wilkinson had gone back into the American army. The "Spanish Conspiracy" in which he had played a prime part had fallen through, and his private ventures in the way of trade had not turned out as he wished. So the convivial General took to soldiering again. Congress gave him the rank of brigadier general at once, and when Anthony Wayne died in 1796, Wilkinson became commander in chief of the armies of the United States. In Madrid he was known as "Secret Agent 13." [10]

Then came the years of international upheaval following the French Revolution. War between France and Spain was one consequence, giving the Baron de Carondelet, who had followed Miro, considerable worry over this French province which was Spanish in name only.

But while the choleric little governor was building miniature forts and keeping galleys on the river alert for any sign of interlopers, an almost unnoticed event took place on a plantation near New Orleans. Etienne de Boré had his slaves build a fire under a big pot, and in this pot the juice of the Louisiana cane finally sugared. Strange are the ways of history: she notes battles, the marching and countermarching of armies, but a pot of boiling cane juice is beneath her notice. So also was the work of a young man named Eli Whitney then experimenting with a box having an ingenious arrangement of toothed saws, designed to pull cotton from its seed. But Boré's pot and

Whitney's gin were to mean more to Louisiana and the world than all the orders of Carondelet or the wars of European kings.

For at that very time the upriver trade in indigo mysteriously died away, and cotton and sugar came in. The rich alluvium of the Mississippi Valley proved an ideal place for cotton, as did the warm soil of Louisiana for cane. Sugar secured a market slowly at first but went to over a million pounds in 1799.[11] Other materials leaped accordingly. The few barges that had drifted down in the early nineties had become a fleet doing a big business by the close of the century.

The immediate cause of this jump was the final signing of a treaty between the United States and Spain. It had been put off too long as it was, but in 1795 Thomas Pinckney succeeded in getting the boundary agreed upon by the government in Madrid. This was to be at the thirty-first parallel instead of the line from the mouth of the Yazoo River, and so the new American nation got Natchez. But Pinckney, anxious to conclude the matter, acknowledged the Spanish contention that the navigation of the Mississippi was rightly under the control of Spain. He afterward admitted that he never dreamed in 1795 that the western trade would amount to much! [12] One valuable concession was secured by the Americans, however—the right to use New Orleans as an entrepôt or a port of transfer and reshipment.

VI

There was immediate need for someone in authority to represent American interests in Louisiana and to protect the rights of the merchants under the 1795 treaty. But the securing of a consular officer proved far more difficult than was expected. President Washington before his term ended attempted to handle this matter by appointing a consul for New Orleans but for some reason the man he selected never came. This left the appointment in the air. Daniel Clark complained to Coxe early in 1798: "We are here without a consul and his presence is highly necessary to prevent and put a stop to numerous abuses which the Spanish government forces the Americans to submit to." [13]

Clark himself had become more of an *Américain* as time went by. Though Irish-born he had early begun to admire the United States, and his partnership with Coxe and the downright American partisanship of his uncle, Colonel Clark, won him completely. He had no idea that he should ever live under the American flag, but the young merchant of New Orleans was now looking hopefully at the fast-growing Anglo-Saxon nation to the north. After all, these aggressive people were of his own blood.

Colonel Clark was now spending more and more time on his plantation near Natchez. Property values were increasing, and the estate in Mississippi needed looking after. The place also provided the Colonel with a life which he found agreeable. Daniel Clark would often ride up from New Orleans to Clarksville to talk with his uncle of their business affairs, and to spend a few days with him after the leisurely manner of young businessmen and planters of the old South.

On an occasion early in 1798 Daniel Clark interested himself in a few American seamen who had been caught in the Spanish toils. Soon thereafter he received a letter from

Andrew Ellicott and Captain Guion, United States officials then in the Natchez country, thanking him for his efforts in behalf of their countrymen, and asking whether he, Clark, would agree to act as American vice-consul in New Orleans pending the appointment of a regular consul. The suggestion was extremely irregular, as Clark was not even an American citizen, but the idea pleased the young merchant, and the request was brought before the Spanish governor.[14] That official proved compliant and Clark notified Guion and Ellicott, "Gayoso has acknowledged me as vice-consul." [15]

After a short time the pro tempore vice-consul decided that he should like to be regular consul himself, and got his uncle, Colonel Clark, to write General Wilkinson urging him for the place.

But on the same day on which Gayoso in New Orleans agreed to allow Clark to act as vice-consul, the Secretary of State, Pickering, had selected Dr. William Empeson Hulings of Philadelphia for that position. John Adams promptly sent his name to the Senate and confirmation was quickly given. Forthwith, Hulings set off to take over the vice-consular activities of the United States in that "foreign" city which is today one of our largest ports. He was appointed vice-consul—not consul, it should be noted —and the Executive at Washington took more time in searching for the right man to occupy the regular consulate. He might have spared his pains. The Spanish government had no intention of allowing either consuls or vice-consuls to step into the New Orleans office, and when Hulings arrived Gayoso flatly refused to receive him in any official capacity.[16]

By what means Daniel Clark was permitted to function is not clear, but it was evidently due more to his own personality and his relations with the leading men of the city than to any influence which the seal of the United States gave to him. Never was our nation considered less a power than during those years.

VII

Irregular as was the position that the pro tempore vice-consul occupied, he at once gained from Morales, the Spanish intendant under Gayoso, two helpful concessions. Clark, by "tactful and cogent representations," persuaded Morales to permit American vessels to export the produce of the colony by paying the same duty as did the Spanish,[17] and at the same time to allow Louisiana and Spanish vessels to export American river produce elsewhere than to Spain by paying the same export duties. This was a great advance over previous regulations, and a noticeable increase came to American trade. The entrepôt was used more and more, and the flatboats kept coming.

Clark made a visit in the late fall of that year to see Guion and Ellicott, as well as to spend some days on his uncle's place. General Wilkinson was then in camp near Natchez, keeping an eye on the survey settling the boundary between the two nations, the line that is today the southern boundary of Mississippi. So Clark rode over to spend two or three days with the General.[18] Wilkinson was most hospitable toward the younger man, whom he called "Dan" with bluff familiarity.[19] On his part Clark was flattered, as he afterward confessed, by the attentions of the commanding General. Good fellowship reigned su-

preme, until at length Wilkinson, who became loquacious
at times inopportune for himself, admitted to the young
visitor from New Orleans that he really had a deeper connection with the Spanish government than a commercial
relationship.[20] Clark was not greatly surprised at the admission, but as Wilkinson created the impression that the
liaison was ended, the younger man soon forgot all about
it.

Guion and Ellicott, and possibly the General also, encouraged Clark to take a step which he had weighed for
some time—that of becoming an American citizen. So,
late in 1798, the youth who had been born in Ireland and
educated in England and who was then rising to prominence as a merchant of the Franco-Spanish city of New
Orleans, took the oath of allegiance to the Constitution and
government of the United States. Years afterward, Daniel
Clark said with simple sincerity: "This gave me a title I
had endeavoured by previous service to merit, and which
no subsequent conduct has tended to disgrace." [21] The
vice-consul could now go back to New Orleans and represent the United States as one of her own sons.

This move was very timely in another way; ill feeling
was growing over the situation in New Orleans. The treaty
of 1795 instead of settling the Mississippi question had
made it more acute. The entrepôt angered the Spaniards
as they saw an alien race becoming rich through their trade
and resources. The increasing number of flatboats and
barges from upriver, the growing number of seagoing vessels, should have meant something for their colony, but it
was perfectly evident that the uncouth people to the north

were growing rich and that his Catholic Majesty's trade was at a standstill.

VIII

Meanwhile with the export of sugar booming and entrepôt rights accorded, with the vast valley to the north awakening, other nations began to recognize the strategic position of New Orleans. Spain held it and was directly concerned; France had founded it and for sentimental reasons felt that Louisiana rightfully should be hers. England was in and about the Great Lakes of the upper valley for no one knew exactly where the Canadian and Louisiana country joined. British traders and trappers doing business about the headwaters of the streams which flowed eventually into the Mississippi would not fail to urge their government to claim as much as possible.

The United States was, of course, vitally concerned. Its own expansion depended on the Mississippi. The eastern states were not excited over the doings of a horde of trappers and flatboatmen and certainly would refuse to go to war about their river rights, but the West was gradually becoming wrought up to a dull-red heat and openly talked of taking what was wanted, Spain or no Spain.

Clark's friends had now presented his name to the State Department for the full consular appointment, but he was passed over for another, Evan Jones, formerly a prominent man of the West Florida colony. But Jones, on arrival in New Orleans, fared worse than Hulings, being threatened with a Spanish court-martial. He had for a time held a commission in the Louisiana militia (Spanish, of course) and had left the colony without formally resigning. This left Daniel Clark still the acting representative of the United States.

To further his own interests in securing the appointment, Clark sent a long memoir to Pickering in which he took great pains to outline the entire situation respecting American trade and interests in the Mississippi Valley. The original of this memoir is yet preserved and it is easy to see that the merchant spared no trouble to secure helpful data and to translate such documents as would give the President and Secretary of State full information.[22] General Wilkinson had suggested that such a paper, if well done, would give Clark a standing with the authorities at Washington, and this proved to be the case. So it came about eventually, after Hulings and Jones had both been rejected by the Spanish and the demand for a consul grew imperative, that John Adams named Daniel Clark to the consulate in New Orleans by a recess appointment.

About this time Colonel Clark, who had been in failing health, died. He left his large cotton plantation and the greater part of his property to his nephew and namesake, and the very name of the older Clark has been obscured by that of the younger. Officially at the head of the fast-growing American party and naturally a leader in any group was this intrepid young man who combined a quick and resistless will with a dominant elegance of person and presence. James Parton, the historian, calls Daniel Clark the "merchant prince" of old New Orleans. At that time he was a merchant prince thirty-two years of age—and unmarried.

Zulime

*H*ER real name was Marie Julie Carrière, and the priest who baptized her so wrote it in the book, but by family and friends she was known by the simpler sobriquet, Zulime. Her people, the Carrières, had originally come from Provence in southern France and, after residing for a time at Biloxi on the delightful Gulf Coast of our own land, had at last settled in New Orleans. There they were quite at home by the time this history opens, though whether both father and mother were then living is not clear. It is certain, however, that there were four daughters, remarkable for their dark, dynamic beauty. Some say a strain of gypsy blood was in the sisters, and it is remembered that a small colony of Romany folk had come into Biloxi in the early days of that little city. The lovely clear-cut features, olive complexion, and grace of form and movement of the Mlles. Carrière unmistakably betrayed this Oriental tinge.[1] By all accounts the girls were unusually handsome. There was Rosa, then Sophie, another who became Madame Lasabe, and Zulime. The last, although she lacked somewhat the positive nature of the others, sur-

passed all the sisters in appearance. She possessed a voluptuous beauty indescribably compelling.

As children the Carrière sisters grew in the sequestered
old-world atmosphere which the girlhood of that age knew,
with chaperonage in everything and custom binding more
heavily than law the daughters of the Creole populace.
Young men might be allowed their fling, but not young
ladies. They were to be maidenly, say their prayers, be
obedient to their parents, accept for a husband the man
chosen for them, raise a family as their mothers had done,
and preach to their daughters the same maxims which
they had painstakingly learned. So Creole maidens were
taught, and the Carrière sisters were doubtless no exception.

The years sped by and the slender, dark-eyed Zulime
began to flower into that conquering beauty which was to
startle even New Orleans, city of handsome women. She
had no more than passed into her teens when a rather impressive suitor came to the Carrière home and sought her
hand in marriage.

Among those who arrived from France following the
wildest outburst of the Revolution had come a person
named Geronimo DesGrange. He "made some pretensions
to nobility" in his own country—a game of make-believe in
which many a penniless *émigré* took a hand—but with the
guillotine swiftly ending the lives of so many in France,
DesGrange wisely decided to flee the sans-culottism in his
native land and so came to Louisiana. He was of an inde-
terminate age, perhaps in his thirties, when he arrived in
New Orleans. Shortly thereafter he set himself up in a
modest way as a wineseller and confectioner, keeping a

little shop on St. Anne Street, between Royal and Condé. The winery prospered and a little later DesGrange became a distiller on a somewhat larger scale.[2]

There is always something mysterious about this Des-Grange. He was in the city but never seems to have become a part of it as did others, Daniel Clark, for instance. No one knew anything definite about his past, and the Frenchman was not especially communicative. But as he went about his own business troubling no one, what more could be asked of a stranger in that port which had admitted with no question more than one man who kept his lips closed about his former life? Be that as it may, the wineseller, DesGrange, saw Zulime and fell madly in love with her. He soon paid his addresses in the timeless Latin way, and the Carrière family went into council on the matter.

He was much older than Zulime and not particularly attractive, but that was a secondary matter—to be considered, of course, when arranging a daughter's marriage, but—there were other things. This DesGrange, was he not doing well? Would it not be an honor to be associated with him in France? In short, the family approved the suit. That settled it, of course. The arrangements were completed, the banns published, and on December 2, 1794, the beautiful Zulime became the wife of Geronimo Des-Grange, as the records of the old Cathedral show. She was but sixteen years of age.

II

Over the little confectionery shop in St. Anne Street the couple made their home. Evenings were spent in the wineshop, DesGrange greeting customers as he served them, and Zulime busy helping about amid the chatter that the French always enjoy at table. The place gradually became popular with the young bloods of the town, and not because of the wines or *pâtés* of DesGrange. It was Zulime.[3] In a place as small as New Orleans, it was impossible that a beauty so rare would be unnoticed by the young Creole gentlemen who vied with each other as connoisseurs of feminine charms, and they did not fail to mark the wine-seller's wife. In the city of pleasure and of handsome women, young Madame DesGrange came to have few peers.

Whether happiness ever completely made its home in the little apartment over the wineshop no one knows. DesGrange was apparently much in love with his young wife, but her attitude is enigmatic. And then among the crowd of gallants who arrived each night came one who was as naturally a leader in a social group as anywhere else. The time was near the turn of the century, and the man was Daniel Clark.

After that the young merchant was constantly to be found among the group of gay roisterers who made their lounging place the DesGrange winery, and Clark came to know the Frenchman and his beautiful wife quite well indeed. To be sure, there was something of a social gap between the confectioner and a personage of the pride and consequence of Daniel Clark, but the town was small and, in a primitive community, social intercourse of the type the St. Anne Street establishment saw each night was not altogether barred. DesGrange came to look upon Clark as

more than a patron and to esteem him as a true friend.
What Zulime thought no one knew.

Meanwhile at the turn of the century another young
man had come into power—Napoleon Bonaparte. To
French hearts beating in Louisiana it became clear that at
last above the storm of the Revolution one had appeared
who could curb its fierce energies and bring order to long-
distracted France. To the expatriated wineseller in New
Orleans, the promise of established government in his native land meant a chance to salvage something of the property he had left so hurriedly when the creak of the guillotine and the shots of the sans-culottes were sounding
behind him. The prospect pleased DesGrange. It called for
a voyage back to Bordeaux and some time spent in that region and in Provence, but it might prove a trip worth
while. In addition to looking after his own interests, it was
planned for him to attend to those of the Carrières, who
also had business in relation to titles and property in southern France. The wineseller decided to go. To further him in
taking care of the family business, the Carrière sisters gave
him their power of attorney, naming him as their "dear
brother-in-law," and empowering him to arrange everything for them in the faraway homeland.

All plans were finally made, and the day of departure
came. Did the Carrière sisters go to the river to see the boat
which was to bear their "dear brother-in-law" away? Did
Zulime? The records are silent. They are as sphinxlike as
the great water itself that on that spring day in 1801 bore
Geronimo DesGrange down to the Gulf, to the ocean, to
France. The attractive Zulime was left alone in her youth

and beauty. She was just twenty-three years of age and
Daniel Clark thirty-two and desperately in love with her.

III

The young American consul at New Orleans had no
sooner been appointed by President Adams than he found
on his hands a problem whose international complications
reached far past Kentucky flatboats and Spanish governors.
Across the ocean a small but tremendous figure had suddenly shouldered his way into the fight over Louisiana.
Napoleon had already effected a secret *traité préliminaire*
with Spain [4] (October, 1800), whereby the province was
to be ceded to France in return for certain concessions made
to the Bourbon princes. But Godoy and the Spanish minis-
ters had made one strict stipulation: If they ceded Louisiana
to France, Louisiana must never be alienated from France.
His Catholic Majesty very decidedly did not wish the
Americans next to his rich Mexican provinces. This condition was agreed to, but the *traité préliminaire* was as far
as the matter went except to loose a flood of rumors concerning the pending transfer. The young consul at New
Orleans was on the alert endeavoring to gauge the meaning
of each rumor.

Flatboats and pirogues continued coming and schooners
arrived from the Atlantic; also an occasional brig from
Havana or Bordeaux. The American consul found plenty
to occupy his mind. Spanish resentment at all Americans
was growing, with an open threat that the river would be
closed against them when the Spanish chose. Clark had his
own business affairs to look after also, for his wealth and

influence were increasing amazingly. To further his private business he formed a partnership about this time with
two of his youthful associates, Beverly Chew and Richard
Relf. So "Chew & Relf" came into being. The concern took
over the partnership of Daniel W. Coxe in the former
Daniel Clark company, but Coxe was kept as the Philadelphia member of the new organization. The Coxe-Clark
partnership was not dissolved, save in certain particulars.

Both Beverly Chew and Richard Relf were younger
than Clark. Relf had acted as a clerk for him when he first
arrived from the North, and Chew was a promising young
merchant of an old aristocratic colonial family. The three
men were close friends as well as business partners. Clark,
of course, was the dominant figure in the combination,
and his money, everyone knew, was the backbone of the
business. The agreement and business articles, however,
were kept secret following the custom of the day. Chew
& Relf prospered.

The American vice-consul at New Orleans in 1801, it
will be observed, was a versatile individual interested in a
number of things. There was his own growing business,
there was the consular activity of the United States in a
difficult port, and there was Zulime. How well Daniel
Clark kept separated these various facets of his brilliant
career time alone was to demonstrate.

An enemy once charged that Clark prided himself on
his ability at intrigue, and the charge must be sustained
within limits. Certainly it is unusual to find a man so
imperiously outspoken and jealous of his own name as was
Daniel Clark, one whom every gentleman of New Orleans
ever avowed to be the "soul of honor," often depending

upon adroitness to accomplish results when his own native force and courage would have been more than sufficient. This appears, indeed, to have been more a game with him than a flaw in character, for nowhere except in respect to Zulime can Daniel Clark be charged with any lack of honor. Even his relations with the lovely Madame DesGrange, according to the code of the day in a Latin port, were viewed lightly, and the secret partnerships and silent business agreements did not violate the established custom of mercantile firms of the time. Nevertheless, in all this there was concealed that which was to bear a bitter fruit.

Late in the year 1801 Clark decided to sail for Philadelphia to see Daniel Coxe and to attend to matters of their common business. He felt it imperative, too, to consult the American government about his consular status and duties, as the rumors concerning Napoleon's interest in Louisiana were growing in weight. So, early in November, Clark dropped down the river. He was at Havana in good sailing time, but there the Spanish, it seems, laid an unexpected embargo on his ship. This delayed him for three weeks. Not until January, 1802, did he arrive in the United States to make his stay at the Coxe home in Philadelphia. From that point he could attend to business as well as keep in touch with Washington. His consular appointment had not yet been confirmed by the Senate.

IV

And now while Daniel Clark was spending the winter and early spring of 1802 in the comfortable house of his

partner, Daniel Coxe, occasionally visiting his parents in
Germantown or awaiting word from the Senate in Washington, Zulime at New Orleans quietly took ship with her
sister Sophie, now Madame Despau, and also sailed for the
North.

For some time there had been floating about New
Orleans intangible rumors concerning Zulime's husband,
the absent DesGrange. It was reported that the wineseller,
who had represented himself as a single man when he
married Zulime, had in reality another wife living in New
York. How these stories originated no one knew, but they
became so persistent that they finally reached Zulime.

She had now given herself passionately and completely
to Daniel Clark, while he for his part was so infatuated
with her that even before he left her to sail for Philadelphia, in spite of the social gulf between them, they talked
of the chances of open marriage and a life together.[5] The
DesGrange rumors came at the time of their wild and
clandestine affair. But Geronimo DesGrange, though
absent in person, was nevertheless represented in his
marital rights by a potent institution—the Church,
speaking through the governor and the alcalde. Clark,
though fatuously in love, knew the inexorable code, and
he soon impressed Zulime with the idea that before they
could make an open move toward matrimony, the proof
of DesGrange's prior marriage must be absolute. Otherwise, consul or no consul, it would be stripes and the
galleys.

So it came about that while Clark was waiting in
Philadelphia for the Senate of the United States to con-
firm his appointment as consul in New Orleans, two re-

served Creole women sailed from their home city, with New York as destination.

Arrived there they spent some days in turning the pages of the marriage registers of various churches and looking through old records to see if they could find any mention of a DesGrange marriage. They found none, and were greatly disappointed; but at last, after some days spent in pushing their inquiries, they were told that a certain Monsieur Gardette, then living in Philadelphia, might be able to tell them something. This decided the sisters, and they determined to go to Philadelphia to see Monsieur Gardette.

The gentleman in question turned out to be a dentist of sorts, who apparently belonged to the little French group which was quite an entity in the Philadelphia of that day. He naturally received the ladies from New Orleans with the courtesy born of his nativity, and—who knows?—may have marked with admiration the magnificent Zulime. His information was of the highest importance. He stated that he had indeed been present at the marriage of a Monsieur DesGrange to a lady in New York some years before and that he afterward knew DesGrange and his wife by this marriage.

For the two women this settled it. DesGrange had deceived Zulime and was not legally married to her, nor was she bound to him. Zulime now felt free to look to a greater and far more attractive man than Geronimo DesGrange. *And that man was then in Philadelphia.*

The information given by Monsieur Gardette was quickly passed to Clark. He was delighted. "You now no longer have any reason to refuse to marry me," he cried.

Zulime was willing and had been for some time.
Madame Despau went with them and Clark invited a
Mr. Dosier and another gentleman to attend him. They
found a Catholic priest, whose name unfortunately has
never been discovered, and presented themselves before
him. The State of Pennsylvania required no banns to be
published, as their own Catholic Louisiana would have
done, nor was even a civil license needed at that time. The
Society of Friends, who had organized the civil government of Pennsylvania, did not believe in outward formalities and symbolic ceremonies, holding that all that was
necessary for a valid marriage was for a man and woman
to take each other publicly as husband and wife in the
presence of the gathered Society. The commonwealth
founded by William Penn continued this practice and for
many years refused to demand a civil registration for its
married couples. So Clark was not forced to pay a fee to a
civil clerk for his Zulime or to have any record entered in
an official book. Nevertheless, according to the solemn
rites of her Church, and before one of its priests, Zulime
Carrière and Daniel Clark were married in Philadelphia
in the spring of 1802. The reader is at liberty to doubt
this if he chooses. In fact, all subsequent events narrated
in this book can be better understood if a heavy question
mark be placed against the assertion that there was a
regular marriage between the two parties as declared
above. One may wonder, for instance, why Daniel Coxe,
the partner of Clark, was not called as a witness to the
ceremony and may be surprised to learn that Coxe not
only was kept in ignorance regarding the marriage but
declared flatly that such a wedding could not possibly have

taken place without his being informed of it. Others later asserted that Zulime's visit to Philadelphia had more to do with the great obstetrician, William Shippen, than with wedding bells. But these things were said years afterward, and by people who had something to gain by saying them.

V

On January 6, 1802, Thomas Jefferson sent the name of Daniel Clark to the United States Senate for confirmation, and four days later that body approved him as its choice for consular representative in the remote Spanish city. But when Clark's commission, duly made out and signed, arrived at his address in Philadelphia, the new appointee was much disturbed to find that in it he was styled a "subject of Spain." [6] This, though trivial, was extremely distasteful. It was not true, and Clark felt that it might mitigate against his effectiveness in New Orleans. So deeply concerned was he that he set off almost immediately for Washington to have the parchment corrected.

The President and other officials of the government received their New Orleans representative with cordiality and promised to attend to the error in the consular commission. So warm was his welcome that Clark was led to unbosom himself to Jefferson and to the Secretary of State concerning what he called "certain combinations for the dismemberment of the Union" [7] then fermenting in the West. The New Orleans man called no names but had in mind the old Spanish Conspiracy in Kentucky and the trouble men like Wilkinson could make in fomenting dis-

satisfaction among the frontier states. The intimations of
Clark did not greatly impress the "officers of the govern-.
ment," as he termed them, but he went back to Philadelphia expressing himself as well pleased with his visit to
Washington.

The government itself had become concerned over the
Southwest, but not on account of internal dangers. It had
become more and more certain that France and not Spain
was to have the chief voice regarding Louisiana. Spanish
control was bad enough, with the intendant in New
Orleans threatening to shut the port and take away the
all-important right of entrepôt, but even the Francophile,
Thomas Jefferson, was becoming afraid of France. As
early as May 14, 1801, the new President had written:
"It is feared Spain is ceding Louisiana to France." [8] But
ceded or not, it had become manifest that Paris and not
Madrid would have the final voice. Robert Livingston,
the American ambassador in the French capital, was
making unwearied efforts to find out something definite
but learned nothing except that "there never was a government where less could be done by negotiation than
here. There are no people, no legislature, no counsellors.
One man is everything . . . he seldom asks advice
and he never hears it unasked." [9]

What that one man intended about Louisiana only his
own inscrutable mind knew. It might have consoled
Livingston and Jefferson, somewhat, had they known
that Godoy and the Spanish King in Madrid were quite
as uneasy about Napoleon's intentions toward Louisiana
as were they.

What France would do in the Mississippi Valley no

one knew. With Spain there was a treaty, holding the door open, as it were, against pressure, but nevertheless keeping a not-quite-strangled outlet for the western markets. When Spain would close that door was problematical, but everyone believed that France would shut it at once.

VI

As the winter passed and spring began to warm the cold waters of the Delaware, Daniel Clark, waiting for his consular credentials in Philadelphia, became more and more impatient to be off for New Orleans. Business affairs were worrying him and it was evident to both Clark and Coxe that their financial undertakings were not prospering as they had hoped. But they entered into a new commercial agreement, made some ambitious plans, and hoped for better times.

Clark served notice on James Madison, the Secretary of State, that he would be compelled to return to New Orleans as "business of a private nature" [10] demanded his presence. Clark's letter apparently hurried matters, for the consular credentials were sent almost at once by Madison, and the new consul was instructed to furnish his bond. This was done, and Clark left on his schooner *Eliza* on the twenty-second of April.

He had no sooner landed in the Creole city than he felt it necessary to write Madison concerning the New Orleans situation. During his absence Evan Jones and William Hulings had both been forbidden to function as consuls. The regulations requiring a Spanish pilot to be on every ship entering or leaving by the passes kept shipping idle for days; the highhanded arrest and seizure of American citizens and property was an everyday affair. Clark told it all, and with undiplomatic heat.

His letter produced an immediate effect in Washington. A copy of it was shortly made for James Monroe, whom Jefferson was considering sending to Paris to see what could be done. The President had just learned definitely that Spain had really ceded Louisiana to France.

Clark felt that matters were approaching a crisis. His own large business was in jeopardy from the Spanish threat to close the port, and a keen appraisal of the attitude of Morales, the intendant, made him feel instinctively that the time of the dreaded closure was at hand. At the same time, with his young partners, Relf and Chew, he was entering upon a much greater venture in shipping cotton to England. Whitney's gin had arrived, and the rich alluvium of the Mississippi Valley was beginning to bring forth its snowy wealth. The few tentative shipments of cotton made by Clark had convinced him of the vast profit in exporting the fiber on a large scale, though foreign merchants were proving timid traders. Peace between France and England had cleared the seas of privateers, but the hesitant attitude of the English merchants toward the unknown house of Chew & Relf in New Orleans was yet to be overcome. Fraudulent contractors had imposed on the British before. So important did Clark consider the securing of English credit and standing that he decided on a voyage to Europe himself, where he could see the Liverpool and London firms in person and satisfy them of his integrity. He would also have an opportunity, he felt, to go to Paris as an American consul, and find out something definite regarding the Mississippi trade, now that France was in control.

His powerful and impulsive nature was not one to wait. Just five days after he had penned the long dispatch to Madison, he was at the Plaquemines below New Orleans, impatiently waiting for the exasperating Spanish inspection of the ship to be completed. "Hoping to get to sea tomorrow," he wrote.[11]

In one month he was at Wilmington, Delaware, en route to Philadelphia for a meeting with Coxe, and possibly with Zulime. Next he got in touch with Washington and not only obtained the consent of the Department of State but secured the credentials necessary for his proposed diplomatic mission to Paris. Late in August, writing from New York, the New Orleans man informed his partner in Philadelphia that he would "embark tomorrow" [12] on the ship *Lydia* for Grenock.

It was the summer of 1802.

VII

In the meanwhile Zulime in Philadelphia had received a letter from her sister Rose, now Madame Caillavet, informing her that DesGrange had returned from France, but, so Sister Rose reported, there was an astonishing story going the rounds of New Orleans. The Frenchman was said to have brought back with him the very woman whom he had formerly married! As if this were not enough, Madame Caillavet added that an even more amazing report had it that a *third* Madame DesGrange had come to light in the person of one Maria Soumeylliat, who was

also said to be in New Orleans.[18] Zulime was urged to return at once and find out the truth.

These tidings were more than sufficient. The two
Carrière sisters hastened to take ship for home and were in
New Orleans in the early autumn.

Apparently the city had grounds for its rumors concerning Monsieur DesGrange and his bigamous tendencies. How New Orleans of that day got its reports on
such matters, no one can say, but regarding DesGrange
they were widespread, so much so that they came to the
attention of the very last person whom DesGrange would
have wished to learn of them: Thomas Hassett, canonical
presbyter of the Cathedral Church and governor of the
bishopric. This official, as an ecclesiastical judge, had
power to try and punish all offenses against the marriage
sacrament, and Hassett at once decided to look into the
scandalous doings of Monsieur DesGrange. He issued a
decree summoning the Frenchman before his ecclesiastical
court, and the alcalde, Don Fran'co Caisergues, at the
capitular house, lent him the secular arm to support the
trial.

The Church had stepped in and DesGrange was in
prison.

A few days later the Frenchman was brought before
the Church court for an examination touching the charges
against him. Exactly what transpired before this formidable tribunal has always remained a mystery. Some say
that three women, including Zulime, faced the prisoner,
but that she alone admitted being married to him. Some
say that the charges against the Frenchman were dismissed; some, that he was held for further questioning.

What seems clear is that DesGrange, either legally or
illegally, managed to gain his freedom and at once quit
the country. It was commonly reported that Lebreton
d'Orgenois, the marshal, connived at his escape. At any
rate the quondam confectioner hastily left, and at some
point down the river managed to take ship and so fled the
province.

VIII

While these events were taking place in New Orleans,
the *Lydia* was nearing the coast of England. It had been
fifteen years since, as a raw Irish laddie, Daniel Clark had
sailed away for America. Now as he landed again in Liverpool, he might be forgiven a feeling of pride in coming
back to his native shores rich and successful through his
own prowess and resource. But any feeling of elation was
destined to suffer a rapid downfall. Relf and Chew had been
badly imposed on in the much-hoped-for cargoes of cotton.
Clark's wrath boiled over against his duped young partners
in New Orleans when he found what had happened.

"Gentlemen: I have been here three days, and am on the
instant of my departure for London. Although prepared
for the horrid tale I have heard, I could scarce stand it, as I
never could bring myself to believe that your culpable neglect would have been so great as to suffer fraud of such an
enormous extent, and practiced with so much deception, to
pass on you. You may congratulate yourself on having
shaken Mr. Coxe's credit, as well as mine and your own.
. . . You were warned of the frauds, by Green, Mr.

Coxe, and myself, and yet so far from attempting to discover them and punish the authors, you make a shipment by the *Mars* which you yourself suspected. . . . Your madness, for such it must have been, has I hope, passed off, and its effects, will I hope, alarm, warn and teach you to attend better in future to your business. I shall send you by the *Creole,* a large parcel of bales untouched, that you may perceive how grossly we have been deceived and injured by all the contractors without exception; and I will probably return in her, to assist in bringing them to punishment. . . . The cotton you ship must be of the very first quality or ship none at all.

"I am preparing a handsome present for the Intendant; it will be elegant and valuable, of which advise him, and shall consist at the same time of things rare and useful. I flatter myself he continues his protection to you, and request you will continue his friendship, and advise me how you stand and how matters are likely to continue, that I may see how far I may venture to rely." [14]

The last paragraph will suggest the means by which the firm of Chew & Relf managed to gain concessions from the Spanish authorities which other American houses sought in vain. An "elegant and valuable" present for Morales— there were more ways than one to cross the Spanish palm with silver.

Clark's sister, Jane, married to a man named Green, lived in Liverpool, and with her and her husband he spent the time, attempting the while to get on a firmer footing with the British merchants. It was a discouraging task owing to the fraudulent cotton. Again he sent a bitter letter to

Richard Relf and Beverly Chew: "I wish it were possible in order to punish you for your negligence, that you should feel half the tortures of my proud heart when forced to solicit favors. Heavens! How humiliating a situation and how unused I have been to it! How painful is the reflection that this is my fate, when I thought myself in affluence; but for the present, no more of this. . . ."

Badly hurt and disappointed by the cotton debacle, Clark was nevertheless alert to the political situation. His next communication sent from London breathes a calmer air and gives a close-up view of the British metropolis during the lull before the storm.

". . . England will not give up Malta; has put a stop to disbanding the army; is fitting out her ships afresh. Couriers are daily passing to the continent; fast sailing vessels are daily sent off at a moment's warning, with dispatches, God knows where, and with sealed orders. . . . I set off for Paris on the 26 inst., to be introduced to the new constituted authorities there, and will be the bearer of the strongest recommendations. After seeing them I shall judge what ought and must be done, and will without delay, return to Louisiana, for which purpose I shall keep one of the vessels now in Liverpool, ready to sail at a moment's warning. The other shall be sent to you in ballast. I shall be a fortnight on my journey from hence to Paris and back. Will stay a week in England on my return. . . . Inform the governor and Intendant of what I have written you, and act with prudence so as to be prepared for the event. . . . I remain, gentlemen, yours sincerely,

"P.S. Sell the ropewalk and Negroes, if you can possibly

do it, with everything else, and as many ships as you have
not immediate use for. Write to the Marquis of Casa Calvo
to pay what he owes, and compel everyone who is indebted,
without any exception, to pay you without delay." [15]

With a final message (October 22) that the *Creole* and
the *Thomas* had arrived in Liverpool, "The former . . .
with another cargo of damned bad cotton," Clark crossed
the Channel and hurried to Paris.

IX

His Catholic Majesty had at last affixed his hand to the
treaty giving Louisiana to France, and upon the day following, in distant New Orleans, Morales did what had
been so long threatened—took away the right of entrepôt.
The Mississippi was now nothing but a trap to float produce down into the hands of the hated Spaniards, and the
greatest American river was worse than useless to the
United States.

The West seethed, but it took a month for the news to
reach Washington. Then Madison ordered Charles Pinckney in Madrid to file a peremptory protest: "The Mississippi is to them [the western settlers] everything," wrote
the Secretary of State. "It is the Hudson, the Delaware,
the Potomac, and all the navigable waters of the Atlantic
States formed into one stream." [16] Pinckney must get the
port open at once. But Madison was addressing the wrong
ambassador. The "man in Paris" was everything.

In that city, Daniel Clark learned the details of the final
transfer of Louisiana to France. The French capital was full

of it, and full, too, of rumors of colossal plans Napoleon was making to build an empire in the Mississippi Valley. The First Consul had already given orders for the organization and government of the newly acquired province. General Victor was to command a strong contingent of troops as an army of occupancy, while Monsieur Pierre Laussat, a former member of the Convention, was made prefect. The French expedition was to sail at the earliest possible date.

Clark saw that no time was to be lost in ascertaining the status of the American river rights now under the French flag, and with the aid of Robert Livingston secured an interview with General Victor himself. The American ambassador and Clark both felt that the consular status of the latter should not be mentioned, and Livingston introduced Clark simply as "a merchant from New Orleans." [17]

Victor wasted no words in disillusioning the American merchant regarding rights he and others might claim through former treaties. Napoleon's commander spoke contemptuously of the treaty affecting the entrepôt as "waste paper." The astute Clark understood at once that the French control would prove even worse than the Spanish, and far more powerful. He did not know then that Morales had already closed the port.

Nothing further could be done, however, except to get acquainted with Laussat, the newly appointed prefect. Finding that certain minor officials of the French army had been detailed to proceed with all haste to Louisiana to prepare for Victor's army, Clark invited them to accompany him and go as guests in his ship, the *Thomas*. This vessel he had ordered to wait for him on the English coast. The French adjutant general, a Monsieur Roustan, with a lieutenant colonel and an ensign, decided to accept Clark's offer, but as it turned out, Roustan was the only one who finally went aboard the *Thomas* with its master.

Two days before Christmas, Clark wrote to Madison from the River Mersey: [18]

"Sir: At the very moment of departure, I have received a letter from Paris, advising that General Victor, the Captain-General of Louisiana, with his *état-Major,* Mons. J. J. Ayme, the *commissionaire de justice,* with all the other officers of administration of that country, had set off about the 11th instant for Holland, to embark for New Orleans without delay. The Prefect had departed two or three days before for Rochefort, to embark in a corvette that he might arrive before and prepare for the reception of the troops, &. . . . I entreat you will favor me with your advice how to act on their arrival. I am in the ship *Thomas* bound directly for New Orleans, and hope to arrive a month before Victor and his army. . . . Your ob't serv't,

"Daniel Clark"

The Flag at the Cabildo

WHILE the *Thomas* was being tossed about by the wintry winds of the north Atlantic, and Daniel Clark on board was listening with anger and chagrin to the boastful words of Monsieur Roustan, or revolving wild schemes in his head in calculation of a possible revolution in Louisiana before Victor's army could arrive, another vessel had set out from American shores bearing a better-accredited envoy. President Jefferson had decided to send James Monroe to Paris with an offer to buy an outlet through the Mississippi.

But before James Monroe could land in France, late in February, the *Thomas* came through the passes and was beating its way up the mighty Mississippi. A short winter's day closed with the vessel many miles below New Orleans, and not until late in the night did the dim street lamps of the Spanish town come into view.[1] It had been a long, tiresome voyage, and Daniel Clark, as he stepped ashore and hurried toward his comfortable home, was no doubt delighted to breathe the air of New Orleans again and to place himself in the hands of servants at his own quarters. A small sailing vessel in the winter season with no modern comforts was a prison from which any man would gladly escape.

But there was no time for rest. During the long hours on the *Thomas,* a daring plan had been fermenting in the mind of Daniel Clark. He knew Louisiana; he knew the temper of the Americans; he knew his Creoles in the city; he knew, from conversations in Paris and with Roustan on shipboard, what the French occupancy would mean; and the American consul saw a chance for a startling coup, something Napoleonic in its own right. Jefferson was going to try gold; Clark believed that the situation called for iron.

He was not at all astonished to discover what Morales had done in closing the port, though he was surprised that the timid intendant took full responsibility for the closure. This was not like the weak Morales, and Clark hazarded the shrewd guess, in a letter to Madison, that an official letter from Madrid was behind Morales' act. He had learned that a dispatch marked *muy reservada* had come into the intendant's possession a few days before he closed the port. Clark was sure that this "very secret" dispatch was behind the order. Long after Clark and all his contemporaries were dead, the archives of Spain were found to corroborate the American consul's keen surmise that the Spanish King and not the easygoing Morales had shut off the American trade.[2] It was found, however, that the King had graciously ordered Morales to accept full personal responsibility for this action and keep the royal name out of it. So the lowly intendant, not his Spanish Majesty, caught the curses of the Kentuckians.

II

Clark permitted himself but a very brief rest in his own home and then ordered horses. He was soon mounted and spurring northward toward the oak-and-vine-covered country where over Fort Adams, its farthest southwestern post, flew the flag of the United States. The journey, short as it is now, then required days, but exactly one week after he landed in New Orleans, Daniel Clark was standing in Natchez in the presence of William Charles Coles Claiborne, governor of the Territory of Mississippi.[3]

Clark saw before him a tall young man with a high forehead and eyes that suggested a theorist rather than a man of affairs. The governor was young, younger even than Clark by five or six years, as the President had given him his appointment over the Mississippi Territory when he was but twenty-eight.

The man from New Orleans at once declared his mission. He wanted Claiborne to have Wilkinson march troops south immediately and take New Orleans before the armament of Napoleon could arrive!

The young governor looked with amazement at the proponent of this daring scheme. He saw that Clark was in deadly earnest. The consul from New Orleans had thought it through, but Claiborne had never dreamed of such a move. He was staggered by the suggestion.

"Will the Government in Washington approve?" he doubtfully asked.

"On the contrary," Clark instantly rejoined, "the whole move will infallibly be disapproved." He hastened to add that he "counted on Washington to take advantage of its success."

This was scarcely the way to persuade a timid governor to try a *coup d'état,* but Clark knew the situation better than did Claiborne. The governor grew still more hesitant, and asked time to consider. Time, Clark knew, was the essence of success in this plan, but he gave the governor until the next day for a final answer.

At the end of twenty-four hours Claiborne proved to be even less in favor of the proposal. Naturally conservative, one who gained his ends by sturdy, honest plodding, he was distrustful of any meteorlike move. Hoping to persuade him, Clark now backed the plan with a pledge of $150,000 from himself and friends. He assured the governor that the project would in reality be easy; that New Orleans was showing uneasiness over the news of the great French army about to be quartered on it; that Creoles were Louisianians and not Frenchmen or Spaniards; and he believed that the populace would hail the governor and his American soldiers as saviors.

But Claiborne again demurred: "If this thing fails," he said finally and with some feeling, "you have your wealth and your estate; but I am entirely dependent on my government and would be ruined."

"I then asked him," Clark himself reported later, "if that was his only objection and if it was removed, whether he thought he could without acting against the wishes of the President, enter heartily into the measure. He assured me he would. I then proposed to him to put my whole estate in trust to be equally divided between him and me in case the expedition failed. He then retracted. Told me he was afraid of consequences, and we parted." [4]

They were simply different, fated from their own diverse natures to be ever incomprehensible to each other. One can no more visualize W. C. C. Claiborne throwing an army into New Orleans and taking it by force in the name of the United States, than Daniel Clark can be imagined as studiously attending to the humdrum details of a territorial government. The two were cast in different molds. But Clark was not yet ready to give up.

III

Spurring back to New Orleans, Clark sent off a dispatch to the Secretary of State himself, urging that the United States seize Louisiana before the troops of the French arrived and give as an excuse either "indemnification for past injuries or security for the future." [5]

Naturally Clark's wild project would scarcely be considered by Jefferson, especially since at that very time James Monroe was trying his gold upon Napoleon in Paris, and to good effect, although America was not to learn of this for many weeks. The plan will, however, make clear the intrepid nature of Daniel Clark. Restless and eccentric he has been called, and undoubtedly some of his movements were beyond the understanding of the ordinary man, but with it all there seems to have been a certain salt of common sense about Clark which prevented him from hazarding everything upon one cast of the die. The New Orleans man was trader and merchant enough to know how far he might proceed as a consul or political leader; his holdings and property were now of such vast proportions that in spite of his Celtic blood and natural impulsiveness he could not but be conservative. It is this which gives weight to his judgment regarding the advisability of seizing New Orleans early in 1803, ignoring, of course, the question of international right involved. Henry Adams, the historian, who is not partial to Daniel Clark, rates him as far superior mentally to Aaron Burr [6] and, while Mr. Adams is by no means a partisan of Burr, yet even he would admit that the Vice-President possessed great talent. With all his quick, hasty speeches and rash movements Daniel Clark seems never to have made a single disastrous mistake, one of the sort into which men of his type—Burr, for instance—usually fell. His mistake lay in another direction, a direction in which Zulime could have told something had she chosen.

IV

Following his rapid trip to Natchez, Clark settled down somewhat and began that correspondence with James Madison which, on file today in the Department of State, gives a graphic picture of international complications as these unwound in 1803.

In March, Laussat, the French prefect, arrived in New Orleans to get everything ready for the French occupancy. He turned out to be a peppery individual who thought highly of himself and manifested a maddening air of superiority toward all Americans. [7] Having investigated possible quarters for the troops and finding the Spanish regiment at home in the barracks, Laussat requisitioned a ropewalk for the use of the expected grenadiers. The ropewalk was managed and ostensibly owned by a young sea captain, Samuel B. Davis, who had not been long in the city. In reality it belonged to Daniel Clark.[8] He permitted the French requisition to stand without apparent objection and reported to Madison: "Victor is hourly looked for." [9]

The spring of 1803 wore on and the summer came, with Monsieur Laussat making himself a nuisance to the Spaniards and an object of intense dislike to the Americans. Then like a bolt from the blue came the news that the United States had bought Louisiana. Clark was overwhelmed at the official dispatch, tersely informing him of the fact and requesting him to prepare a map and a memoir for the State Department. He was asked to send all requisite information about Louisiana, its extent, resources, etc. Jefferson and Madison wished to be fully informed in preparation for any objection which Congress might raise.

As autumn came on details regarding the formal cession of the province were discussed in letters to and from the State Department, to and from Claiborne. The Mississippi governor wrote Albert Gallatin that he was "depending fully on Daniel Clark," and would descend on the city at once if that official should so direct.

The arrangements for taking over the province were giving concern both to Washington and the little American colony in New Orleans. The storm which occurred when O'Reilly received Louisiana from France was not forgotten, and what reaction the excitable Creole populace might show to the American rule was a matter of grave interest. "The President wishes you to watch every symptom which may show itself," Madison wrote Clark. Meanwhile the

Department of State ordered Claiborne and General Wilkinson to get ready to act as commissioners for the United States and receive the province officially.

Clark knew his city and people and, though somewhat excited, wrote Madison reassuringly: "On the whole, I am fearful of little trouble with respect to taking possession. The trouble I apprehend will be more likely to occur afterward when all the evils attendant upon a change of government, *viz*, a new language, new officers, new laws, new courts, new forms of justice, etc. are felt, and before the blessings expected can be realized." [10] This sage observation the future was to verify.

The Secretary of State and all American officials were now leaning heavily upon their consul at New Orleans. That official suddenly advanced the unlooked-for suggestion to Madison that Laussat should be allowed to have a few days to hold the province in the name of France, instead of being asked to make an immediate transfer from Spanish to American authority.[11] Napoleon had commissioned the prefect to turn over the province to the American commissioners in the name of the Republic, but Clark, who had taken the measure of the fulsome Laussat, felt that the prefect would give less trouble if allowed a brief play of authority than if he were pushed entirely outside the scene. Clark also may have felt that a taste of Laussat in power would make New Orleans eager for any change of government—as the event proved. At any rate, Clark's advice prevailed and Laussat was allowed a brief reign.

On a misty, disagreeable day, the last of November, 1803, the Spanish flag came down at the Cabildo and the tricolor went up. Daniel Clark, closely watching the cere-

mony and studying the populace, was able to report that
little enthusiasm greeted the change. The truth was, Spanish rule, like an old shoe, had become comfortable to the
Louisianians.

V

One evening, before this transfer took place, a group of
Americans, Clark among them, were gathered in George
King's coffeehouse discussing coming events. The conversation at length turned upon the fact that with the scheduled withdrawal of Spanish authority, the city would have
no military or police protection, since Laussat had no troops.
Someone suggested that a volunteer company should be
raised and its services offered to the French prefect until the
American troops should arrive.

"We all agreed at once to the proposition," Woodson
Wren, one of the men present, told it afterward, "and
Daniel Clark was requested to raise the company and take
command of it." [12]

Clark took to the idea with his accustomed vigor and
called for the first muster at Davis' ropewalk—his own
building.[13] When he let it be known among the young
Creole gentlemen that the command was to protect and
police their city and announced that all loyal Orleanians
were welcome to join, the young beaux of the place flocked
to the ropewalk to enroll. The company soon mustered two
or three hundred men, many of them of the first Creole
families.[14] Clark they knew and trusted and the whole affair turned out to be a fortunate one. Had this military
organization been composed of Americans only, it might
have been looked upon with suspicion, but when the fa-

thers of the city saw their Pierres and Henris and Jules in the ranks, they felt it to be their own home guard—which it was. Nights at the ropewalk saw much drilling and the walls rang with voluble commands in French. Perhaps Clark's good friend, Colonel Bellechasse, the Spanish commander, occasionally dropped in to laugh at the awkward squads of those whom he was accustomed to meet as social rather than military heroes, or to advise with Clark as a brother commander. As for Laussat, he was delighted to avail himself of the services of the company and during his twenty-day regime it really did good service. Clark was inordinately proud of his "company." There was enough swank about the whole thing to please his vanity and although his report of the matter to Madison is formal and matter of fact,[15] it is evident that he enjoyed being *Monsieur le Capitaine*.

Laussat wisely appointed Bellechasse to be the actual commander of the militia.[16] This was at Clark's instigation, and was a good stroke, though Bellechasse at first flatly refused to accept the place. "I am a Spanish officer," he said heatedly, "not a Frenchman." But Clark persuaded him that his official leadership of the French forces in Louisiana would be a guarantee against any possible trouble. This silenced the Colonel. So, as soon as the flag of the *Republique Française* floated above the Cabildo, the prefect presented Bellechasse as the commander.

The twenty-day reign of Laussat had about it all the elements of comic-opera kingship. The prefect set everyone by the ears. Clark, who held him in utter contempt, did manage to continue working with him during his brief prefecture. In an official dispatch to Paris, Laussat reported:

"For the past few days, I have been on the best footing of intelligence, at request of the American government, with Mr. Daniel Clark, their Consul and a rich planter and merchant, who knows perfectly the country . . . who is extremely jealous for the cession; and whose penetration and talents for intrigue are carried to a rare degree of excellence." [17]

The days were busy ones for Clark, and at night there was the "grand patrol" of his military company. This organization was now "keeping the city in better order than I had ever known it before," Woodson Wren told James K. Polk long afterward.[18] So the twenty December days of French rule sped by, until at last there came riding through the Tchoupitoulas gate a small troop of horse, bearing proudly the Stars and Stripes.

The Creole historians let their imagination take fire at the ensuing scene on the Place d'Armes—Laussat and the American commissioners on the balcony of the Cabildo, troops drawn up at attention, the vast concourse of onlookers. There was silence amid the great throng as the grip of France was felt to be loosening on the city which its brave men had founded amid the swamps of a new world, the colony its people had sustained by their courage and their blood. The instant the American colors started to rise, the flag of France began to come down and the two bits of cloth met at half mast.[19] For a moment they rested together; then to the peak of the staff went the flag with the stars. A cannon boomed. Below, the tricolor was gathered by a grizzled sergeant and a small band of French soldiers who had constituted themselves a guard of honor for the standard of their people—no half-American or amateur band this, as was Clark's gay battalion, but grim-faced soldiers, the last upholders of the glory of departing France. Stiffly they marched out with set faces, bearing their precious emblem, nor did the occasion lose any solemnity when the American troops presented arms as the colors passed. It was over. The flag of the Union was on the Cabildo and a territory of undreamed greatness had been added to the United States.

Thomas Jefferson thanked Daniel Clark for his part in the triumph, thanked him coolly, formally, as a President thanks a consul,[20] as one gentleman thanks another; but it remained for Colonel Bellechasse, who knew much more about Clark than did Thomas Jefferson, to say long after: "The United States owe the acquisition of Louisiana to Daniel Clark." [21]

Myra

*L*ET it not be thought that participation in this international drama had changed Daniel Clark into a professional politician or had made the planter and capitalist forget his business. Far from it. The man was too versatile and alert for that, but when a tense situation called for his utmost attention, he gave it. The cession completed and governmental affairs out of his hands and in those of a regular proconsular representative of the United States, the ex-consul could drop back into his former routine of life. That meant business—and Zulime.

The daughter of the Carrières had all this while been in New Orleans with her sister. The DesGrange *mésalliance* was apparently soon forgotten by all save a few. New Orleans had other interests of more importance than the fate of one deserted beauty. Besides, it was observed, Madame DesGrange appeared to be getting along. She had . . . friends, Daniel Clark, for instance. Rumor definitely coupled the two names.

It was true. Clark had established Zulime in a handsome

residence where he spent much time with her. This the city knew or guessed. What New Orleans did not know was that these visits were known and approved by the Carrières. Sophie had related to them privately what had happened in Philadelphia: that Monsieur Clark and their Zulime had been quietly married by a priest of the Church. For obvious reasons the family was delighted at the news, but a faint trace of worry was appearing on the face of Zulime herself. Why would he not announce their marriage and present her before the world as his wife?

But Clark emphatically declared that this could not possibly be done until they could get definite legal proofs of DesGrange's prior marriage. The flight of the Frenchman had made that well-nigh impossible, but a premature disclosure, Clark insisted, would be ruinous. Think of the Church and its penalties; think of his position, his fortune; think of the scorn of the city. It simply could not be risked. They must wait, and Zulime did the waiting.

II

By this time Daniel Clark had come to be the best-known man in New Orleans, and by all odds the most influential.[1] Chew and Relf were prospering and so was Coxe in Philadelphia. The Natchez plantation was doing well, and to it Clark was adding other holdings. He was rapidly becoming a landowner on a vast scale. Sugar and cotton had both developed amazingly as trade staples, and even before the cession the eyes of canny investors were turning toward the rich bottoms of the Attakapas country and the region now known as the "sugar bowl" of Louisiana. Clark soon purchased the Houmas, a plantation where the cane promised to grow in all the rank luxuriance of the tropics. Cotton, too, was coming down faster from the Mississippi country as Whitney's gin was surreptitiously duplicated without benefit of patent. Everything betokened the prosperity soon to come, and Clark was already far in the lead as a capitalist, trader, merchant, and planter. His ventures in diplomacy merely provided an outlet for his restless spirit, and while he lives today in American archives for his part in national affairs, he lived then as a truly regal person, the first citizen of the old Creole city.

An aura of elegance always seemed to rest about Daniel Clark. His outward manner of living was that of a bachelor of wealth and culture in a city where such talents were held in respect. Characteristically, he seems to have moved his residence a number of times until he built a sort of luxurious town house where he could do as he pleased. Here he stayed while he was in the city, though he was also fond of his countryseat at Cannes Brulées, situated on the river above the city.

The appointments of Clark's bachelor quarters were princely. He had a slave named Lubin who had come to him through Zulime, and the Negro proving faithful, Clark made him his confidential body servant. Lubin thenceforth looked after the town establishment. It was a man's world, for Clark's most intimate friends always declared that they had never seen a woman in his house except the black wife of Lubin. The place, however, was no hermitage and was open at all times to the friends and boon companions of the owner. These were many. From the Spanish officials to the blacks, Clark was liked. The young

Creole gentlemen had long considered him one of them, and lacking home ties, he was often to be found with them of evenings at the coffeehouses or at some social affair. Life was gay, and the austere morality of his native land was not in evidence in the voluptuous society which sipped sherbet under the magnolias in old New Orleans. Nor was more than a shrug of the shoulder given to certain matters of morals having to do with beautiful quadroon girls to whom young Creole gentlemen gave their nights and their money but never their names.

Clark had become more and more attached to Colonel Bellechasse, the erstwhile Spanish commander, and the two men were often to be seen together. Captain Samuel B. Davis, who had been managing Clark's ropewalk until something better opened, had also become one of his intimates. Clark liked the outspoken sea captain and helped him as he could. The time was to come when the sea captain could help Clark.

III

At the very outset of American rule, Clark and Claiborne began to clash. The new governor, trying to get his bearings amid the torrent of French which filled the air, was naturally inclined to lean heavily on the man who had hitherto represented his country in Louisiana. But Claiborne soon concluded that Clark was overbearing and dictatorial. Clark, for his part, decided that the governor was a fool—and said so in his outspoken way.[2] Claiborne's motives were high, his character flawless, and in his quiet, plodding way he eventually did good service for the nation in the Southwest. But although he later married into the aristocratic families of Louisiana, W. C. C. Claiborne was always a stranger to the people whom he had come to rule.[3] Daniel Clark was part and parcel of them.

Matters reached the boiling point when a number of merchants met to protest certain of the new governor's measures.[4] Clark, of course, was the leader, but associated with him were others including Evan Jones, as well as James Pitot, whom Claiborne had named mayor of New Orleans. The distinguished Edward Livingston, lately landed in Louisiana, made a powerful addition to this group. The young New Yorker, a brother of the ambassador who had signed the treaty of cession, left a place of honor in the state where he had "lived like a nabob," in order that he might begin anew in Louisiana. He was soon to marry into the D'Avezacs, and to be henceforth heart and soul a Louisianian. The protest meeting ended with Edward Livingston and Evan Jones on the committee ordered to memorialize Congress for redress.

Claiborne was much disquieted. He wrote Madison, belittling the number of the petitioners but singling out Clark and Livingston as especially formidable "for the standing their talents give them."

Meanwhile the territorial government was formally set up. Claiborne was sworn in as governor on October 3, 1804, by James Pitot, the mayor. Lebreton D'Orgenois, a former Spanish official, was named marshal.[5] He it was who, rumor stated, had connived at the escape of Des-Grange two years before, when the husband of Zulime had fled from the charge of bigamy. Clark managed to advance

his protégé, Captain Samuel Davis, in the turnover, and
the erstwhile sea captain was made master of the port.
This took Davis out of the rope manufactory and gave him
a better standing in the city. Mrs. Davis' brother, Pierre
Baron Boisfontaine, of a distinguished family of the West
Indies, heard of Davis' advancement and soon came to
New Orleans to join the family. He, too, became a friend
and admirer of Daniel Clark.

But marshals and harbor masters were but minor ap-
pointees. What concerned the well-intentioned young
governor from the northern country was the personnel of
the proposed legislative council, that oligarchic few who
were to help him rule the newly organized Territory of
Orleans. Hoping to allay the fast-gathering opposition,
Claiborne wisely nominated on this council several of
those opposed to him. Among these were Boré, whose pot
of sugar-cane syrup we have lately seen boiling; Colonel
Bellechasse, lately in command of his Catholic Majesty's
troops; Evan Jones, planter, officer, and former vice-
consul; and Daniel Clark himself. Whatever may have
been Claiborne's motives in making these men nominees,
they all, with Clark as leader, peremptorily refused to
allow their names to be used.[6] Bellechasse did later consent, and was eventually among the five selected by the
government at Washington to compose the council.[7]
Claiborne blamed Clark for the whole incident, and reported him as "greatly soured with the present administration." [8] He was. The strong-minded Clark expressed himself vigorously to all on the subject of the governor whom
the United States had sent into Louisiana, and of the over-

bearing attitude of the *Américains* toward the new province. He had become much more of a Creole than he imagined.

So matters stood as 1805 wore on. The new American party headed by Claiborne, and the Creoles with Daniel Clark at their head began slowly to draw apart, that is, so far as politics was concerned. New Orleans was too much New Orleans to permit its social life to become upset over a storm in the political teapot. When night came and the balls were given, or when a play was in progress at the theater, truce was declared by common consent.[9] The young city gallants who were of the party of Clark, bowed ceremoniously to the American governor when he sat in his box at the old French theater not understanding a word of the play. Clark kept on in his big, restless way. The rich bachelor was now at the height of his popularity and was adding vast tracts to his property in Louisiana as he had already done in West Florida. Chew & Relf was prospering; life and youth were yet before this man who had come to the city not twenty years before. Fortune had been kind to him.

IV

But fortune, dealing so generously with Daniel Clark, was preparing to be less kind to one close to him. Zulime was now far along the road which women travel, sometimes in honor, sometimes in dishonor, but always alone. The veil which the years were to throw over the coming event is hard to penetrate, and the barrage which countless heated arguments later laid down makes it yet more difficult to follow that lone figure to her ultimate hour.

That Clark was not married to her the city was certain. Those who knew the proud, imperious man of the world would have laughed at the idea, and what the Carrières knew or thought not many cared. In utter secrecy, Clark called his protégé, Samuel B. Davis, now captain of the port of New Orleans, and asked him to find a suitable place where a woman might be privately accouched. Davis thought of a house which his brother-in-law, Pierre Boisfontaine, had leased but had not occupied. The Captain was sure he could manage the affair. Without giving definite reasons to Boisfontaine, Davis asked him for the key to his newly rented house. The place was on Quarter Street, according to report, and at some uncertain time—they say late in June, 1805—Zulime was taken there.

Every birth is a mystery, but surely over the empty house in Quarter Street there hung a very curtain of impenetrability and silence, to be broken at length by a baby's cry. A little girl had been born. Nothing could be less auspicious than the surrounding circumstances: the expectant mother hurried into a vacant house, secret comings and goings, mother and baby soon whisked away to other temporary quarters, as the Boisfontaines wanted their house and told Davis so. Mrs. Aimée Boisfontaine long afterward remembered that they were living in it by the middle of the next month and that the place then gave no sign of prior occupancy.[10] But in the meanwhile, somewhere in the city, Zulime and her newborn baby had been tragically separated.

One account has it that Clark was constantly with Zulime but that he made her realize that she must give up the child until the long-sought proofs of DesGrange's bigamy could be produced. *Then* would come his acknowledgment and *then* they could claim their child and together face the city. But meanwhile, Clark's prestige, her own liberty, the child's inheritance—all demanded a separation. And so it was done.

The tiny mite of humanity was taken away and put with the wife of a coachmaker named Gordon. This woman, who had a child of her own, was induced by a handsome stipend to nurse the newborn baby. So she did, after a fashion, but a hireling is a hireling, and the lusty, full-throated cry of the healthy little infant gradually took on a thin, querulous plaint which would have spoken volumes to a mother. Perhaps the Gordon woman understood it, but what of it? She wanted Daniel Clark's money, not his child.

But, as the storybooks would say, good angels were watching, and so, to do him credit, was Daniel Clark who was by no means an angel. The angels were Mrs. Rose Boisfontaine Davis, wife of the Captain, and her niece, Mrs. Harriet Harper. These Clark asked to go to see the child. Amid impossible surroundings giving every evidence of neglect, the two women found the little baby girl in the coachmaker's house. Mothers both, they were profoundly moved. Harriet Harper was then nursing a child of her own, and without more ado, the women took the baby away and brought her to the Davis home. There under tender, loving care she immediately began to thrive. Clark was delighted with the home his little daughter had found. Characteristically he declared that they must get her everything and was unsparing in his outlay for her wants. He made no secret to the Davis family of his relationship to the child and said again and again that they had put him under an obligation he could never hope to repay. Always generous, his ample means were from that time on at the service of Davis or the Harpers, and he supported the whole household as the need arose. The Davis home was henceforth the little girl's home, and she soon proved to be its life and joy. They named her MYRA.

Aaron Burr Arrives

ONE day, late in June, 1805, the flatboatmen and other sun-tanned children of the river, with the usual array of levee loungers, looked with vast interest at an elegant purple-sailed barge which was making in toward the levee.[1] Several oarsmen were found to be aboard this strange craft which bore every evidence of belonging to a person of consequence. The boat touched and tied up, and there stepped out a small but dynamic figure. It was Colonel Aaron Burr, late Vice-President of the United States. The luxurious vessel in which he had made the descent to New Orleans had been furnished him by General James Wilkinson, now somewhere with the army in the Missouri country; the rowers, it appeared, were ten enlisted men and a sergeant detailed to propel Colonel Burr wherever he would go. The traveler bore with him a letter from Wilkinson to Daniel Clark, requesting that he receive the "great man" cordially, and hinting darkly that Burr would have "matters of importance" [2] to tell him (Clark) which could not be mentioned by letter.

Clark rose to the occasion and received Colonel Burr in his own mansion. Bachelor establishment though it was, Clark, like other Orleanians of prominence, kept open house for friends, and Lubin, his black major-domo could always get enough slaves from the plantations to keep the place properly manned. Clark met Burr on equal terms and was pleased with his society. The Colonel did a great deal of visiting while he was in the city, but must have been with Clark at times in his great library. Here Clark and his celebrated visitor talked freely, though what passed between them has never been disclosed. Clark later declared that Burr "confided nothing to him," [3] and while this visit has always associated Daniel Clark's name with Burr's schemes, nevertheless there is the ring of truth and sincerity in everything Daniel Clark ever said concerning his connection with Aaron Burr.

Whether Burr told Daniel Clark much or little, his New Orleans host aided the "great man" materially when the time came for him to go back to the North. Wilkinson's elegant barge was forsaken, and Clark let him have two horses, with a servant to bring them back, and with these Burr set out for Natchez.[4] At that little town on the bluffs, he was entertained by one Stephen Minor, known to the Spanish as Don Estevan Minor, lately a commander of his Catholic Majesty's troops. Daniel Clark believed that this man was still in the pay of Spain. With Minor, Burr remained a week and then set out for Nashville over the Natchez Trace.

This famous Indian trail had recently been rendered a bit more passable by the energies of a young army officer named Edmund P. Gaines. But at best it was a poor road, blocked by briars, fallen trees, and innumerable dirty creeks. There was no white settlement from the Bayou Pierre in lower Mississippi to the Harpath Mountains in Tennessee. On this long four-hundred-mile trek, through the heat of summer, we may imagine the dapper wanderer riding his horse slowly along and turning over in his mind those schemes of empire and grandeur which were so peculiarly his own. And what were those schemes? Scholars and historians have set in order theories of all sorts. Ere long in Richmond men would hail Burr before Judge John Marshall and accuse him of treason, while others, including Andrew Jackson and Henry Clay, would defend him passionately. Historians are divided in their judgment upon the motives and intent of this little man jogging along through the swamps of Mississippi. Was he trying, as some think, to trick England? Spain? Both? Was he trying to break the Southwest away from the Union and set himself up as a backwoods emperor, à la Napoleon? Was he a patriot, seeking to wrest from Spain new lands for American settlers, as the Texans were to do on their own account before his death? Let the historians puzzle. As James Parton kindly wrote, "It is doubtful if Burr himself knew what he was trying to do."

II

Burr had been gone but a short while when floating down the river came all sorts of rumors connected with his visit to New Orleans. Clark apparently had forgotten Burr as soon as he departed. He had his business, and, besides, he was beginning to take great interest in the little girl at the Davis home. But his friend, Thomas Power, informed him a few weeks after Burr's departure that the Spanish were uneasy about Burr, and that he (Clark) was thought to be connected with Burr's plans. Clark ridiculed the idea. Then on the eve of a business trip to Vera Cruz it came home to him unmistakably that Burr's talk and travel had caused a huge stir in the whole lower Mississippi Valley, and that his own old friends, the Spanish, were indeed looking askance at *him*. Whereupon Clark sat down and wrote to General Wilkinson a letter which has been called by those who connect Clark with Burr, a "masterpiece of dissembling." [5] Others find it no more than it purports to be. At all events it is typically Clark:

"Many absurd and wild reports are circulated here, and have reached the ears of the officers of the late Spanish government, respecting our ex-Vice President. You are spoken of as his right-hand man, and even I am supposed to be of consequence enough to combine with Generals and Vice-Presidents. At any other time but the present, I should amuse myself vastly at the follies and fears of those who are affected with these idle tales; but being on the point of setting out for Vera Cruz, on a large mercantile speculation, I feel cursedly hurt at the rumors, and might, in consequence, get into a hobble I could not easily get out of. *Entre nous,* I believe that Minor of Natchez has a great part in this business, to make himself of importance. He is in the pay of Spain, and wishes to convince them he is much their friend. . . . Inquire of Mr. Burr about this, and let me know at my return, which will be in three or six months. The tale is a horrid one, if well told. Kentucky,

Tennessee, the State of Ohio, and part of Georgia and Carolina, are to be bribed with the plunder of the Spanish countries west of us, to separate from the Union. This is but a part of the business. Heavens! what wonderful things there will be in those days. But how the devil I have been lugged into the conspiracy, and what assistance I can be to it is to me incomprehensible. *Vous, qui savez tout,* can best explain this riddle. Amuse Mr. Burr with an account of it, but let not the great and important objects, these almost imperial doings, prevent you from attending to my land business. Recollect that you, if you intend to become kings and emperors, must have a little more consideration for vassals; and if we have nothing to clothe ourselves with, for we can be clothed by the produce of our land only; and if Congress take the land for want of formalities, we shall then have no produce and shall make a very shabby figure at your courts. Think of this, and practice those formalities which are necessary, that I may have from my Illinois lands wherewith to buy a decent court dress, when presented to your levee. I hope you will not have Kentucky men for your masters of ceremonies." [6]

Having dispatched this letter up the river in the general direction of Wilkinson, Clark then set out for Vera Cruz to fulfill a contract he had signed with a Mr. B. Bosch. A cargo of $105,000 was involved and the merchant felt that it was important for him to take ship on his *Caroline* and accompany the goods.[7] This he did, proceeding to Mexico City during his two-month trip. He was received with extreme courtesy by the Spanish officials and Mexican grandees, who had known of and learned to respect him when his city was one of their ports. The Spanish-speaking Clark, who had well-nigh become Latin-minded himself, was on the best possible terms with the Mexican government and talked freely concerning many international affairs. On departing, he left $56,000 of his money in Vera Cruz, intending to send a ship for it the next year. This fact, together with his visit at the time, serves some historians as evidence that Daniel Clark was an emissary of Burr to Mexico.[8] The same fact was used by Clark himself as evidence that he was *not* implicated with Burr, as he declared that he would never have trusted his money where Spanish confiscation could reach it had he been personally involved in the schemes of the "late Vice-President." [9] Clark, who was in position to know the whole time, felt that Burr's plans were all really aimed at Spain.

III

Not long after Clark had left for Mexico, out of the mists of the Gulf, Geronimo DesGrange—of all persons—came back! The Holy Office had gone from Louisiana with the Spanish flag, and the man who had been tried for bigamy before the Church court with alcalde and soldiers standing by to enforce its findings, could now return and snap his fingers in the face of a Church that could not enforce its penal regulations under the American flag. So DesGrange came back to the city where he had left his beautiful wife. But not to be with her. That is certain. All else respecting his return is hazy.

Zulime refused to have anything to do with her former husband, but what further steps to take she did not know. Beautiful, Creole, feminine—that was Zulime. Aggressiveness even in a womanly way she totally lacked, and apparently in the face of DesGrange's return she simply waited, perhaps wishing for the presence of the stronger character who dominated her.

Somebody acted for Zulime, however, for the November records of the old court of New Orleans of 1805 show that a suit was filed seeking alimony from the returned DesGrange in the name of Zulime.[10] The bill alleged that she had been basely deserted by Geronimo DesGrange from September, 1802, until October, 1805, and prayed monetary redress. It has always been doubtful whether Zulime ever really saw the papers of this suit, and certainly she did not sign them. This was done by her counsel. One cannot but suspect that behind the whole thing was Daniel Clark, perhaps just returned to New Orleans. The immediate object was apparently to get rid of DesGrange and in this the suit was quite successful. Judgment in Zulime's favor was given on the twenty-fourth of December, according to the old court record, which itself has not been unimpeached, and DesGrange again hastily left New Orleans, to disappear forever. Zulime and Clark would be no more disturbed by the former husband's presence. If the alimony suit was filed that they might drive away DesGrange without waiting the long, tedious, and perhaps hopeless process of a civil and ecclesiastical divorce, they had accomplished their purpose. But what they had done had woven a tangled web about some tiny feet just then lying in a cradle in the home of Samuel B. Davis.

IV

Another personage had been busy during the latter part of 1805 in weaving a tangled web. Aaron Burr was threading his way about from place to place through the western country, making friends, broadening his acquaintance, feeling out the minds of men. Nor did he confine his work to the West. He was in touch with important men in the East, including the British ambassador, Sir Anthony Merry. Burr actually convinced Merry that the West was ready to secede from the East and that British assistance would enable him to throw Louisiana and other southwestern territory into the hands of England. Burr had not hesitated to let it be known over Kentucky that Daniel Clark was one of his chief backers, and Clark, writing Wilkinson that he did not know "how the devil" he had been "lugged" into it, was later to find that Burr himself had lugged him in by the free use of his name. So much so that Sir Anthony Merry, who was completely taken in by Burr, wrote Lord Mulgrave in England suggesting that in accordance with Burr's plan the Admiralty should send an expedition consisting of a few frigates, with a ship of the line or two, to lie off the mouth of the Mississippi and wait until "Daniel Clark of New Orleans" should send them word that the "revolution had taken place." [11] Then they could sail up and take possession of Louisiana in the name of Great Britain. This remarkable dispatch remains today in the British archives. Whatever the Burr scheme contemplated, Sir Anthony Merry was certainly willing to be a party to it.

But before this dispatch reached London, William Pitt died and the document fell into the fat, pudgy, but exceedingly capable hands of Charles James Fox, who had succeeded Pitt, the last person whom Merry would have wished to see it. Fox at once recalled Merry and paid no attention to Burr's request. He had other things for British frigates to do in the year 1805 than hide off in the Gulf until Daniel Clark "delivered" Louisiana to England.

By this time matters had reached a crisis between Spain and the United States, and the Burr megalomania, if it was analyzed at all, was thought to be aimed at the Spanish West. As 1806 opened, everything pointed to war with Spain, partly because of the uncertain Louisiana boundary situation, partly because of the Florida question. "Every indication presaged a speedy rupture with Spain, and the whole west was impatient for the collision." [12]

On the brink of this, Daniel Clark went back to Vera Cruz to get the money he had left there the year before and to bring home another cargo. Again he traveled the tortuous way of cactus and mountain from Vera Cruz to Mexico City, but this time took care to make observations along the way and even to draw a rude map of the country through which he passed, thinking it might be helpful to the United States in the event of war. Again Clark was graciously received by the Mexican officials, and finally departed in peace, this time leaving $40,000 in Vera Cruz.[13] He did not get this amount until the next year. The *Patty*, one of his ships, brought back the $56,000 which had been there during the winter.

V

Early in the spring the party conflict in New Orleans came to a head in the election of a territorial delegate to Congress. Clark himself decided to stand for the place. His opponent was a Dr. Watkins, who enlisted the support of Claiborne and the American element. But Clark had the Creoles and, as it turned out, the votes. He was triumphantly elected, to the intense mortification of the governor. Claiborne reported the matter to Thomas Jefferson and at the same time assured the President of his own regret at the attack of John Randolph of Roanoke who was then making himself a thorn in the flesh to Jefferson. Not long after this, the governor reported to the President those persons who had been nominated to be "counsellors" for the Territory, among them a Mr. La Croix who "was one of the partisans of Clark and if appointed would probably be directed by him." [14] This was a gubernatorial way of advising the President that Mr. Delacroix—as the name later came to be written—should not be appointed. Jefferson took the hint, and "Mr. La Croix" was not named to help Claiborne direct the affairs of Orleans Territory. We shall meet the Chevalier Delacroix again in this story— and again.

Gentleman from Orleans

CLAIBORNE was not the only one writing to Mr. Jefferson during 1806, or talking to him either, for vague reports and half-stated implications regarding the wanderings and intentions of Aaron Burr began to dribble into Washington. Burr was busy indeed, going from place to place, hearing from friends, writing letters and keeping in touch with Wilkinson all the while. The General was hand in glove with him in all his plans, and this was Burr's undoing.

Whether Daniel Clark in New Orleans completely fathomed the intentions of Burr is uncertain, but certainly he knew enough to be alarmed. Fearing the effect of Burr's rumored expedition on the excitable Louisiana populace and knowing that he must speedily leave for Washington, Clark called together a number of his friends and supporters for joint consultation and advice, Bellechasse and Derbigny among them.[1]

Clark "informed them of some of the views and intentions imputed to Burr . . . and he advised them all to exert their influence with the inhabitants of the country to support the government of the United States, and to rally around the Governor although he thought him incapable of rendering much service as a military man." So Bellechasse described this meeting in the public print a few days after it had taken place. But long afterward, when Claiborne was dead, Bellechasse said that it was the *weakness* of the governor, not his lack of military experience, that had made Clark fearful.[2]

The political situation thus diagnosed and safeguarded and business affairs put in order, there remained for Clark one further interest—Zulime. He and the beauty who was the mother of his little girl had all this time remained in the most intimate relationship. To her he had given everything she might wish, everything that riches could furnish, but not his name. The DesGrange bigamy was yet to be proved, and the divorce waited upon that. But as the day drew near on which he was to sail for the nation's capital to take his place in the charmed governmental circle which claimed him, who can tell what was in the heart of the woman he was leaving so lightly? As she saw this dominant, attractive man for whom she had suffered so much, now in his restless way turning to other toys—a seat in Congress, for instance—did a premonition come to her that he would never acknowledge her as Madame Clark? But fret as she would or plead as she might, Clark had his way with Zulime as he did with everyone. He left the wife of his black Lubin to be Zulime's personal servant as the husband was his own; he told her good-bye in whatever mood was upon him, and sailed away to be the first delegate from the Territory of Orleans to the Congress of the United States.

II

After a short stay with Daniel Coxe in Philadelphia, where he had an opportunity to see his parents also, Clark proceeded to Washington and in December took his seat in the Sixth Congress.

Washington then was but a straggling hint of the magnificent capital of today. Georgetown, on its hill, with its aroma of old Maryland substantiality, had about it a far greater air of permanence than the newer town springing up in the mud and flats on the river below. The members of Congress clung together in groups at their respective boardinghouses, eating together at some common mess which served both as a social club and political meeting place. The gentleman from Orleans soon found himself at home in a Federalist mess, where he made warm friends with his usual impetuosity. Chief among these was a young senator from Delaware, Samuel White, recently appointed to fill a vacancy.[3] Sam White and Daniel Clark soon became boon companions. Their alliance seems to have been more social than political, and it was reported that they spent more time in the drawing rooms of Georgetown than they did in the halls of Congress.[4]

It will not be difficult to guess that Daniel Clark was a Federalist and was compelled to be a Federalist by every possible motive. His English and aristocratic training, his pride of family and fortune, would be challenged directly by the proletarian and antiaristocratic tendencies of Jefferson. He was already in opposition to the President as represented by the inane government of Claiborne in New

Orleans, and he well knew that the letters of the governor had put the party in power against him even before he arrived. No sooner had he started his congressional career than Samuel White and other more prominent Federalists discovered in the man from New Orleans a willing recruit. He was soon to prove a vigorous ally.

One day into the Federalist mess where Clark was at home, there came a gentleman from Baltimore by the name of Robert Goodloe Harper, and another of those strong friendships for which Clark was famous sprang up between the two men, a friendship destined to last. Harper had been the leader of the Federalists in the Fifth and Sixth Congresses and both John Adams and Alexander Hamilton had learned to lean heavily on him. But when Jefferson and his ideas triumphed in 1801, Harper was swept out with his party. He then took up residence in Baltimore and continued to keep in touch with the group he had formerly led in Congress, finding solace for his defeat in marrying Catherine Carroll, a daughter of the rich and influential Charles Carroll of Carrollton. His political reputation, in spite of his defeat, was undimmed among the Federalists, and his name was potent in Washington.

III

Clark spent his first winter in Washington making more of a stir in the social than in the political realm. The bachelor delegate from Orleans, with his wit and spirit, his courtesy and elegance, in combination with soft foreign manners and a reputation for immense wealth, made a tremendous impression upon the rather provincial "court circle" of the new Republic. He became something of a sensation in the drawing rooms of Georgetown, and even in Annapolis and Baltimore. With the gay young senator from Delaware and other gallants of the same type, Clark found himself in a congenial coterie. The rumors of his part in the Burr imbroglio Clark brushed aside in his out-spoken, half-jesting way. For him there were other things to think of than an "impractical" scheme of empire build-ing in the West.

And by this time the impractical scheme had collapsed. The whole story of the Burr episode would take us too far afield here—how he prepared his expedition; how he was betrayed by Wilkinson and arrested by Jefferson's order at Bayou Pierre in Mississippi; how Wilkinson sent his aide, Lieutenant Walter Burling, to Mexico City asking for $116,000 in Spanish gold for having stopped Burr; and how at the same time Wilkinson was hailed in Washing-ton as the savior of the United States; how the General went on to New Orleans, issued proclamation after proclamation, suspended the civil courts, locked up the harbor and had the Creoles believing that a British fleet was coming up from the Gulf and a vast armada drifting down from the North, and that he alone could save their homes; how Burr attempted to escape and was arrested near Mobile by a young lieutenant, Edmund P. Gaines, in command of Fort Stoddert; how Gaines took his prisoner to Richmond, Virginia, where Thomas Jefferson ordered him to be held for trial; and how Mr. Burr waited there in ward, and the whole nation waited with him, as the greatest legal drama that the young Republic had ever seen was about to be enacted.

IV

Daniel Clark at Washington was filled with wrath when he heard what Wilkinson had done in New Orleans. He was under no illusion concerning the General. To his intimate knowledge of Wilkinson obtained in the early Spanish years, Clark had added further proof that the liaison between the General and the Spanish had never been broken. But he had paid small heed to this until the Burr expedition ended, and the news from New Orleans told of the strong-handed measures Wilkinson had adopted there. When these tidings and news of Burr's arrest and confinement in Richmond were reported to Clark he saw what had happened. Wilkinson had been as traitorous to Burr as Clark thought him to be to his own country.

The delegate from Orleans lost no time in saying so to his Federalist colleagues. They were already so opposed to Jefferson that they were ready to believe that the Burr arrest was nothing more nor less than a Democratic plot. Jefferson himself soon complained: "The Federalists appear to make Burr's cause their own, and spare no effort to screen his adherents." The President, on his side, was becoming anxious to convict Burr. The nation awaited the trial.

Meanwhile during the winter and early spring Daniel Clark was doing other things besides enlightening his colleagues on the character of General Wilkinson. Robert Goodloe Harper, upon a long-remembered occasion, had presented him to some of the members of his family, and for the first time Daniel Clark bowed before Louisa Caton.

The daughters of Richard Caton of Baltimore were then in the first flush of a triumphant social career. Already they had cut a wide swath in Maryland circles. As grand-daughters and heiresses of Charles Carroll of Carrollton they assumed by right of birth a first place in society, though their own charm and beauty might have obtained this for them had they been less favored in lineage and wealth. As it was, the Caton sisters were the rage of Baltimore and Annapolis, as they were one day to be the toast of London.

Richard Caton, their father, was from the British Isles and, like Clark, had arrived in 1786.[5] When the handsome young Englishman married "Polly" Carroll, somewhat against the wishes of her distinguished father, his fortune was made. The gentle, dark-eyed Mary Carroll, or "Polly," as the family called her, was quite a beauty her-self and enjoyed taking part with her daughters in the life and activities of the social season. After the coming of the children, the Catons established a home at Castle Thunder, known as Catonsville today, a suburb of Balti-more; and another seat at Brooklandwood in the famous Green Spring Valley a few miles to the northeast. Amid the restful surroundings of Brooklandwood the four famous daughters of the house—Mary Ann, Elisabeth, Emily, and Louisa—grew to womanhood, though the Catons spent considerable time in the well-known home of their grandfather on Lombard Street, Baltimore, the old Carroll residence that still stands in vacant grandeur above the roar of city traffic.[6] The Signer was exceedingly fond of his grandchildren and liked to have them about, either in his town house or in the more stately Carroll home in Annapolis, with its garden sloping down to the Spa.[7] Of course during the winter the young ladies found life more attractive in the city than at their countryseat, and frequently moved about following the drift of social festivities.

The Catons used to say that Louisa was more like her father than were any of the others. There was the same tinge of hauteur in face and bearing, the same suggestion of English aloofness, and it is hinted that more than one tropical disturbance occurred in the Caton home, with Louisa at the center of it. But in the early spring of 1807 the young lady was all smiles, especially in the presence of the distinguished Mr. Clark who began to spend more and more time in her presence.

Naturally the girl was flattered. Clark easily outshone the younger gallants of her circle, and the close friendship which had developed between himself and her uncle, Robert Goodloe Harper, gave the former an additional luster in her eyes. Louisa was soon profoundly interested. So for that matter was Polly Caton, her mother, and when the time came for Congress to adjourn in the spring, Clark was on the best of terms with the whole family. Even old Charles Carroll, though no one suspected it, was studying this man who was paying such marked attention to Louisa. The family did not fail to take into account the stories of his immense wealth.

And what of Zulime all this time, while Mr. Clark of New Orleans was attending balls and routs in Washington, Georgetown, and Annapolis? He had promised to write her, and had given her instructions how she might forward and receive letters through his partners in New Orleans. But as the winter wore on his own letters became fewer and shorter—if indeed any were sent. New Orleans was one place; Washington was another. Clark had grown more and more interested in the charming girl of Baltimore and, in a word, Zulime was forgotten. The messages he had promised to send never reached her, and a timid inquiry she is said to have made of Richard Relf concerning a hoped-for message from Clark drew a cold negative. Neither of Clark's confidential partners bore Zulime any good will, as she well knew, and their attitude added distrust to her suspense. As ship after ship came in, day after day passed, and no word reached her from Clark, the distracted Zulime imagined all sorts of possibilities. Her marriage to him had never been made public. Would it ever be? At times her feelings expressed themselves in futile anger; again she was melted with contrition at holding suspicion against the man she loved. But for all that, no letters came. One story has it that at length Zulime poured out all her heart in a long letter to her absent husband and gave it to the men of his firm to forward to him, but that later alien eyes coldly studied the tender missive meant for Clark alone. Or was it sent at all? [8] The possibilities of interference of this sort easily suggest themselves. Zulime could eat her heart out in secret, she could inquire hopefully, but there was "No message." She could imagine anything, and Richard Relf and Beverly Chew let her do so. They had heard something of Clark's social exploits in Washington and were not sorry. Clark's business partners had scant patience with him in the whole affair affecting Zulime, Myra, and all connected. They wished heartily that the head of their firm would forget the DesGrange woman—something that Clark was apparently doing very successfully under the smiles of Louisa Caton.

V

Congress adjourned sine die on the third of March, 1807. Some were going to the Burr trial in Richmond but Clark was going home to New Orleans.

As he paced the deck of the ship which bore him southward, one might have seen a man in the prime of life, rich and powerful and at the pinnacle of success, with future brilliant, a person of note and culture, holding as friends some of the foremost men of the nation. Extraordinary versatility marked him also, for Clark had a mind which could easily turn from the type of tea that might best be marketed in New Orleans to an appraisal of the clothes he should wear to an evening function in Georgetown, from the value of an arpent of Louisiana land to the discernment of motives behind the parties in the Burr embroilment. He understood how to talk to a Spaniard, a Frenchman, or an Englishman in his own tongue and idiom, or he could turn and address one of his ship captains in the language of the forecastle. But with all this rare manifold of personality, "Daniel Clark was in some respects a very peculiar man," as Coxe, his best friend, put it long afterward. Force was governed by a certain restlessness; common sense was strangely mingled with eccentricity; and honor, that for which he would have fought to the death according to his code as a gentleman, was suspended when it came to a beautiful woman. This the world of that day would forgive; certainly New Orleans would scarcely have considered his lapse with a lovely woman as reprehensible. Even the brilliant, exclusive circle in Washington and Baltimore might not have held against the rich Mr. Clark the ever old, ever new transgression of the social law. Society forgives its men. But what the figure on the ship did not then know, could not know, was that while society forgives and God forgives, Nature never does. As Clark slept on the ship bearing him home, had he been able to hear through the sound of the waves at night the cry of a little child, it might have told him something; had the sunlight glinting on the water of the Gulf shown him his own eyes looking back at him from the face of a little girl, he might have learned even more.

The Duel

CLARK was not prepared for the tumultuous welcome that greeted him on his return. The imbecilities and swashbucklering of Wilkinson had angered rather than injured New Orleans, and many who were not his partisans had longed for the presence of the fearless, outspoken Clark. He had scarcely landed when there began to pour into his ears a torrent of excited French giving him the whole story of the recent fiasco.

As soon as possible, Clark hurried to the Davis home to see little Myra. She was just at that interesting age when personality gives a first hint of what its ultimate unfolding will be. The child was strong and vigorous. Perhaps Daniel Clark saw, as did others, that she bore a decided resemblance to him. He was vastly proud and pleased, but something deeper began to assert itself in the heart of the bachelor father. He cared for her more perhaps than he had dreamed. Madame Davis and Harriet Harper were greatly pleased. They, too, loved the child and knew that this man whose wealth was ever increasing, could well afford anything he wished for their little girl. But what would Miss Louisa Caton in faraway Maryland have thought of all this had she been able to observe the visits of her lover to the Davis house?

Clark presumably had some opportunity now to go over his affairs with his partners and to ask about the plantations. These were thriving. The vast purchases of land which he had made at the cession were doubling in value with the increasing immigration to Louisiana. The political situation, however, left him little time for other activities. News of the Burr trial began to filter into New Orleans during the early summer, and the excitement throughout the Southwest was intense. Then Clark got hold of definite information that made clear the actions of Wilkinson.

He learned that as late as 1804 the Marquis of Caso Calvo had given the American general $10,000, no doubt for "services rendered." Clark later said that this "gave him a different view" of Wilkinson.[1] What it actually did was to put together for him all the odds and ends of half-formed suspicions and the many enigmatic actions of the General, and there came back with convincing force the old conversation under the General's marquee in the Natchez woods. Now all was clear. Wilkinson had been *then* and Wilkinson was *now* in the pay of Spain. He had betrayed Burr for Spanish gold, and yet even then was being hailed in Washington as a patriot and was at that very moment the chief witness for the government against Aaron Burr. Clark's wrath rose.

He resolved that he would take Thomas Power, his informant, and proceed to Richmond to accuse General

Wilkinson of treachery. But before anything else could be done, trouble broke upon Clark from another quarter. He was served with a challenge from Governor Claiborne.

II

This was unexpected. Clark was of course familiar with the code duello, and sympathetic with it, if the truth be told, but for Claiborne to challenge *him*—that was astonishing. The pacific governor was not of the truculent type and in fact was known to detest dueling ever since his brother-in-law, Micajah J. Lewis, had been killed on the field of honor. Furthermore, Claiborne, as head of the Territory, was sworn to observe the law, which, in letter at least, forbade dueling. Clark more than suspected that behind it all lay the machinations of other men who had prodded the slower governor to action. But in the meanwhile there was the Claiborne challenge, and while Clark respected neither the governor's intellect nor his ability, he knew that if Claiborne challenged, Claiborne would fight. So much for plodding Saxon earnestness.

It was agreed that the two men should meet outside the Territory, across the Iberville. This would save Claiborne's official reputation as far as the law was concerned. The governor was to set off first in order that suspicion of the event might not be aroused. Clark was to follow later with his second, Richard Reynall Keene, a personal friend.

According to plan, Claiborne left with his party on the third of June, but after his departure a rumor of the impending event leaked out. It became evident that the sheriff would stop the affair if he could, as interested persons of both parties felt that an armed conflict between the two men would be disastrous. Clark learned that he would have to move speedily if he were to avoid arrest. He decided to wait no longer than the next morning and to set off at daybreak. That would give him a few night hours in which to put his affairs in order before he left to face the governor's pistol.

An unusual pause came to this man who until then had swept all before him. The thought presented itself to him with peculiar force: What if this were the end? Suppose his life should be snuffed out by that stupid young governor? Whose then would be his vast landholdings, his business, houses, slaves? His parents were living in Philadelphia, but curiously enough Clark passed them over. The infant at the Davis home took his whole mind. He had already told the Captain and Mrs. Davis that everything he had was to go to Myra, but for the greater part of that June night Daniel Clark sat up putting upon paper the most important measures that he felt should be taken in the event of his death. Whatever happened, the child must be looked after. The gray dawn of Louisiana was breaking over the moss-hung swamps to the eastward before he finished. Then he took horse, not without risk of arrest, and spurred rapidly northward toward Bayou Manchac.

III

One week later Clark was writing to Coxe from his plantation, the Houmas, in Ascension Parish:

"My Dear Friend—When I wrote you last, I mentioned that I was on the point of setting off for Natchez, and you must naturally conclude that I have had time enough to get there by now. My departure from the city was caused by other reasons than business, and I shall now detail them.

"Governor Claiborne, stung to the quick by the few words I said in Congress respecting his conduct to the militia, and driven to despair by the flattering reception I met with on arrival, since when the most unbounded testimonies of affection have been heaped on me,—thought fit, after some preliminary correspondence, to challenge me. To this step I believe him to have been spurred by one Gurley, Attorney General, who has always hated me for my contemptuous treatment of him, and who preferred the Governor risking his person in a quarrel with me rather than to put his own in danger. We set off, therefore, for Manchac, in order to be out of the Governor's jurisdiction, and, immediately on crossing the Iberville, we fought and decided our quarrel, on Monday, the 8th, at one in the afternoon. The aforesaid Gurley accompanied the Governor as his friend; Mr. Keene, a gentleman of the bar, and an intimate friend, was mine. We fired almost at the same instant, at ten paces, and the Governor fell, shot through the thigh, and with a most severe contusion on the other. I have received no injury. I look upon this business as settled, and will return to Orleans in three or four days. I keep away from it merely to avoid the congratulations and exultation of the public on the occasion. You will, doubtless, have some account of the affair from thence, and, on my return, I will forward you the correspondence which took place previous to it. Wherever I have appeared since then, the inhabitants have mixed with the proofs of a most affectionate attachment, some bitter reproaches that I should have dared to risk a life, which, they think, ought to be reserved for them; and the pain of his wound is not the only smart my unfortunate adversary will suffer under. I have not written a line to Orleans since the affair, but my second will reach the city this morning, and should misrepresentation of facts take place, he will correct it.

"On my return to the city, I shall determine, without delay, what I shall do during the summer, and will advise you. Let my parents know the fortunate result of this business, and that it will end here.

"I have found my plantations in better order than I expected, and with appearances of excellent crops of sugar and cotton. Present my respectful compliments to the ladies." [2]

Poor Claiborne! Forced to nurse a dangerous wound all summer and see his opponent congratulated on all sides. But perhaps the congratulations were not quite so widespread as the exultant Clark fancied. The governor had his friends, and, even more significant, they were increasing with every new American family moving in. Clark definitely belonged to the old order, to the Creole regime, not the American. The city was beginning to show the effect of the increasing immigration in a burst of business prosperity. New faces had appeared; new signs were painted over stores in the city, with a heavier percentage of English names among them. Out to the westward, sugar plantations were being opened in new, rich land, while the old ones were increasing their yield. Certainly those of Daniel Clark were flourishing.

And then suddenly the owner of these plantations

found his summer vacation ended. Aaron Burr had summoned him to his trial in Richmond. The former Vice-President declared in open court that he "expected testimony from New Orleans to prove that both himself and the country had been sold." He referred to Daniel Clark.[3]

These words of Burr alarmed Wilkinson. The General forthwith began to write Clark a series of messages which appear somewhat frantic in view of future developments. But long before the letters were written, Clark had sailed.

IV

Before doing so he and Zulime had a stormy and violent parting. Exactly what were the relations between these two during the exciting summer of 1807 does not appear, but it is certain that the old status was quite strained if not altogether broken. "Interested parties" had overlooked no opportunity to bring about an estrangement between Daniel Clark and this woman to whom he had been bound by such tender ties. "Interested parties" had apparently succeeded. Richard Relf, the inscrutable young partner of Clark, has always been thought to have had a hand in this, and Clark's own actions while in Washington gave a diabolically effective lever for prying the two apart. Stories of his infatuation for Louisa Caton of Baltimore did not fail to reach Zulime and to her jealousy was added the bitter realization that the man she loved continued to put off every suggestion that their marriage be acknowledged. It was intolerable for the proud, discarded beauty, and the gypsy blood finally flamed in Zulime. A violent quarrel was the result. The jealous resentment of the woman,

breaking forth in angry, perhaps almost incoherent,
French, was matched by the deeper scorn and the more
deadly wrath of Clark. In anger they parted, the woman to
weep at home, the man to sail away to be a witness at the
trial of Aaron Burr.

On the long sea voyage an unusual incident occurred.
Clark was traveling, as he usually did, on one of his own
ships, the *Comet,* Captain Dixey in command. It happened that as the *Comet* swung past the Bahama Bank, a
little boatload of sailors was discovered adrift and helpless.
They were taken aboard and proved to be a part of the
crew of the ship *Argo,* bound from New Orleans to Philadelphia. The *Argo* had struck and bilged on the Bahama
Bank, the seamen declared, and the rest of the crew had
taken to the longboat and were thought to be not far away.

Although the *Comet* carried a $100,000 cargo belong-
ing to Clark, and the waters there were exceedingly dangerous, there was no hesitation on the part of the owner.
He at once ordered Captain Dixey to cruise about until he
should find and save the men in the longboat. For four
long days and nights the search was pressed, until at length
on the fourth day the stranded mariners were located on
the Great Isaac Rock. The *Comet* took all aboard and the
men ever after declared that they owed their lives to Daniel
Clark.[4]

V

Richmond, Virginia, in the summer of 1807 was a little
city overrunning with heat, excitement, and visitors. Men
of note mingled with teamsters, and mountaineers from
the western settlements rubbed elbows with the blue

bloods of the eastern cities. On one corner it was reported that a loud-mouthed, swashbucklering man from Tennessee was haranguing the crowd and breathing out all manner of threats against the enemies of Burr. His name was Andrew Jackson.

The grand jury had finally brought in its indictment and Burr's trial for treason began in earnest early in August. This was before Daniel Clark arrived—indeed, the trial was almost over when he got there.

His arrival in Richmond proved a staggering surprise to Wilkinson. The General rushed up to Charles Hay, one of the lawyers for the prosecution: "That man can ruin me," he exclaimed in great agitation.[5]

Clark might have ruined Wilkinson, as the General feared, but nothing developed between them at the trial. Clark was not put upon the stand, because John Marshall ruled that no examination of General Wilkinson's conduct unconnected with his testimony against Colonel Burr could be permitted. Wilkinson said afterward that Clark came to see him while he was in Richmond during the trial and that their relations appeared to be friendly.[6] This may or may not have been true. Clark's fault, now a deeply rooted trait of character, was the old readiness to dissemble. In reality he had lost all patience with Wilkinson.

When the drama in Richmond was ended and Burr was released to continue his wanderings over the earth, Clark made his way northward to Philadelphia, there to stay with Coxe until Congress should open. Incidentally he stopped over at Baltimore.[7]

It is almost certain that Clark did not fail to see Louisa Caton while he was that near her during the autumn of

1807. Perhaps she was then in her father's home at Brook-landwood, and it may have been that Clark rode out amid the autumn foliage then clothing the Green Spring Valley, to bring gifts to the young lady who had come to occupy so much of his thought. During the entire summer he had kept in touch with her by letter. The affair was prospering.

Philadelphia Clark found ringing with his praises for saving the sailors of the *Argo*. Charles Biddle and Henry Pratt, leading citizens, decided that he should be honored by a public dinner. Clark demurred at the praise, saying that he had only done what any other man would have done, but he consented to the dinner. This event was set for late in October and went off in fine fashion. Charles Biddle afterward recalled with pride that his son, William, gave the first toast: "Our distinguished guest: The wreath of honor belongs to him who saves his fellow men." [8]

During his Philadelphia stay Clark presumably had time to visit his parents and to go over business affairs with Coxe. Coxe was an excellent trader and kept an eye on the main chance in business, leaving politics to Clark, but the steadier northern man lacked that intuitive perspicacity even in commercial affairs which his more brilliant partner had to a superlative degree. Just at this time, or a little later, Clark reasoned strongly against Coxe's plans for attempting a wider market in northern Europe. The Napoleonic wars were then devastating almost the whole of that continent, and with American commerce preyed upon by both sides, it was decidedly no time for consigning valuable cargoes there. So thought Clark. Better stick to Louisiana sugar, cotton, and land. But Coxe later decided to disregard this sound advice.

VI

Congress met late in October amid a great stir. Earlier in the year the *Leopard* of the British navy had caught the United States *Chesapeake* off guard, and, although the two nations were supposedly at peace, had poured in a destructive fire and forced the larger American ship to strike its flag. The British had then taken from among the crew four American sailors claimed as British. The nation was yet smarting under the outrage while daily the intense death grapple in Europe brought destruction and expense to neutral shipping. Jefferson was considering his Embargo Act. Many of the men arriving for Congress had come directly from the Burr trial whose details were providing conversation at every crossroads. Altogether the legislative assembly of the nation found quite a situation on its hands when it met, but Daniel Clark was not present at the opening session, nor for six weeks afterward, all this time presumably remaining in Philadelphia. When he arrived early in December, it was to find himself suddenly made the focus for the eyes of the whole country. It happened in this way:

John Randolph of Roanoke, as foreman of the grand jury which indicted Burr, had come to feel great contempt for Wilkinson, and when, as a backwash from the trial at Richmond, a flood of rumors began to come up from the western country concerning the General's liaison with Spain, Randolph listened. When Daniel Clark arrived in December he was immediately approached by the queer but honest character from Virginia, who asked directly what he knew of the General.

Clark on his own account had finally decided to expose

Wilkinson's perfidy. He had made the attempt before to
get a hearing on what he knew but had been brushed aside
by the President—and he felt the slight keenly. He well
knew the danger of attacking a man so firmly entrenched
in executive favor as Wilkinson, unless he had his proof
well in hand. But Clark had taken the precaution to get
certain documents and letters from Thomas Power, as well
as to secure other written evidence which he knew he could
use to support his allegations of treason. Encouraged also
by a message from Robert Goodloe Harper of Baltimore,
who as a leading Federalist was not unmindful of the political consequences of the disclosures,[9] Clark, soon after his
arrival in Washington, put into John Randolph's long, lean
fingers the incriminating documents.

On the last day of the year the virulent Virginian rose
in his place and read the papers Clark had given him—old
dispatches from Gayoso, telling of money sent to Wilkinson, and also Thomas Power's letter and charges, with
much other evidence. Randolph's high-pitched voice carried consternation with it, and he closed by moving that
the President be requested to "cause an inquiry to be instituted into the conduct of Brigadier-General James Wilkinson, commander-in-chief of the armies of the United
States, in relation to his having at any time while in the
service of the United States, corruptly received money
from the government of Spain or its agents." Randolph
further observed that it would be a waste of time to comment on what he had read, but that there was a member of
the body who could give the house "much more full, important and damning evidence."

"I allude," he said, "to the gentleman from the Territory of Orleans (Mr. Clark) whom I now have the pleasure to see in his seat."

But Clark demurred with pretended hesitation. He explained later that if he had replied "off-hand" his allegations would simply pass as another speech. A resolution to compel him to speak was something else, and that John Randolph, who had arranged the whole scene with Clark beforehand, immediately offered. A tremendous debate broke out at once on the Randolph resolution, and it was not until the next week, after much wrangling, that the House formally ordered Clark to make his statement.

It was a rather formal one, subscribed under oath and designed to be presented with other documents to the investigating authorities. It began with Clark's arrival in New Orleans, told of his clerkship in the Spanish treasury, and of his learning there of the American General's pension from the Spanish; then came the conversation he had with Wilkinson under his marquee in Mississippi, when the General had admitted to him that he had himself been in the employ of that country; and finally it centered with great particularity upon the more recent disclosure concerning the Caso Calvo dollars.

Clark's account was clear and strong, though necessarily somewhat involved. It was laid on the desk before the Speaker of the House and caused a tremendous sensation.[10]

VII

Wilkinson, with all his double-dealing, was no coward. The General did not intend to take this attack lying down and, without waiting for Congress to act, promptly demanded that the President appoint a court of inquiry to examine into his official conduct. Then he challenged John Randolph. The latter, who was a noted duelist, refused to meet him, on the ground that he would not demean himself by "fighting with a traitor" on the "field of honor." Upon this, Wilkinson posted Randolph, to the great glee of the Jeffersonians.

However, it is significant that Wilkinson did not challenge Clark, who, while not the dead shot that his friend Samuel White was, was a fair marksman, as Claiborne had found. The Orleanian would certainly not have been afraid to meet the corpulent Wilkinson.

But Clark was challenged in a different way, and by no less a person than the President of the United States. Thomas Jefferson addressed Congress with a presidential message (January 20, 1808) in which he clearly manifested his favor for Wilkinson, and informed the House members that before their resolution had been passed, a committee of inquiry at the request of the General had begun to function. The President then took up the allegations of Clark and furnished Congress with a copy of Clark's old memoir to Pickering describing the commerce on the Mississippi when Wilkinson was a leading trader with the Spaniards. Jefferson suggested that this might throw some light on the alleged receipt of Spanish money by the General, indicating that it was simply a case of commercial trade.[11] The President noticed Clark's statement that he had informed the President of treason in the Southwest, and said that Wilkinson's name was not even mentioned to him by Daniel Clark, whom he styled "at that time (1802) a subject of Spain." Jefferson closed by expressing his desire to assist the House in any further way.

This message left Clark in a decidedly bad light before the whole country. The President, in fact, firmly believed Daniel Clark to be an ally of Burr, and Jefferson's followers throughout the country were soon asserting it. Clark suddenly found himself assailed, his motives impugned, and his influence jeopardized by the ill wind that blew steadily from the White House. He learned what weight a President's displeasure can have even in a democratic country.

End of Romance

THE political tempest now roaring around his head kept Clark from running the social career which he had begun the previous season. It did not, however, interfere with his affair with Louisa Caton, to whom apparently he gave all the spare moments at his disposal. More and more the charming girl of Baltimore had taken his thought, and matters had come to that delightful pass where a mutual understanding existed before actual fixed promises had been exchanged. Zulime had been forgotten. She was out of sight, out of mind, and what Clark thought of the child, Myra, while he was courting Louisa Caton, no one can say. Men were long afterward to ask if Daniel Clark would have courted the daughter of the house of Carroll if he had ever really married Zulime Carrière.

On one occasion during the winter, whether before or after the Wilkinson exposé is uncertain, Clark was in Baltimore visiting Louisa Caton. Upon the evening in question, near the appointed time, he left his hotel and gave crisp orders to his coachman to drive down to the town

house of Charles Carroll of Carrollton. The horses bore the
fashionably attired Clark from his hotel through the quiet
streets of Baltimore down toward the harbor. Had Clark
looked back he might have seen another vehicle following
his at a respectful distance. At length a bridge over a little
stream was crossed and his conveyance stopped near a
great brick house. The man from New Orleans went in
and was lost behind the walls of the hospitable mansion,
then alive with the coming and going of guests.

Meantime the other vehicle came near and was halted
by a soft foreign voice from within giving an order to the
driver. Obediently the man stopped his hackney coach
across and at some distance from the house. Well wrapped
against the winter's chill, a single passenger, with strange
fires contending in her dark eyes, sat motionless, intently
watching the windows and the occasionally opening door.
It was Zulime.[1]

II

Clark had forgotten but Zulime had not. The wounds
made by the bitter quarrel of the summer insisted on heal-
ing in spite of the mistreatment which this woman knew
she had suffered at his hands. Furthermore, concern for
the sacred tie which bound them was insistently present in
her mind. New Orleans did not know of their marriage,
perhaps would never learn of it from his lips, but could she
not herself obtain proofs of that marriage, proofs which, in
spite of all calumniators, she might present to the world?
Why not go back to Philadelphia and secure from the
priest who had performed the ceremony a certificate that
would settle the matter forever for herself and her family?

Perhaps she might even see *him*. Vanity added that if Clark could see her once more, he might forget that fairer, colder beauty of the North. She might yet save him for herself.

So Zulime doubtless reasoned, and not without hope. She was in the full flower of youth, not yet thirty years of age, and men called her surpassingly beautiful. She had conquered before, she would conquer again. To get to Philadelphia became the insistent desire of the distracted woman.

Madame Despau—Sophie—ever the faithful sister, agreed to the plan. So once again the two women took ship and made the long voyage, sailing a second time into the waters of the Delaware. Once more they were visitors in the city of William Penn, where they secured for themselves a modest lodging on Walnut Street with a Mrs. Rowan.

But the sisters met with disappointment in their efforts to locate the priest who had married Zulime and Clark in 1802. They were told that he had gone to Ireland. A further search failed to locate any of the witnesses who had been present at the ceremony. This was disturbing. Zulime and Madame Despau did, however, get in touch with the same Monsieur Gardette who had on their former visit furnished them with information in regard to the Des-Grange marriage. Monsieur Gardette, now a widower, was extremely agreeable, especially to Zulime. He later called upon the ladies several times. The two women, far away from home and alone in the northern city with its alien tongue, were grateful for the suave courtesy of Monsieur

Gardette, and came to depend on him. Then Zulime sent for Daniel Coxe.

The merchant came, rather against his will. He neither liked nor trusted this handsome foreign woman. He knew too much about her, for one thing, and had always resented her relationship to Clark. Coxe himself was a typical, none-too-broad Yankee merchant, rather correct in a hard, exact way. He had little use for Clark's foibles and failings, especially where women were concerned, and did not hesitate to upbraid him for them. Clark always laughed at him and went on in his lordly way.

Coxe answered Zulime's summons and came to see her in Mrs. Rowan's modest boardinghouse. She at once asked him about the truth of the rumors regarding Clark and Miss Caton. The merchant said that he knew these accounts to be true and that Clark did intend to marry the Baltimore heiress.

Zulime did not understand English, but there are moods and symbols that transcend language. She saw by Coxe's icy satisfaction that the rumors concerning Clark's proposed marriage were based on truth and she was deeply disturbed. Concluding the interview, the merchant suggested that she should take legal counsel and later sent a Mr. Smith, an attorney, to offer his services to Zulime. This gentleman had in his possession a letter signed by Clark which purported to be a private admission to Coxe that he was getting ready to propose marriage to Louisa Caton. This letter Smith read to the uncomprehending and frightened woman. Mr. Coxe after this felt that he had done his full duty and gladly washed his hands of the

whole affair. He reported long after that while he was concluding his interview with Zulime, "a Mr. Gardette came
in." So Coxe took his leave.[2]

This then was the end unless she could see Clark and
that Zulime decided to do. As the story has it, she made
the long journey to Baltimore hoping and praying that
sight of her in person would reclaim Clark. But as fate determined, just as she was driven up to the hotel where she
proposed to lodge, she saw Clark himself come out and
spring into a carriage. It was in the early evening and from
his manner and dress she concluded that he was going to
some function of importance. Zulime, for reasons best
known to the feminine mind, at once determined to follow
him without making her presence known. Her order to the
driver of her conveyance was to keep the other vehicle in
sight until it reached a destination. And so it came about
that outside the palatial residence of an old gentleman who
had once fixed his name to the Declaration of Independence, was the woman from New Orleans.

Within was gaiety, wealth, aristocracy, pride—all that
went with the ancestral fortunes and powerful name of the
ancient house whose daughters were then reigning as social
queens. Outside was the discarded Zulime. The bitter
thought was driven home to her as she watched that Daniel
Clark was too far above her now for her to think of him
more—and then suddenly through the window she saw
the well-known figure of the man she loved. On his arm
leaned a beautiful girl looking up at him as Zulime herself
had looked in days gone by. He had eyes only for his companion, and the couple seemed definitely set apart from all
the others.

With the sight the inevitable truth seemed clear to Zulime. She had seen enough and gave orders to her driver to return. There was no use in remaining longer and with a leaden heart she made her toilsome way back to Philadelphia. Clark never learned of her presence in Baltimore.

During the days that followed, one person alone, besides the ever faithful Sophie, seemed to sympathize with Zulime. It is not strange that the omnipresent Monsieur Gardette should soon gain the good will and then the affection of the beautiful, injured woman, still nursing her wounded feelings. Perhaps it was woman's weakness, perhaps it was spite, but the fact remains that in a few weeks Zulime stood in St. Joseph's Church in Philadelphia and *was married to James Gardette.*[3] The record can no doubt be seen there today. Long afterward it was truthfully observed: "When she did that, she forever sealed the calumny of her enemies."

III

Early in 1808 Coxe had received a letter which may have been the very one read to Zulime:

"Washington, 9th February 1808
"My Dear Friend:
I shall set off this evening for Annapolis and shall pass two or three days there. If I find Miss Louisa Caton as favorably inclined toward me as you have hinted, I shall endeavor so to secure her affections as to permit me to offer myself to her, at my return to this country in the course of the ensuing winter. I shall first go home to settle my affairs. On this subject I have never yet spoken to her, and I now

communicate my intentions to you that you may inform
Mrs. Coxe, who will, I hope, as well as yourself, keep the
affair quiet. At my return I shall inform you of the result.

> "Yours affectionately,
> "Daniel Clark" [4]

So Clark had fully determined to marry the daughter of
the house of Carroll. But romance had small place in the
mind of Coxe. A cold question was before the Philadelphia
merchant: What would such a marriage mean to the affairs of their firm? How would it affect his own interests?
This was the chief concern of the business partner. But
within a week came a quick, businesslike dispatch from
Clark:

"My Dear Friend:
"Previous to setting off for Annapolis I informed you of
my intention. I am sorry to have now to mention that not
only has it not been effected, but that the affair is forever
ended. The reasons I will give you when we meet although
they are too trifling in themselves to have caused the effect
produced by them. I beg you to state this to Mrs. Coxe,
and if you are spoken to on the subject, to state that you
have had no knowledge of the affair.

> "Yours sincerely,
> "Daniel Clark" [5]

What had happened? Something assuredly between
the riding forth of the hopeful lover and his subsequent
curt direction that the whole affair be consigned to oblivion. Coxe was forced to wait to learn the details, but the

reader can get them from another source. It was Wilkinson!

The General himself tells quite a story about it in his later memoirs, though he lived and died with no idea what devastation he had spread by a random remark. It seems that he had gone over to Annapolis late in the previous year, even before congressional attention had been called to his conduct. With him were a Dr. Carmichael of Mississippi and a certain minor officer of the army, and the three travelers made quite a stay in the little Maryland capital. While there, Wilkinson had been invited to dine and visit with one whom he terms "a very distinguished and prominent person," in reality, Charles Carroll of Carrollton. In the course of his visit in the Carroll home, apropos of nothing, the old Signer suddenly asked the General if he knew Mr. Daniel Clark of New Orleans.

"Yes," said the General, "I know him very well."

"What is the real truth about his standing and credit?" asked Charles Carroll.

Wilkinson afterward said he thought Clark must be trying to borrow some money from Mr. Carroll and felt it his duty to warn his host. Of the character of the General's motives the reader can be the judge. But he affected a judicial and impartial air and in his deceptively frank way said: "Daniel Clark was left a cotton plantation by his uncle, and with judicious management this ought to bring in about $12,000 a year; but his credit is so low in New Orleans that I myself during the previous month was offered Daniel Clark's note marked down to a discount of one-third."

"A very bad sign," laconically muttered the Signer. In

the room, listening to everything, was Richard Caton.[6]

Thus it came about that when Clark went to the little town on the Severn to ask the hand of Louisa Caton in marriage, he was met by such pointed inquiries as to his personal affairs, and with such thinly disguised suspicion regarding his words, that the ardor of the lover turned at once into the affronted pride of an imperious man of affairs. In truth he was cut to the quick. That he should discover the family of his intended wife so doubtful of his honor as to take the word of James Wilkinson for his present standing was too much. The stipulations which the Catons intimated that they wished as a guarantee of his financial integrity aroused Clark's wrathful scorn, and through the chill of February he made his way back to Washington nursing his wounded pride. The affair was forever ended.

Long afterward when the sting had gone out of the Annapolis affront, Clark is reported to have said that he might have married Louisa Caton if Wilkinson had not "blabbed too much." Perhaps. But "blabbing" was one of Wilkinson's weaknesses, unfortunately for himself as well as others.

IV

By this time Clark was feeling the full force of the tempest he had stirred in denouncing the General in Congress and was not finding the situation pleasant. The Federalists were with him, and Randolph, a hard fighter, was insisting that the matter be sifted, but the hostility of the President and his party was no light thing. The end of the rosy dream concerning Louisa Caton found Clark in the midst of political turmoil, and there are signs that at times he wished himself well out of it. He made sporadic visits to Philadelphia, saw Coxe, saw his parents, and planned with Coxe a better-directed and well-publicized effort to clear his own name before the nation as well as to complete the evidence of the General's duplicity. But when the spring adjournment of Congress came, Clark was glad to get away and sail for home. He was no half-hearted fighter, however, and on the very day of adjournment brought forth several other accusing documents which he laid before the House. John Randolph promptly moved that these be printed as had been Clark's other evidence.[7]

Smilie, a Democrat of Pennsylvania, objected. He was willing for the papers to go to the court of inquiry, but he had "had enough of this business of denunciation."

Randolph called for the yeas and nays, and the motion to print carried 52–30. That day Congress adjourned, and with it ended Daniel Clark's career as a legislator.

Defeated

FROM this time there began a slow ebb in the tide of fortune for Daniel Clark. He had been brilliantly successful, had risen, meteorlike, from an humble clerkship to the most influential position in New Orleans. At every point he had imposed his will, and the towering intellectual and personal strength with which he dominated his own group had made him a noted figure in national circles. But when he landed in his home city in the summer of 1808, he found that an almost imperceptible change had taken place in the public attitude. A newspaper war was raging over his actions in Washington,[1] and its virulence indicated that the forces opposed to him were bolder and stronger. What Clark scarcely realized was that he himself belonged to the old order, to the regime that was passing, and that the ever increasing power of the *Américains* in Orleans was to be at the expense of himself and the party he led. Claiborne, weak as he was, had behind him the vast weight of the great people to the northward. The new settlers were supporting the new order.

During the summer Clark learned the result of the court of inquiry sitting on the case of Wilkinson. The General was cleared with scant ceremony. The President and his party, with the ranking officers of the army, were anxious and determined to see that the slur cast on the loyalty of their commander in chief by the territorial delegate from Orleans should be wiped away. Clark refused to remain behind to press his charges before the army court.[2] He had made his statement to Congress. Now let Congress act for the nation.

The court gravely found that Wilkinson had "sold a great quantity of tobacco to the Spaniards" for which they owed him $10,000. It was the exact amount of the Casa Calvo dollars and neatly took care of that charge. Irony was added by the fact that Clark's own memoir to Pickering of years before had explained that the General was "trading" with the Dons. Jefferson himself had pointed this out to Congress. The argument had a telling effect upon the court of inquiry, and the President had the satisfaction of signing his approval of the court's finding on July fourth. His General was cleared.[3]

II

Clark heard with chagrin the result of the Wilkinson inquiry. He had dropped back into his old life, looking after the plantations, consulting with Relf and Chew, buying more land. But the storm he had roused made its effects felt in various ways, and peace was not to be had. He soon found it advisable to make a more pretentious arrangement of the anti-Wilkinson documents, and in correspondence with Coxe in Philadelphia began to arrange his *Proofs,* as

he was to call them, in an attempt to convince the nation
that he was right. His friends cheered him on. Robert
Goodloe Harper wrote from Baltimore: "All not blinded
with prejudice agree with you." Harper added significantly, "Louisa often gets her aunt to ask whether I have
heard from you, and when I expect to hear."

Harper was one member of the Carroll family who had
been disappointed when the affair between his niece and
Clark was broken off, and now made a series of efforts to
renew it.[4] But Clark proved more wary than before, and
Miss Caton not quite so desirable now that he was back in
his old carefree bachelor life.

Letters came occasionally from Senator Samuel White
also, one almost before he had landed, asking with solicitude whether he had reached New Orleans in safety. The
question was not out of place, for, besides the usual perils
of the deep, British frigates were not proving helpful to
American sea travel in the tense days of the Embargo.
"Had the pleasure of hearing from your sweet but capri-
cious little Miss L——a. She is well. You must hasten
back my friend, and improve these fleeting hours of life,
for they are no-where well spent but in the bosom of love
and beauty." [5]

So wrote a senator of the United States to a fellow congressman in 1808. One wonders what the good Methodist
Bishop Asbury, at whose Cokesbury College young White
had been schooled, would have thought of this letter as a
working philosophy of life. White added: "Bayard is well.
The Embargo is operating gently but firmly. . . . Eight
Federalists have been elected. . . ."

Eight, or two dozen, Federalists might be elected in the

North but as the year passed it became increasingly evident that the one in New Orleans was going to have a battle. In addition to the Wilkinson affair, Clark's uncertain connection with Aaron Burr was telling heavily against him, as it did against all who were ever involved with the late Vice-President. Andrew Jackson found this out a score of years later.

Toward the end of the year Governor Claiborne had the satisfaction of writing James Madison: "One thing is certain—Mr. Clark will not be reelected." [6]

The governor was right. Indeed, Clark withdrew from the contest toward the last, as he saw clearly that the opposition was too much for him. To counter it as best he might he put forward as his candidate Dr. Watkins, at that time mayor of the city. But in spite of Clark's personal influence and the loyal support of the old Creole party, Watkins failed of election, and Julien Poydras became the second delegate of the Territory in Congress.[7]

III

Defeat was unprecedented for Daniel Clark. He had been so self-assertive, so confident and conquering, that failure in his own home city brought a deep bitterness to the proud, high-spirited man. Characteristically he began to lose interest in public affairs except as they touched his own name and fortune. He was not, after all, a professional politician, simply a man of wealth who had taken up politics as a game. Now he turned to other things. He had learned, too, the cruel truth that the huzzas of the populace are always on the side of the victor.

His devoted friends, of course, remained faithful. The Davises, James Pitot (now Judge), Baron Boisfontaine, the fiery Bellechasse, these all believed in him and were proud of his friendship. Bellechasse was such an intense Clark partisan that he refused to work longer with Claiborne and so resigned as Colonel of the First Louisiana Regiment of Militia.[8] The Colonel sent in his resignation with polite expressions of formality and the governor accepted it with equal assurances of "respect and esteem." Bellechasse was admired even by his foes.

As if in compensation for the loss of his seat in Congress, Clark found a deepening interest in the toddling infant down in the Davis home. Little Myra was proving to be a much larger part of his life than he imagined.

Many afternoons found Daniel Clark riding under the moss-covered trees down to "the coast" below the city where two old Spanish houses of a certain Mr. McNeill then stood side by side, like twin sentinels watching the river. In one lived Captain Samuel B. Davis; in the other a young clergyman, Reverend Philander Chase, rector of the recently established Christ Church in the city. Between the two households there was little in common, but the minister often watched the figure of Daniel Clark riding up to the adjoining home, or saw Mrs. Davis or a nurse lead little Myra out to meet the visitor.[9] Clark would pick her up and kiss her, or perhaps put into her hands some pretty present. Such visits were often repeated. The bachelor father found in the little child's affection something he had missed all his wayward life.

Clark gave more attention to business, too, especially to ventures in land. His plantations were doing well, but Jefferson's Embargo was disastrous to all outside trade and was bitterly condemned by every merchant. Clark had always opposed it and in Washington, with the other Federalists, had heaped scorn upon the measure when first proposed. But for all that, the President had it passed. Now the boats were tied up at the levee, and Captain Davis had much less to do as Captain of the Port. There were few ports in 1808.

The land ventures, however, were promising and usually paid well. About this time, General Wade Hampton, who had been stationed on the Louisiana border watching the Spanish forces across in Texas, became interested in the Houmas plantation, and, although Coxe was its real owner, Clark advised and managed a sale. The distinguished Carolinian gave his note for the place, and the transfer was duly recorded.

Another large plantation, the Sligo, and still another, the Desert, were also acquired by the Clark-Coxe partnership. Perhaps some of the slaves put to work on them were surreptitiously furnished by the brothers Laffite down Barataria way, but if so, what of it? New Orleans shrugged its shoulders. The land must be cultivated, and pirate slaves were as black as any.

Thus life for Clark became again what it had been before, something of business, something of pleasure, but not quite so gay and carefree. The past was the past. Zulime had gone, and gone forever. Yet there was little Myra, and life was still before him.

Robert Goodloe Harper wrote again: "We have your elegant present. The medals handsomely framed in our parlor. . . . Betsy has returned yesterday from Philadelphia . . . she and the family are well."

The Marylander was trying desperately to renew the

Clark-Caton alliance, and through Harper's influence the Carrolls once more proved gracious. But the financial stipulations still remained of great weight. Clark toyed with the idea. Then the colder, more canny Coxe in Philadelphia threw the strength of his influence against the match.

"He relinquished it," Coxe drily reported later, "in part, in consequence of my disapprobation of it, and my belief that it might affect both him and me injuriously."

Business was business. So the affair was dropped and letters from Robert Goodloe Harper after a time ceased. Sam White wrote again in his usual rollicking vein, twitting Clark on his inaction: "L——a has it in serious contemplation to take the veil." [10]

But both men knew that the daughter of the house of Carroll would never grace the inside of a convent. She was destined for a greater career, in London and Paris, rather than in New Orleans. And not with Clark.

IV

In 1809 with Coxe's aid, Clark brought out in book form his *Proofs of the Corruption of Gen. James Wilkinson, and of his connexion with Aaron Burr*. The greater part of the book is in the shape of documentary evidence gathered from many sources. Part of it Clark had already laid down before Congress; the rest he had secured from various persons who stated under oath the facts bearing on the case. The language is strong and clear and bears about it that suggestion of sweep and clarity in prose which the educated Englishman always seems to possess. Copies of

the book are to be found today in the older libraries of the
East, but as it was a polemic for the time, it perished with
the situation that called it forth. The volume, after all,
does not seem to have caused much comment in the nation,
though it was in large part the reason why Wilkinson was
forced to stand a regular court-martial two years later.

After the *Proofs* were published, Clark began to draw
further and further aloof from national and state politics.
He gave himself more to business and friends, and more
and more to little Myra. To the small girl, the bachelor
father became the most indulgent of parents. He ordered
from Philadelphia a little coachee which must have been
the admiration of other children and gave this to her when
she was old enough to ride; he had a Choctaw pony
purchased for her and continued his almost daily rides
down the coast to see the child. Politics became less and
less important and Myra more so. The restless, ungov-
erned man had at last found an object in life. It was something he had always lacked.

So the days passed. A new president came to power,
but Clark was no longer greatly interested. His opponent,
Claiborne, in one of his gossipy dispatches told the
government with righteous satisfaction that the "influence
of Mr. Clark is about at an end." But uneasy lies the head
that governs a Territory. The brothers Laffite on Barataria
Bay were becoming a sharper thorn in Claiborne's side as
the more direct Clark became quiescent.

Business, too, absorbed the former congressman's
thought. About this time he laid out a great tract of land
behind the city toward the Bayou St. Jean, and began to
sell blocks of it in a modern real-estate manner. The city

was growing and with the end of the Embargo had come renewed trade. The flatboats were still coming, but so also were barges and packet boats and vessels of considerable size from near and far, with new settlers continually arriving. Altogether the St. Jean property appeared a promising development. Clark himself made plans to build an elegant mansion out toward the Bayou.

Until then he had lived in the city spending much of his time with one or the other of his partners, as he seems to have closed his former establishment during his congressional term. He now had a regular room at the Richard Relf residence and took meals there whenever he pleased. The Relfs, and later the Chews, considered him one of the family and admired him tremendously. The men certainly must have known of little Myra and, while they did not approve of Madame DesGrange, looked with more favor upon her pretty child. Richard Relf long afterward recalled that he had enjoyed fondling the little girl.

In 1810 Beverly Chew came in by ship from Virginia, bringing his sister, Miss Caroline Chew, and a niece, Julia Brockle, both quite young and pretty. The girls were to go to school in New Orleans and learn French, as accomplished young ladies of that era were supposed to do. The Chews as well as Clark all stayed in the Relf home for a time; then Relf married and took another place, while the Chews continued to reside in the Relf house. Clark kept his room there also. He liked the society of the girls —they were mere children to him; but it was a home, and a home was something Daniel Clark had never had.

The comparative ease of this life was suddenly broken by disastrous news from Coxe. Clark had warned his

Philadelphia partner against speculation in northern
Europe. Now his advice was seen to be only too good.
Coxe was forced to report heavy losses and urged Clark to
collect at once from General Wade Hampton, who had
bought the Houmas. Hampton in turn was suffering
financial reverses and asked time to meet the obligation
Coxe held against him; Coxe wrote frantically to Clark
to see Hampton, to do something, anything, to save his
credit. The New Orleans man was himself greatly worried
for fear that Coxe's losses had also involved him ruinously
and so decided to sail for Philadelphia and draw up a final
settlement of their joint affairs. In his rapid way, Clark
made preparations to leave for the North.

His own fortunes were somewhat involved, though
Clark knew that in Louisiana, at least, his great investments and holdings were, or eventually would be, of
enormous value. Relf and Chew he might trust to look
after these. But as a three weeks' voyage in that day was
always hazardous, he felt that he should leave a formal
will, or at least a memorandum drawn up in case of any
mishap. He had great property; he had parents living; he
had partners; he had Myra.

The small child with her piquant face had now become
precious beyond measure to Daniel Clark. He loved her,
but he had never publicly acknowledged her. How could
he? She was the daughter of a woman who had never been
officially divorced from another man, a woman whom he
had never claimed as his wife, a woman now married to
another man; and when the proud Clark thought of the
scornful laughter of the coffeehouses and sarcastic grimaces
of old Creole acquaintances, he saw how hopeless a toil

this made. He could imagine the ribaldry of a city which would never believe him in earnest or, if it really believed he had married Zulime, would despise him for permitting another man to have her as wife. His pride and reputation could never survive it.

But there was another side, a less selfish one. Think of little Myra herself, a fresh-faced innocent to grow up with the smirk of New Orleans at her back whenever she passed —that is, if he should declare publicly that she was his child. It was too great a price to pay. He must make it up to her in some less public way. He would go to see Edward Livingston, who was to write the Louisiana Code later adopted; and he would see Etienne Mazureau.

We have no record of Clark's conversation with Edward Livingston, but he certainly called on Mazureau, one of the foremost Creole lawyers of the city. Before the swarthy attorney Clark laid his whole problem, except that he made no mention of a marriage. The irascible Mazureau was somewhat impatient with Clark and told him plainly that he, Clark, knew the law himself, and certainly knew that the Code did not permit an illegitimate child to inherit any part of a father's estate, even by will. It simply could not be done in Louisiana.

What then could be done?

This: If he had any trusted friends to whom he might leave property in trust for the little girl, do it, and these friends could then protect and hold this property until such time as the child came of age. They could then give it to her themselves. That was the only way.

"That I'll do," exclaimed Clark and left.[11]

Colonel Bellechasse was certainly a "trusted friend,"

and so the Colonel suddenly found himself besought to receive from Clark a number of lots in the new St. Jean settlement, all to be kept in faith and trust for little Myra. The Colonel, for Clark's sake, agreed. But real estate was not enough. Clark also saw Captain Samuel B. Davis and put into his hands some money for Myra's use to be held strictly for her. All was done in confidence. None knew of the secret conveyances Clark thus made. Secretly he had done wrong; secretly he would do right.

With Relf and Chew, Clark left a short but very formal document drawn up in the form of a will leaving everything to his mother, Mrs. Mary Clark, and appointing Richard Relf and Beverly Chew his executors. Then he sailed.

The next day he wrote Davis for a last time from the Balize. He seems to have had some sort of presentiment concerning that voyage and wished to emphasize to the end his private wishes concerning Myra. He repeated his instructions to the Captain, and then pursued his way with an easier heart. In due time he arrived in Philadelphia.

There he stayed with Coxe and after a short visit agreed with him upon a final dissolution of their partnership. The terms of the agreement were somewhat involved and need not concern the reader here, save that the partnership was amicably ended. Coxe was no longer to be formally associated with Chew & Relf. All was done by consent and to mutual satisfaction and the partners separated with affection unbroken.

The Will

IN SPITE of the fears that made Daniel Clark set his affairs in order before he sailed for the North, he landed again on the familiar levee in his home city without mishap. No summer hurricane out of the Caribbean, no British cruiser, blocked his return. The time and worry over the disposal of his property had been wasted after all.

Colonel Bellechasse, who had not been overanxious to be the custodian of the property which Clark had made over to him for Myra, came to him soon after his arrival and insisted on giving back the lots now that the owner was home safe and sound. But Clark refused, telling the Colonel to continue to keep the land for Myra as he had directed. Bellechasse said no more about it, and the matter was apparently forgotten. The Colonel was proud that he enjoyed the implicit trust of Clark.

The Philadelphia agreement with Coxe eventually forced a change in the house of Chew & Relf in New Orleans. It was through Clark personally that the two firms had all along held together. Clark was becoming more and more anxious to drop out of active participation

in business, preferring leisure to enjoy his wealth rather
than the continual struggle to add to it. His younger
partners, Richard Relf and Beverly Chew, were ready for
anything but retirement, quite at home in the faster pace
which business was setting in Louisiana since the American advent. Soon after Clark's return, therefore, the three
men met and drew up a private agreement. This meeting
seems to have been stormy—Clark against the two—but
at length a compromise was reached. It was agreed that
as soon as possible the concern, which the three of them
had carried on under the name of Chew & Relf, should be
liquidated. It turned out that liquidation was not possible
for two whole years, but the terms which they agreed upon
in 1811 were carried out when 1813 rolled around.[1]

Somewhat before this time Clark had secured a
magnificently situated plantation called Cannes Brulées,
about seven leagues above the city on the left bank of the
river. Clark turned this area into a splendid estate, furnishing the house in palatial style, enlarging the slave quarters,
and providing for the various needs of an up-to-date
plantation.[2] In charge of it, he put his good friend and
confidant, Pierre Baron Boisfontaine, who had for some
time been looking after the Sligo, the Desert, and the
Havana Point, other estates of Clark. Some called Boisfontaine an "overseer," but Clark, recognizing the culture
and breeding of "the Baron," as he called him, not only
received him as an equal but took him into other homes of
prominence—to Judge Pitot's for instance, where they
dined quite often on Sundays. It will be remembered that
Boisfontaine was the brother of Mrs. Davis, nee Rose
Boisfontaine.

About this time Clark also completed a residence designed for his own use and situated on the Bayou St. Jean. By all accounts this mansion was an elegantly appointed one. Built of brick, the house contained on the first floor a great hall or *grande salle,* as it was called, with two other large rooms and two fireplaces—something worthy of comment. Running across the whole front was the inevitable porch or gallery. Upstairs were the living rooms and bedrooms, perfectly equipped in their private arrangements. But it was the library that became the special pride of the owner.[3] Ancient classics in the original sat side by side with French novels, while the works of many a writer in that famous galaxy of eighteenth-century English men of letters graced the shelves of the New Orleans home. The student of Eton had not forgotten the lessons of his youth. One is amazed today to glance over the list of books which Daniel Clark had in those early days. With the necessary house servants to look after the place and the capable and omnipresent Lubin ordering them about in soft but authoritative "gumbo," the lord of this manor on the Bayou Road might well feel that he now could receive his friends in a manner agreeable to his wealth and position.

II

Taking up residence in this house, Clark withdrew more and more from civic and business affairs. The old restlessness and wanderlust had somewhat quieted and, although he was in the prime of life, there seems to have been shadowing him an intangible atmosphere of foreboding not at all congruent with his energetic and vivacious disposition. His pride had felt keenly the loss of public favor after the Wilkinson incident, and business, as has been indicated, had lost its savor, but there was something else. He was realizing more and more the toils into which he had placed little Myra. Daniel Clark, who was considered the soul of honor in all other particulars, began to see that after all there was something more to honor than fighting duels and keeping a gentleman's word. There was such a thing as the rights of a child, little as he had realized it before, a child, too, whom he loved profoundly.

He was now leading a strange life as we view it long afterward. The Beverly Chews came out to spend the summer with him in his new house, and of course charming Miss Caroline was along.[4] The big front gallery during the long evenings, when the mosquitoes were not too active, would doubtless hear the conversation and laughter of the owner and his guests, but these guests seem to have been unconscious of the deeper interest of the man who was their host. Perhaps they knew of little Myra, certainly Beverly Chew did, but it never seems to have dawned upon these associates that the Daniel Clark whose strength of character they so much admired, might be centering all the force of his powerful personality upon that one child. To them, the women as well as the men, such lapses as Myra represented were but a part of New Orleans life. The Creole city forgave its sons and overlooked their easy morality, relying for its social integrity not upon masculine virtue but upon the iron law of its Latin Code which visited the sins of the fathers mercilessly upon the children. Had it not been for the bar, sinister yet effective, which the Latins set up against illegitimacy, the quadroon caste, represented by women of great beauty, would long ago have taken the city. While the slower-witted Nordics were endeavoring to make the tree good that the fruit should be good also, the Latins ignored the parent and punished the child. But, *pouf!*—young men will be young men. What would you?

So Daniel Clark might have reasoned once. But the time had long gone since a newborn child was left to cry in a vacant house near the Esplanade. The face of little Myra was now preaching with a dreadful innocency what no Code had the power to express. Then she had been but a troublesome event in the life of a lovely woman to whom perforce he owed something out of common decency; now she was blood of his blood and bone of his bone. The Chews and the Relfs may have known something of all this, knew indeed some very intimate things about him, but they did not know everything.

There is a story that at some time during these later years, Zulime, now Madame Gardette of Philadelphia, returned to New Orleans for a brief season and paid a visit to her sisters. In spite of a none too cordial reception at the Davis home, she went there, perhaps several times, to see her child. It was upon one of these occasions while watching Myra romping about in the shrubbery, that Daniel Clark, so they say, suddenly appeared. The two were again brought face to face.[5] Time had done its work with both, and after the first start of surprise they began to speak quietly in the presence of their child. Both realized that they could not and should not meet again, and that there were things to be said then or not at all. So Zulime let Clark know of the letters which never arrived, of the carefully calculated messages she had received from sources hostile to herself, of the plans which had been carried out only too well to effect their separation. Clark saw all and divined even more. Soon they parted, forever, as both well knew. But from that moment Daniel Clark changed toward Richard Relf.

The time had now come for a more difficult parting. Samuel B. Davis was making plans to leave New Orleans and return to his native Delaware shores. He had by this time acquired interests in Philadelphia and in Lewes, Delaware, and furthermore the war clouds of the fast-approaching conflict with Great Britain were beginning to lower threateningly as 1812 opened. Captain Davis, ex-privateersman, smelled the battle from afar. He hated the English with a deadly and personal hatred. He had spent a considerable part of his life fighting them and was ready to do so again at any time, especially at the call of his country. He planned to return to Philadelphia, taking his family along, and, if war came on, to offer his services to the United States.

Captain Davis had much for which to thank Daniel Clark, both as patron and friend, but a coolness had slowly grown between the two men. This was partly caused by their opposing political views. Clark with un-measured regret saw the second war with England coming on, brought about, he firmly believed, by continual mismanagement at Washington. He was a Federalist still, in spite of his apparent political quiescence, and with his party in the North was hoping mightily to avert this war. Furthermore, with valuable cargoes at sea which he would surely lose if the British cruisers were unloosed on them, he

knew that he would become an actual sufferer. Last but
not least, he was Irish born, and English bred, and after
all, the Britons were his own people. It is small wonder
that as the national crisis during the spring of 1812
brought war, Daniel Clark expressed himself with great
bitterness, and between himself and the Anglophobe
Davis there came about strained relations.

There was a further cause for difference between the
two men—Myra. As the Davis family made preparations
to leave for the North, the Captain, a kindly if explosive
type, approached Clark concerning the little girl, now six
years of age. Davis and his whole family had come to
love the child, and her foster father told Clark plainly that
he ought to acknowledge Myra openly and keep her in
New Orleans with him.[6] To this Clark responded that he
would be delighted to keep her but could not possibly give
her his name. She might have everything else, but he
simply could not make the acknowledgment. He would
do anything for her, but not that.

Davis, blunt as always, refused to let Myra go from
under his roof if she were to be treated in that way. Forthwith the Captain informed his family that Myra was to
sail with them and to continue to be one of them. The
Captain remained firm in his intention, to the unmeasured
joy of Mrs. Davis.

Daniel Clark now went through a fearful inner
struggle, but pride won again. Living as he did in his new
home, surrounded by the families of his partners. with
associates of wealth and education, he persuaded himself
that it was better to let Myra go into a home where she was
loved and where he knew she would be properly cared for,

than to expose her to the certain gibes of New Orleans and to the uncertainty of a future with him. But there was selfishness in this also. Always weak before woman's beauty, he was paying marked attention now to Caroline Chew, the sister of his partner, and to another New Orleans lady also, it was rumored. He loved his daughter, but pride was stronger than affection.

According to plan, Mrs. Davis was to sail first with Myra, and the Captain was to come on later in the year. Clark did nothing to prevent them. So on a day early in 1812, Madame Davis took Myra to the levee and then onto a ship making ready to drop down the river. Myra Clark was then allowed to float down the mighty Mississippi, away from her father and his riches, away from her native soil, away from the inheritance that might have been.

And Daniel Clark let her go.

Death on the Bayou Road

WAR broke, complicating everything. Captain Samuel B. Davis followed Mrs. Davis and Myra and, after a few weeks, offered his services to the government. He was soon drilling Delaware militiamen, as Colonel of the 32d Infantry, U. S. Army.[1] Myra and Mrs. Davis had landed at Baltimore but after a time went to Lewes, Delaware.

In the city on the Mississippi Daniel Clark continued to live in his handsome new house, to entertain friends, and to move about in that small group which he had come to prefer to the wider social life of the years gone. Colonel Bellechasse he had always liked, and the years had deepened the affection between them; Judge James Pitot was another intimate. Clark was often at Pitot's home, which was not far from his own. The Chevalier Delacroix, a gentleman of taste and culture, was also much in company with Clark. He it was whom Claiborne had asked Jefferson *not* to appoint to the Orleans legislative council, because he was a "partisan of Mr. Clark."

But to Pierre Boisfontaine, Clark came to be drawn by

even stronger ties as the months passed. The two men spent hours together, sometimes out at Cannes Brulées where Boisfontaine was manager, sometimes at Clark's own house. It was to Boisfontaine alone that Clark finally admitted the marriage with Zulime. He not only admitted it but went so far as to express regret that the affair had been broken. Clark confessed that he himself would long ago have acknowledged the marriage with Zulime but for her action in marrying Gardette. That made a "barrier," so he called it, which effectually prevented any acknowledgment on his part. Boisfontaine heard and remembered.

More and more as the months lengthened after little Myra had gone, Clark felt that he had not dealt fairly with her. The absent child occupied a larger part of his thought than he had ever dreamed would be the case. When his vast property holdings came to mind and he took account of what the years might bring, the idea came to him that through his wealth he might be able to do what he could not do by open acknowledgment. The project of a will took shape in his mind, a testament which would secure for the child all her rights and at the same time efface the stain he had placed upon her birth. He had heard Livingston and Mazureau upon the provisions of the Code as respected illegitimate children, but Daniel Clark, too, knew something of the civil law and something about Myra which he not told these men. He planned to make a will that should be her charter and warrant for a new, unshadowed life. He told Colonel Bellechasse that if he could but live to bring Myra up, it would be the greatest blessing under God that could be given to him.

Outwardly life went on as usual. Clark was said to be

paying court to Miss Caroline Chew (she certainly thought so), while others believed that he was engaged to a handsome Creole divorcee who lived just outside the city. But to Mrs. Harriet Harper, who had always had his confidence ever since she nursed Myra, he said positively that he "never would give Myra a step-mother." The city might think what it pleased; only Daniel Clark knew Daniel Clark. The truth is, he had become so used to leading a manifold career, that one feels he is dealing with two. or even three separate individuals, when tracing Clark's history.

For instance, there was the Daniel Clark who had his room at the Chews, who entertained them at his house, who joked with Miss Caroline, who drove his cabriolet to Madame Florian's school to bring Julia Brockle home for week ends; the Clark who was the partner of Relf and Chew; the old enemy of Claiborne; the former congressman; the rich owner of the Houmas, the Sligo, the Desert. the Havana Point plantations; the master of many ships and slaves; the courtly bachelor and man about town of old New Orleans. And on the other hand there was Daniel Clark, the thoughtful father of a little girl in the North; the confidant of another group of friends, including that child's foster mother; the intimate of a former Spanish Colonel, of an overseer on his place. How did he keep these existences apart, as he went to and fro among all these individuals, each of whom was ready to swear to the day of his death that Daniel Clark was the "soul of honor"? Or did he keep them apart?

Certainly he told Mrs. Harper the particulars concerning the will he intended to make and talked often with her of plans for Myra's future. He wanted his child educated as befitted her station and had decided that France would provide the proper atmosphere and school for that purpose. Meanwhile, his good friend, the Chevalier Delacroix, had consented to act as her tutor and promised to oversee her education when she grew beyond him. So the wealthy, careful father planned, and after a time, somewhere about the spring of 1813, he reported to Mrs. Harper that he had begun making his will.

The Chews left for the North early in the summer of that year, and Miss Caroline and Julia Brockle went with them. Madame Florian had taught Julia something of the ways of French mademoiselles, and the sisters in the convent had given Miss Caroline the correct accent for her French. Now they were going back to Virginia. The days and summer evenings at Clark's home had been pleasant for all, and he felt the tug of parting when it came.

The day the young ladies sailed, he was at the boat with cards, books, and flowers. He himself had been planning a trip to the North, which they had talked over many times, and Clark's last word to Caroline Chew reminded her of that fact.

"God bless you!" he exclaimed, remaining by her side until the vessel had actually cast off. "I hope to see you soon in Virginia."

So another friend departed. But was it the fourteen-year-old Caroline Chew or the six-year-old Myra who was furnishing the motive for Clark's anticipated voyage northward?

II

All during the early summer of 1813 Daniel Clark continually employed himself in writing his will. He planned that it should be olographic, that is, done in his own handwriting, and his small slanting script soon began to fill page after page. After the Chews had gone, Richard Relf came out to stay with him in his house on the Bayou but, although the relationship between the two men was apparently cordial in the extreme, and yet Clark in making his will begged his executors, Judge Pitot, Colonel Bellechasse, and the Chevalier Delacroix, *to say nothing of it to Richard Relf*. He had secured the consent of these three gentlemen to act as executors, and knew them to be persons of consequence who would carry out its provisions in case of his death; but for reasons known only to himself, he begged of them to keep its existence to themselves. His friends promised and, as they were gentlemen of honor, he relied upon them.

Pierre Boisfontaine, "Monsieur le Baron," as they called him, was also aware of the will. Occasionally when they were riding up toward Cannes Brulées or over the great plantation, Clark would speak of the progress he was making on it and regretfully mention the past. Boisfontaine listened, respecting the confidence of this man who was more than an employer to him.

So the midsummer of 1813 came on, the hot, humid summer of the lower Mississippi. Daniel Clark was apparently in the best of health, planning that visit to

Virginia and the North, but all the while continuing to work on the will.

There is something of pathos in the spectacle of this strong man whose life had lost itself in shallows when it should be at flood, now at the last attempting to set for himself a course which he should have steered from the first. He was yet in the prime of life, in his forties, with wealth, huge estates, slaves, friends, admiration, and luxuries. But as Daniel Clark set his house in order in 1813 against he knew not what, there is undeniably something of failure, of shortage, about the man, more of a psychic flaw than anything belonging to the ounces, pounds, or plantations in which he dealt. As has been the case with other men who have succeeded too rapidly, a certain savor had gone out of life for Clark by reason of his early victories. These had come naturally and inevitably. Then when failure struck him in the withdrawal of public confidence after the Wilkinson episode and the onslaught of the President, he took refuge behind a high pride and scorn. He had tasted popularity, then lost it, and found the loss not unbearable. Rather than the uncertainties of popular favor he preferred the fiery loyalty of Colonel Bellechasse, the quiet of a visit at Judge Pitot's, or the fellowship of the Baron as they rode down from Cannes Brulées after a day on the plantation. What, after all, was the approval of the Jeffersons or Claibornes, or of the rabble they led?

The war gave him something else to talk about. It had now begun to affect the city through the shutting off of its shipping, and there were rumors of a great British armada to be launched at the Gulf Coast. Clark continued to rail

against the insanity of the government and the senseless-
ness of the conflict, but his mind was not on these things.
He was devoting himself to the paper he was writing, list-
ing all his property, his slaves, his plantations and financial
dealings so that he might secure everything to the child
far away. He knew now that he had wronged Myra and
wronged her deeply, but vowed to God he would atone.
The pride that had never given way before the hostility of
Presidents or governors or generals, which had met on its
own terms the house of Carroll in Maryland, was now dis-
solving before the love of a little girl. The city might say
what it pleased; he would do right—and in this he found
a partial redemption.

One day in July, Clark strode into the house of Mrs.
Harper in his impetuous way and seeing her cried: "My
will is finished!"

In his hand he held a bulky document. Mrs. Harper
took it, but, as she was pressed for time, Clark agreed to
leave the paper with her until the next day. She then read
through the whole thing, noting that Mrs. Mary Clark,
his mother, was remembered with an annuity; that a five-
thousand-dollar bequest was to go to the son of Judge
Pitot; that Lubin, the faithful black body servant, was to
be given his freedom; and that many other persons were
mentioned; but the whole estate was to be Myra's save for
minor exceptions. The executors were the three persons
Clark had named.

Some days after this, the Chevalier Delacroix and
Boisfontaine happened to be at Clark's home. They were
all sitting in a sort of small office room or perhaps a part of
the library downstairs, when Clark suddenly reached over

and opened with a small key a little black case. From this he drew a sealed packet, and handed it to the Chevalier Delacroix saying, "My last will is finished."

Delacroix looked at the paper packet curiously. On the outside written in Clark's hand was, *"Pour ouvert être en cas de mort."*

"It is in this sealed packet with other valuable papers," continued the owner of the house. "As you consented, I made you in it tutor to my daughter. If any misfortune happens to me, will you do for her all you promised me?"

The Chevalier agreed. Clark replaced the papers in the small ebony case and locked it with a little key, one of a bundle of keys which he kept on his person.

III

With the completion of the will, a strange sense of finality seems to have come over its maker. There was no special reason for him to have been so interested in outlining a final settlement at this time. He was in middle life and should have looked forward to many years of vigorous existence. Men of his age usually do. But driven by an inner urge, he found no rest until he had completed the will. Strange to say, when that was done, a vital chord seems to have snapped somewhere within Daniel Clark; some inner nexus between himself and the world had been destroyed, and he may have realized beforehand what others never dreamed, that soon, for him, ships and slaves and plantations would have no meaning. Whether the completion of the will assisted in bringing this about or not we do not know. What is certain is that a very few days after the scene in the little office, Daniel Clark lay desperately ill in an upstairs room of his house on the Bayou Road.

Richard Relf, that enigmatic young partner of his, took charge and summoned a physician, but it became evident as the hours passed that Daniel Clark was a very sick man. Boisfontaine came in from Cannes Brulées to see him on business, and, to his surprise, Clark admitted that he felt very ill.

Boisfontaine wished to know if Clark wanted him to remain with him.

The sick man signified assent, so the Baron rode rapidly out to the plantation, hastily arranged affairs there, and came back into the city on the same day to take his place by his friend's side.

Colonel Bellechasse, totally ignorant of the illness of Clark, accidentally dropped in to see him a day or so after this and was astonished by Relf's statement that Clark was too ill to receive him. The doughty Colonel, whether suspicious of Relf or anxious to see for himself, strode straight upstairs and into the room where his friend lay.

He found Clark very ill indeed, but, with a shadow of his old spirit, the sick man roused at the entrance of his faithful friend.

"How is it, Bellechasse, that you have not come to see me before since my sickness? I told Relf to send for you."

Bellechasse, surprised, replied that he had received no message at all from anyone in Clark's house and added: "My friend, you know that on various occasions I have been your physician, and on this occasion I wish to be so again."

Clark merely gazed at him and pressed his hand. The Colonel was afraid that his presence might not improve the prospects of the patient and so withdrew. Finding Richard Relf he offered to remain in the house to attend Clark and be of further service. Relf replied briefly that there was no occasion for his so doing. The doctor had given orders that his patient was to be kept quiet and allowed to talk to no one.

Bellechasse expressed fears for his friend's safety, but the younger man took a more hopeful view. As he promised to send for the Colonel should any turn for the worse come, Bellechasse went on to his home.

He had seen Daniel Clark for the last time.

That very afternoon the final scene in the life of this strange man of old New Orleans was being enacted. Under the blazing summer sun the rich merchant was breathing his life away in the magnificent house which he had built for his own comfort. As the hot midafternoon wore on, Boisfontaine and the others about him realized that the end was fast approaching. Then, as the moments ticked by, the real interest of Daniel Clark, the man who had played so many different parts, came to the surface, and he cried out for Myra. Forgotten was wealth, business, scenes of fame and conquest: he thought only of his child. Solemnly he charged Pierre Boisfontaine that he wished above everything that his last will should be taken to the Chevalier Delacroix as soon as he was gone. Then he called for Lubin.

The black slave had come to mean something more than a well-trained servant to the man who lay dying. Lubin had been faithful to his master through the years and had come to love him with the unquestioning fealty which his kind often bore to those who were merciful to them. Between master and man there was something almost of affection. Obediently the servant moved to the bedside of the man who owned him, and waited for a last command. With an intense finality Daniel Clark told Lubin that he must, as soon as he was dead, take the little black case over to the Chevalier Delacroix. The slave signified assent and after that Clark seemed content.

Life was now fast slipping away in that upper room. But before Daniel Clark died, there began to take place in the house on the Bayou Road a mysterious series of happenings which were to provide speculation for the entire American nation in days to come.

Boisfontaine, sitting by the bedside, afterward said that he saw Richard Relf take "a bundle of keys" from an armoire in the room where Clark lay and, carrying the keys, descend the stairs. One of these keys, Boisfontaine knew, unlocked the little black case. The Baron remained by his friend's side, but Lubin, who had seen the action of Relf, followed him downstairs as though upon other business. The Negro saw Relf go into the office room, heard him turn and lock the door behind him. The slave crept nearer to listen and, as he furtively took his position outside the office door, heard somewhere within the sound of the *rustling of papers.*

Boisfontaine came down later and saw the closed office room door. He did not know that it was locked.

Upstairs Daniel Clark had ceased to breathe. It was the thirteenth of August, 1813, about five o'clock in the afternoon.

Mist on the River

As Daniel Clark was known to possess great wealth, Monsieur Preval, an officer of the law, came out as soon as he learned of Clark's death, in order that he might affix the procès-verbal in accordance with the Code. This was a very important step always. It consisted in making an inventory of effects and of sealing and securing papers, with such testamentary evidence as might be found. In the case of Daniel Clark it was doubly important. Richard Relf himself recognized that fact and sent for Monsieur Preval within a few minutes after his partner's death.

The notary was at the Clark mansion before the sun was down [1] and made a hasty examination of the boxes, papers, etc., instituting a search for evidence of the will which the late owner was supposed to have made. He had made rather a careful examination without finding any evidence of such and was getting ready to leave when Richard Relf came in and gave Notary Preval a packet which he said was marked as Mr. Clark's will. It so proved to be, and Preval, after glancing at it hastily, put it under seal and departed. The will was short and *bore upon its face the date of 1811*. Mr. Relf's plans were apparently working very well.

The news of the death of Daniel Clark spread rapidly, but not until the next day did Colonel Bellechasse learn of it. When he did, the stanch Colonel was much hurt that he had received no previous message informing him of the demise of his friend. Bellechasse went hastily to the Clark house but did not tarry, pressing on to the residence of Judge Pitot near by. There he found the Judge also grieved at the death of Clark and irate at the treatment he felt he had received in having been kept in ignorance of his late friend's condition. The Judge regretfully declared that if some of Clark's friends had been present, they might have prevented the "fraudulent suppression" of his last will.

"What!" exclaimed the Colonel. "Has Clark's last will disappeared?"

"Yes, my friend. It was not in the case in which he had placed it, and the short and provisional will of a dozen lines, which he had previously made when sailing for the north has been brought forward by Relf." [2]

Both men were concerned even during the preparations then in making for the funeral. These ceremonies proved to be in keeping with the station which Clark had occupied in the life of the city and state. Full justice to his pride and position was done. Governor Claiborne, his old opponent, let death settle their long feud and came in person to do honor to the man whose bullet had once nearly ended his own life. To Bellechasse's disgust, the Colonel found himself assigned to a place in the cortege side by side with

Claiborne.³ This was Relf's doing, as Bellechasse well knew, and he held it as another count against the man who had so completely taken over his late friend's affairs. The procession filed into the old St. Louis cemetery, and in one of the vaults of that silent city of the dead the body of Daniel Clark was placed at rest.

On their return from the ceremonies incident to the interment certain of the gentlemen taking part came back to the Bayou Road mansion. There Bellechasse, with Judge Pitot and others, brought up again the strange disappearance of the will which they knew Clark had made.

"Gentlemen," exclaimed the Colonel, "this mysterious occurrence surprises and afflicts me." He went on to tell how, before the making of the apparently lost will, he had received from Clark certain lots which he was to hold for Myra and how Clark would never let them be reconveyed. But talk as they might, there was apparently no will but the one Richard Relf had produced. The Chevalier Delacroix, however, who was to have been the tutor of little Myra under the new will, decided that he would make a try at getting something more tangible if possible. Realizing that there was a slight chance that Clark had made a duplicate of his lost will, Delacroix went before Judge Pitot himself, then in charge of matters of Probate, and entered this petition. It can be found in the records today:

"To the honorable, the judge of the court of probates of the parish of New Orleans.

"The petition of Frances Desuau Delacroix, of this parish, planter, respectfully showeth that your petitioner has strong reasons to believe, and does verily believe, that the late Daniel Clark made a posterior will to that which has been open before your honorable court, and in the dispositions thereof he thinks to be interested.

"And whereas it is to be presumed that the double of the last will, whose existence was known by several persons, might have been deposited with any notary public of the city, your petitioner therefore prays that it may please your honor to order, as is the usual practice in such cases, that every notary public of the city appear before your honorable court within the delay of twenty-four hours, in order to certify on oath if there does or does not exist in his office, any testament or codicil, or any sealed packet, deposited by the late Daniel Clark." [4]

The Judge thereupon issued the following order:

"It is ordered that the several notaries of the city do appear before this court at the office of their register of wills, tomorrow, the 19th instant at 9 o'clock precisely, in order to comply with the prayer of this petition.
     "New Orleans, Aug. 18, 1813 JS/Pitot *Judge*"

The notaries came, but they had no "testament, codicil or sealed packet" of any sort. Pierre Pedesclaux, Claude Dejan, Estevan de Quinones, Marc Lafitte, Michel De Armas, Narcissus Broutin, and John Lynd appeared and disclaimed all knowledge or possession of such a paper from Clark. The will was gone.

Then, before Judge Pitot himself, Richard Relf produced the procès-verbal and proof of the will of 1811,

". . . Paul Lanusee and Louis Sere, being duly sworn . . . say that a packet folded up as a letter, sealed with a red wafer, which I presented to them, and bearing the following inscription: *This is my olographic will, New Orleans, 20, May 1811, Daniel Clark*, that the same is the proper handwriting of him the said Daniel Clark.

(Signed)

"Whereupon, I, the said Judge, caused the said packet to be broken open . . . and ordered it to be deposited and recorded in the register office of this court, that copies thereof may be delivered to all persons it may concern.

"JS Pitot, *Judge*"

And this was the will which Judge Pitot then allowed to be probated and wrote his *ne varietur* on it:

"In the Name of God, Amen! I, Daniel Clark, of New Orleans, do make this my last will and testament.

"Imprimis, I order that all my just debts be paid.

"Second, I leave and bequeath unto my mother, Mary Clark, now of Germantown, in the state of Pennsylvania, all the estate whether real or personal, which I may die possessed of.

"Third. I hereby nominate and appoint my friends Richard Relf and Beverly Chew my executors, with power to settle everything relative to my estate.

"New Orleans, 20, May, 1811

(Signed)   Daniel Clark

"*Ne varietur*   JS/Pitot, *Judge*" [5]

Then Richard Relf took oath that he would "well and faithfully perform all and singular the duties of a testamentary executor, So help me God."

This gave him full charge of the property, houses, lands,

slaves, personal effects, papers, and, most important of all, the correspondence of Daniel Clark.

He could save what he would and destroy what he would, sell or settle as he pleased. Beverly Chew was away in the North where Clark had hoped soon to see him, but his partner in New Orleans was able to act for both, and proceeded with vigor to finish what he had begun.

II

And what of the friends of Daniel Clark while his vast fortune went into other hands than those to whom with dying breath he had consigned it? Where were the Spanish Colonel, the Judge, the Chevalier?

The tale is not a happy one. A strange apathy suddenly fell upon Judge Pitot and the Chevalier Delacroix. The one allowed the will of 1811 to go to probate as we have shown; the other after a few days ceased to be concerned over the missing will. It must be recorded, moreover, that when the slaves of Daniel Clark were offered for sale by Richard Relf, Monsieur Delacroix got $50,000 worth of them! Nothing more was heard from him concerning a lost will, for after that the Chevalier apparently seemed to feel that the will under which Mr. Relf was acting was an eminently satisfactory one.

The part Judge Pitot played in all this is the more remarkable as he was universally esteemed as a man of probity and honor. He had acted as mayor of the city and was an intimate friend of Clark. He had expressed his indignation to Bellechasse in private at Relf's suppression of the lost will; and his own son was remembered by a bequest of

$5,000 in the will which was destroyed. But long after-
ward it was indicated that the Judge had bought from
Clark a very valuable tract of land a short while before
this, and if he had never paid for it, as possibly he had not,
he was then in debt to the Clark estate quite heavily. It
may be that Mr. Relf gave the Judge to understand that
if he be allowed to probate the will of 1811 he would thereafter know nothing of this debt to the Clark estate! Perhaps this supposition does the Judge an injustice, but he
certainly allowed Richard Relf to get all Clark's property
and he certainly knew that he himself was an executor of
the lost will of Daniel Clark.

Colonel Bellechasse, the remaining executor, was a man
of a different stamp. But as fate ordered it, the Colonel was
called away from New Orleans just at this time and was
forced to sail for East Florida. There a series of misfortunes
and family troubles breaking about him brought him to
the verge of ruin and into great mental dejection. When
the Colonel, having settled his own affairs as best he could,
was ready to return to New Orleans, a significant letter
reached him from Richard Relf.[6] The Colonel was informed by Relf that the city believed him, the Colonel, to
be in league with the English! As by this time the war had
come to the Gulf Coast and it was known that a British
armament was making ready to descend upon New Orleans, Relf's warning alarmed Bellechasse. Excitement was
then at fever heat in the city. With Spain and England
allies in Europe, and Bellechasse, a former Spanish officer,
off somewhere in the Gulf, it is easy to see how the Creole
populace was ready to jump at once to the view that their
former commander was probably then telling Sir Edward

Pakenham ways and means of taking New Orleans. Whether the city actually believed this or not is beside the point. Bellechasse thought that it did, after the "friendly" letter from Richard Relf. He well knew the excitable temper of the New Orleans mind, and when he thought of returning to face the sticks and stones of a wild, senseless mob on the levee, the aging officer, broken in fortune and dejected in spirit, decided that he would quietly retire to Cuba. There in that island, soon to be the last remnant of the once great Spanish empire in America, Bellechasse took service once more as an officer of Spain. He never saw New Orleans again.

The other dramatis personae fell apart, as it were, to go their several ways, now that the man whose life had been the nexus between them was no more. Zulime lived for some years in Philadelphia; then she with Dr. Gardette and their growing children went to the doctor's native France and took up residence there.

Daniel Coxe, Clark's erstwhile partner, lived on and prospered in his shrewd, canny way. The Randolphs and the Claibornes, the Carrolls and the Harpers and the Wilkinsons ran their several careers, carving for themselves in the nation's history the particular niche in which each stands.

But the Caton sisters swept on to triumph. In 1816 they made what was called a "transatlantic invasion" of England.[7] There the three of them met with unparalleled social success, and were toasted in London as the "Three American Graces." Nor was "Grace" a term misapplied. Each of the girls married a title. Elizabeth wedded Baron Stafford. The widowed Mary took as her husband the

Marquis of Wellesley, brother of the Duke of Wellington.
Her first husband had been Robert Patterson of Baltimore,
and it was his sister, the famous Betsy, who married
Jerome Bonaparte. Thus it came about that the two American sisters-in-law each married a brother of the two captains who had faced each other at Waterloo.

Louisa, the once beloved of Daniel Clark, gave her hand
to the elderly Sir Felton Bathhurst Hervey. When he died,
Louisa married again, this time the young Marquis of
Carmarthen. He, upon the death of an older brother,
eventually became the Duke of Leeds. So Louisa Caton had
the distinction of being the first American girl to wear the
ducal strawberry leaves.

The war and its attendant excitement contributed very
much to the complete triumph of Richard Relf and Beverly Chew, who had by this time joined him. Property
rights were likely to be forgotten, with the British fleet
hovering in the lakes below the city, Andrew Jackson arriving, and a motley army of backwoodsmen marching
posthaste down the Natchez Trace to save New Orleans.
Laffite, the pirate, was making common cause with Claiborne and putting his outlandish Baratarians in line against
the invaders. Then came the battle and the complete defeat
of the English, kilted lads from the highlands of Scotland
bleeding out their lives in the dark mud and mists of Chal-
mette, brave men sent in formation against the terrible
rifles of our frontiersmen entrenched behind cotton and
earth, New Orleans going wild at the victory, and Andrew
Jackson already becoming in the Creole mind the bronze
man on the rearing bronze horse that the old Square shows
today. It is no wonder that men then had scant time to pay

attention to routine matters in a probate court, or the disposal of a lonely bachelor's property. At any rate, they did not. Clark's former partners saw to all that.

And they saw to it with merciless effectiveness. Cannes Brulées eventually was "struck off and sold for $120,000" to the Messrs. Fortier, with certain slaves thrown in.[8] Among these, third on the list, is *negre nombre Lubin*. Wretched black! It was his own freedom he had heard torn to shreds in that locked room.

The grand mansion on the Bayou Road, with its orchards, gardens, flower parterres, kiosks, and statues, remained for a short while in its pristine glory; then, as though following the fortunes of its owner, it began to deteriorate rapidly. Negligent tenants completed its ruin, and, left vacant for a while, it became the prey of marauding neighbors. In the course of time it was rumored that the place was haunted, and Henry Castellanos tells how "ghosts had been seen stalking in the dead of night along its corridors." No respectable family would then take it, and at length every vestige of brick and lumber was carried from the dilapidated building. Like the hopes of its master, the place simply disappeared.

One thing more remains to be entered in this record of blasted hope. One would think that the "executors" now had all that they wished. Everything Daniel Clark had left was at their disposal, except one thing, the comparatively small amount of money, $2,500, which they knew Clark had given to Samuel B. Davis in trust for little Myra. Relf and Chew had all the rest of her patrimony—they would get that. So while Samuel B. Davis, as an officer of the United States army, was in Albany, New York, serving

on a court-martial trying Isaac Hull for his disgraceful sur-
render of Detroit, he was astonished and angered to learn
that suit had been entered against him in New Orleans to
secure the meager $2,500.[9] Colonel Davis, as he had now
become, could do nothing about it, and Relf and Chew got
judgment against him *and collected!* Diabolism had come
to flood tide.

Then at the head of the grave of Daniel Clark, Richard
Relf had these words graved, in Latin:

HERE LIES
DANIEL CLARK
A NATIVE OF SLIGO IN IRELAND,
AND AN INHABITANT FROM BOYHOOD
OF LOUISIANA AND OF THIS CITY.
WHILE IT WAS UNDER THE SPANISH GOVERNMENT
HE WAS CONSUL OF THE UNITED STATES,
APPOINTED ON ACCOUNT OF HIS ILLUSTRIOUS VIRTUES.
AFTERWARD BY THE UNANIMOUS VOTE
OF THE PEOPLE OF THE TERRITORY OF ORLEANS,
HE SAT AS THE FIRST DELEGATE
IN THE CONGRESS OF THE AMERICAN PEOPLE.
HIS GREAT WEALTH,
ACCUMULATED WITHOUT FRAUD,
HE USED IN RELIEVING
THE NECESSITIES OF THE POOR;
NEVERTHELESS BECOMING RICHER,
BY HIS LIBERALITY.
HE DIED, WEPT OF ALL GOOD MEN,
AUGUST 13, 1813,
IN THE FORTY-SEVENTH YEAR OF HIS AGE.
A FRIEND TO A FRIEND
HAS ERECTED THIS MONUMENT.[10]

Book 2

Myra

Delamore Place

ON THE upper portion of Delaware Bay near the little
city of Wilmington there might have been seen, about the
year 1830, a splendid mansion-house, as it would have
been called then. It was a superb country place, uplifted
above the bay and commanding one of the finest prospects
in the whole region. Picturesque and broken scenery lay
all about in rude luxuriance, while close around the dwell-
ing reigned the most perfect cultivation. Parklike groves,
lawns fringed with choice shrubberies and flowers, might
be seen from every window, while stables, lodges and lesser
buildings, kept in perfect repair, indicated a rare degree of
wealth as well as that atmosphere of colonial self-sufficiency
which the older mansions of the South and East ever
seemed to enjoy. The spacious front veranda commanded
a view of the distant bay and the broken shore line for miles
on either side. In the whole state of Delaware there could
not have been found, at that day, a gentleman's residence
more perfect in itself or more luxurious in its appointments.[1]

Such was Delamore Place in its earlier days, a house destined to last with its fame undimmed until very recent years. Its owner, at the time of which we write, was Colonel Samuel B. Davis, a retired army officer and a gentleman of wealth and influence. The Colonel, who was a member of the legislature of Pennsylvania, kept another residence in Philadelphia during the winter season; but with the coming of spring he enjoyed moving down the bay to the site which long ago he had chosen as his home and upon which he had built his luxurious country house. There within the walls of Delamore Place, Colonel Davis delighted to entertain his chosen guests, and sometimes for them he would unbend and tell of his adventures by sea and land. These had been many and interesting. Men of prominence, many of whom were proud to count themselves his friends, often mused on the varied life the Colonel had led.[2]

He had been born at Lewes on the Delaware coast, March 25, 1776. His father served as a colonial soldier but was captured by the British early in the war and was so brutally treated by them that he died thereafter, a sacrifice to his country's cause. From this bitter experience, Samuel B. Davis inherited a hatred of the English which was to persist throughout life. As a mere boy he took to the sea, after a time going into French service, eventually signing on board a privateer. His courage and skill made him an officer, and running down the English shipping proved his particular delight. Young Davis developed into a typical hard-fighting seaman and soldier of fortune and bade fair to continue so until the end of the chapter. But in one of his maritime forays he ran into Santo Domingo, where, in some way, the rough privateersman met Rose Elisabeth, daughter of the Baron Boisfontaine, a French nobleman broken in fortune. He was charmed at once by the gentle beauty of Santo Domingo, and they were married. Misfortune had overtaken the house of Boisfontaine, but Davis loyally assisted his wife's people, and they learned to trust and admire his rugged, if sometimes tempestuous, strength. After a time, Davis with his family went to New Orleans as has been seen, and there he found opening for him a new and much more profitable life. His fortune and prestige gradually increased. He secured property not only in New Orleans but in his native state and managed all his investments wisely. Then the War of 1812 came on and Davis sailed for the North and entered the American army.

In the second year of the war Davis had an opportunity to carve a name for himself. Early in 1813 a British fleet had come north from the Indies for the purpose of harrying the United States coast and anchored in the lower Delaware. Sir John Beresford, the English Commodore, sent a message in to the little American village of Lewes, Delaware, commanding its inhabitants to provision his ships at once or he would be under the necessity of destroying the town. Governor Hazlet of Delaware answered by throwing a thousand militia into Lewes, and putting Samuel B. Davis in command.

Events moved rapidly. When the message of Beresford was ignored, the British frigate *Belvedere,* Captain Byron commanding, moved close in to the town and sent a further threatening message to Davis. But by this time the blood of the Delawareans was thoroughly up, and Davis himself had smelled British powder before. He peremptorily refused all demands and to Captain Byron's somewhat hypo-critical expression of grief for the distress that Davis' conduct was going to cause the women and children by the English bombardment, Davis returned the laconic an-swer: "Colonel Davis is a gallant man and has already taken care of the ladies," a message which has a Gallic tang about it, reminiscent of his privateersman days.

At this the *Belvedere* and other ships moved in and threw eight hundred round shot into the town as well as a quantity of Congreve rockets, much dreaded then in naval warfare. But for all this furious and, as it turned out, famous bombardment, no damage was done, and one his-torian gravely informs us that the boys of the town dug out the balls where they struck the sand and gleefully bore them to the American gunners to fire back. During the night of the bombardment, Davis sent for more ammuni-tion, and the "Du Pont Mills" in Wilmington forwarded a supply at once. But there was little need. All this can-nonading did no damage and a force attempting to land in small boats the next day was driven back. No American was hurt and Britannia had never ruled the waves if Eng-lish cannon balls had been fired to no better purpose than they were on April 6, 1813, against the sandspits of Dela-ware. The *Belvedere* moved away and Davis was the hero of the occasion.[3]

Late in the war Colonel Davis was ordered to proceed with his regiment, now the 44th Infantry, to New Or-leans, then menaced by Pakenham. The sea route was of course cut off. His march was from Sandy Hook into his own state again, en route to Wheeling, in what is now

COLONEL SAMUEL BOYER DAVIS

West Virginia, where he was to take boat to the south. The Colonel with his men camped one evening on a piece of rising ground near Wilmington. The place was beautiful for a homesite and Davis vowed that he should desire nothing better than one day to have a house upon that very spot.

The Colonel arrived in New Orleans with his men the day after the big battle. It was all over and peace had been declared. There was nothing for him to do but wait at Fort St. Philip down the river until he was honorably discharged.

Not long after his return to Delaware, the Colonel sought out the owner of the land which had so pleased him when he had camped on it. A house had been begun on the hill but was not finished. Davis bought it, and Delamore Place was the result. The splendid home which he completed remained until the year 1921 as one of the show places of that section.*

The Colonel continued to engage in business and alternated for a time between New Orleans and the North where he became more and more engrossed in public affairs. By 1830 he was a member of the legislature of the state of Pennsylvania, and Delaware was preparing to present him with a handsome sword for his part in defending her coasts in 1813.[4]

II

During the years between the War of 1812 and the first presidency of Andrew Jackson, there might have been seen running about Delamore Place a slip of a girl who was

* It was destroyed by fire.

called Myra, a member of the Davis family. Besides Myra, it was known that the Colonel had a grown son, Horatio Davis, in New Orleans, and two other children.

Friends of the Davis family believed that there was a difference between Myra and the other Davis children. She did not resemble either the Colonel or Madame Davis, and intimate friends had found out that she was an adopted child. Myra herself knew nothing of this and had been taught from infancy to call the Colonel and his wife father and mother. To Philadelphia and Wilmington acquaint- ances she was always known as "Myra Davis."

The Davises were indulgent parents and, although the Colonel had a temper which often played out of hand, the children all admired and loved him. His gentle wife proved a gracious queen for Delamore Place, and it could easily be seen that there was perfect love and trust between her and the girl, Myra.

So Myra grew. Delamore Place was her playground in summer, and a select school for young ladies in Philadel- phia her home in winter.[5] The years sped by; the child be- came a girl, the girl a woman, and an amazingly interest- ing one.

Myra was small of stature. Of feminine beauty she had her share, though her distinguishing trait was a charm of manner and a vivacity indescribably compelling. It was early discovered that when Myra was present, the center of social gravity shifted at once to this small but dynamic person.

As the daughter of the wealthy Samuel B. Davis it will be guessed that she was not allowed to reach the age of twenty-five without having what our grandmothers would have called "attention." But Myra in her positive way preferred to send her admirers about their business, apparently not at all interested. It is hinted that Colonel Davis was not displeased at this, as he destined her for a man of his own choosing. But the Colonel was to learn that his little Myra had a will of her own.

III

Upon a long-remembered occasion when Myra was in her middle twenties, it happened that she went on an excursion to Washington, D.C. This sounds prosaic enough now, and in fact the very antithesis of romance is a hot and harried excursion crowd of today, getting off its stuffy trains in packed mass. But in that era a stately excursion boat provided thrills in plenty, especially to young ladies whose emotions were supposed to be laced in as tightly as their bodices. Of the details of this particular trip, there is no record. Doubtless Myra was heavily chaperoned, as were all other young ladies of good breeding; but however that may be, it is certain that she came back from that trip having made the acquaintance of a tall, dignified young man from New York state, who bore the substantial name of William Wallace Whitney.

He, it seems, had business in Philadelphia a little later, and asked permission to call at the Davis home. The Colonel was away in Harrisburg at the legislature, but Mrs. Davis permitted the visit. She, too, was impressed by Mr. Whitney. That Whitney was interested in Myra there was no doubt whatever, and so the days passed. Then the Colonel came home.

For apparently no reason whatever, Colonel Davis at once took a violent dislike to young Whitney. It is said that even before he saw the young man, he was set against him. Perhaps he really had made other plans for Myra's future. Be that as it may, Mrs. Davis was alarmed at the symptoms of brewing anger which she knew only too well in her tempestuous husband. In a frightened attempt to pour oil on troubled waters, she explained that Mr. Whitney's visits had been merely formal. Her husband responded that he was sure this new acquaintance was seeking to marry Myra for his money, and challenged both wife and daughter to give any definite information regarding him. They admitted that they knew little but had come to believe in his sincerity.

William Whitney himself, who, if truth be known, had come to be much in Myra's thought, now found it necessary to return to his home, but, before doing so, called and asked to be allowed to present to the Davis family letters testimonial in order that they might feel him worthy of acquaintance and no social impostor. Thereupon the young visitor produced a packet of papers declaring his family and standing. Such recommendations and endorsements were then often a part of a gentleman's portmanteau when away from home and were vastly serviceable in an age that had no telegraph nor rapid mail service.

The papers Myra's friend produced showed that he was the son of General Josiah Whitney of Broome County, New York, a name of the highest standing in that section. General Whitney had served in the Revolutionary army and later settled with Colonel Bingham, the founder of Binghamton, in the town named for the latter. It was therefore with a pride matching Davis' own that the young scion of the house of Whitney proffered his credentials merely as a warrant for his social standing, that and nothing more.

But the Colonel viewed them coldly. He later explained to Myra that they might be forgeries. Davis was determined to believe no good of the young man who had so strangely affected Myra, and he evidently deemed the matter ended when William Whitney left for home. Shortly thereafter he was himself called away again.

But the affair was not ended. Letters were exchanged. The summer came and with it days at Delamore Place where Myra could dream her daydreams and write often to her absent admirer. Parental objection had served, as it often does, to center the thought of the girl on the man frowned upon. It was the old story of the forbidden lover, and Myra was peculiarly a person whom opposition called to instant attention.

Then Colonel Davis came back to Delamore Place and to his astonishment and wrath found that William Whitney was still in the mind of Myra and that she had actually been corresponding with him. More than this, Whitney was then en route to Delamore Place to see her. At this the pent-up fury of the old sea captain broke forth in one of his angry spasms, and before he could gain command of himself, Davis, in the presence of the girl, thanked God that no drop of *his* blood ran in her veins! Myra's spirit had been roused to meet his wrath, but these deadly words, hot as they were, fell like a chill upon her. She cried out to know what he meant, and saw that, while her father regretted his haste, he had, in a fateful way, spoken truth. She rushed to her mother. Mrs. Davis, always in awe of the Colonel when he was angry, at first clasped the girl close, then as quietly as possible told her the truth. She was not their child. She was Myra Clark, daughter of Daniel Clark of New Orleans.

Myra had had a curious intimation of this sometime before when she found certain old papers in one of the family's trunks. But that was nothing to the revelation that Davis' anger now made.

At any other time such news would have made an epochal change in her life, but something mightier had now come into play. The Colonel was not by nature a bad man or even an unfair one, but this time he was possessed of an all-devouring anger toward a youth whom he scarcely knew and who was committing no offense other than to come down to Delaware to see a young lady. But Samuel B. Davis was the slave of his own will. He swore that if Whitney presumed to come to Delamore Place, if he came as near as Wilmington or New Castle, he would challenge him—he would shoot him dead on sight! Myra knew that the Colonel's anger would blow over, but she also knew his pride and iron will, and the sickening realization came to her that he would keep his word.

It was now Davis' time to learn something about Myra. He had been so used to commanding in his own house that perhaps her sudden independence with regard to Whitney accentuated his wrath and anger. He could not bear to be thwarted by this child whom he loved. But when he delivered a threat against the life of her lover, the Colonel found that he had aroused a personality suddenly grown as powerful as his own. The blazing eyes looking at him were those of Daniel Clark, and the injustice of Davis' attitude called forth the strength as well as the deeper emotions of the girl. After a startled gasp of horror at his announced intention, she left his presence and began to resolve on a desperate plan. She would fly from Delamore Place and warn her lover.

Today such action on the part of a young woman would be commonplace, but at that time it was the height of maidenly indiscretion, especially for one in Myra's prominent social position. That this would compromise her name never daunted her. She persuaded herself that she was going to save human life, her father's or her lover's, and the consequences to herself she could disregard.

She did not know it, but at that moment Myra Clark was setting out on her career.

IV

Myra had some young lady friends in Wilmington and to them she wrote a hasty note saying that they might expect her to be their guest that night. She informed them that she would arrive quite late but that she would surely be there. At Delamore Place she made feverish though secret preparations for her departure. She managed to secure one little trunk without lock or key and into this put such belongings as she felt she must have. Her next step was to cajole an old servitor of the family, who was a devoted admirer, into promising to drive her into Wilmington late in the night. He, like everyone else, feared the wrath of Colonel Davis, but the darkness, they hoped, would protect the old man from discovery. There was one tollgate on the road and this caused them much concern, as the keeper knew both carriage and driver, but it was hoped that he would be asleep when the vehicle drove by.

The night came on with a sweeping rainstorm, drenching the whole countryside but helping Myra's plans for flight. The storm drowned all lesser sounds, and the carriage was drawn forth as prearranged and brought to the rear of the house. It was about midnight when the servant saw Myra appear at the back entrance, having brought her little trunk downstairs herself. She turned it over to the old man and, with the rain pouring about her, stepped into the carriage. She told the driver that if the tollgate were down, he must crash through it. She remembered that the barrier was old and rotten.

This daring advice proved sound. The alert gatekeeper heard above the rain the noise of the approaching carriage, but Myra's servant followed her order and put the horses into the barrier with a rush. There was a crash of weak timber, and the lumbering vehicle swept on into Wilmington bearing a wet and bedraggled but dauntless little figure to the appointed home. Myra's friends were waiting for her and she was taken care of for the rest of the night.

But there was no time to lose. Before day had well broken she was away again, driving on toward New Castle, escorted by the father of her friends. Morning dawned bright and clear. The New Castle road, winding down the coast, soon brought her where she could see Delamore Place with its majestic pillars and massive bulk outlined against the green background of the countryside, fresh after the night's rain. With mingled emotions Myra looked across at the home she had left, but she had no idea of turning back.

At New Castle she was put in the care of another friend's father, who offered her asylum under his roof. A quick investigation showed that no person named Whitney had as yet landed from the Baltimore boat. Her lover was coming via Baltimore, it should be explained, because the Susquehanna and Chesapeake then furnished the most convenient route from Binghamton to Wilmington.

As any moment might see Colonel Davis ride furiously in and any boat might bring William Whitney, Myra decided that she would herself take the next boat going to Baltimore and stop her lover there before he could sail for Delaware. Her chief worry was that perhaps he had already sailed or was even then leaving on a boat scheduled to pass the one she was taking for Baltimore. But this contingency must be risked. Leaving a message for Mr. Whitney in case she missed him, she and the New Castle gentleman sailed for Baltimore, only to find when they arrived that a person named Whitney had indeed taken passage on the very boat which had passed them en route. There was nothing to do but to sail back and hope that Colonel Davis and Whitney had not met at New Castle. And this was the best communication that could then be had between two cities as close as Baltimore and Wilmington.

Back at New Castle, Myra found that the Whitney who had arrived from Baltimore was not her Mr. Whitney. The wisest course now seemed to be to wait for him. A kindly clergyman took her under his roof and she began to count time by the incoming boats. Then Colonel Davis found her.

V

It might be thought that the wrath of Davis would now have reached the point where he was ready to offer physical violence to the girl who had fled from his home, but it turned out otherwise. The empty chair at his table and the eloquent silence of a deserted room had soon driven all anger from the Colonel. Samuel B. Davis was at heart generous and forgiving. His unaccountable dislike for young Whitney was born more of pride and love for Myra than of anything else. The thought of his little daughter escaping from his home during a storm at night, as though from prison, showed Davis to what lengths his tempestuous spirit had taken him. He resolved to leave no stone unturned to find Myra and to make restitution. Naturally it was not hard to discover her location.

Her foster father did not go to her at once, as he was at first persuaded to let a relative act for him and intercede with Myra to return. But it is said that this relative, having reasons for wishing Myra well out of the Davis household, played the Colonel false and artfully dissuaded Myra from returning to Delamore Place, giving her the impression that her foster father was still bitterly determined against Whitney. This part of the story may perhaps be legendary. The account of Myra's flight has been passed down in various versions, so that a critical judgment upon its minute details proves almost impossible.

At last William Whitney landed from the long-awaited Baltimore boat, and then Myra came to a sudden realization that she was desperately in love with the young man for whom she had braved the wrath of her foster father and fled her home. Her choice was not unworthy. That William Whitney was her devoted admirer she had known, but it remained for him to prove the depths of his devotion after she had told him that she was not Samuel B. Davis' daughter, but an adopted child.

It was Whitney's turn to be surprised. He had known Myra as the daughter and heiress of a wealthy and influential man. Now he found she was not the daughter of Samuel B. Davis and, since her flight, might perhaps be forever alienated from him. But William Whitney was no fortune hunter. He heard all, but declared that he loved Myra for herself alone. He pleaded with her to marry him at once and go with him to his own country and kinspeople.

This Myra refused. She felt, for one thing, that it would not be fair to Whitney nor to his family and urged him to get the consent of his parents, even if she could not secure that of Colonel Davis. So it was agreed that her suitor should leave her for the time and arrange matters with his own people before he came to claim her. Whitney returned to Binghamton, Myra to Philadelphia.

There in the home of friends she suddenly became desperately ill. The strain through which she had passed had told on her, and she was put to bed with a raging fever. But this was the last of her immediate troubles. Samuel B. Davis could stand the separation no longer, and during her convalescence made his way with unaccustomed timidity into Myra's sickroom. All doubts were swept away at once when father and daughter came together. Everything was forgiven and to Myra's stout declaration that she would return only on condition that nothing should prevent her marrying Mr. Whitney, the Colonel struck his flag like the sea-fighter he was. Never one for halfway measures, Davis declared that not only William Whitney but the whole Whitney family must come to Delamore Place for the wedding!

So to the joy of all, Myra went back to her beloved home.

Early in the autumn the fires were lighted on the hearth of the great house, bedecked for the occasion, and the wedding took place. One of the bridesmaids years after told of a strange hitch that occurred in the ceremony when it was found at a late moment that the license had not been properly made out. The whole company was compelled to wait until one of the gentlemen could go to Wilmington and have the papers correctly drawn, but through some mistake, the gentleman in question was given an old, broken-down horse. This kept him stumbling along the road and through bypaths until the hour had grown late. It had been raining, but after the apparently unfortunate delay, the moon came out clear in the sky as if to harbinger happiness for the couple.

Then at last Myra came down the great stairs arrayed in her bridal robes and put her hand upon the arm of the young man from the North. The papers the next day made this announcement:

"Married Thursday evening the 13th inst. at Delamore Place, Del; by the Rev. Pardee, William Wallace Whitney, esq., of New York, to Miss Myra E. daughter of Colonel Samuel B. Davis." [6]

The child of adoption at last had a home of her own.

VI

William Whitney proudly bore his bride back to his native heath, to the straggling town that his own family had helped to carve out of the wilderness. Binghamton itself was but an isolated, rural community where the arrival of a new bride would be a matter of more than nine days' interest. It will not be thought that Myra lacked a welcome among her husband's people, inasmuch as William Whitney was the ninth son in a family of twelve—nor did she.

William's eldest sister Pamela, who was Mrs. Waterman, gave a ball in Myra's honor that was the greatest social event Broome County had ever seen. Former Governor DeWitt Clinton came to do honor to the Whitney family and to pay homage to the new daughter of the house.[7] As for the brothers and sisters, wives and in-laws of the Whitney clan, they all turned out en masse to welcome—and inspect—the girl their William had brought home. They liked Myra at once, although her slightly foreign ways and spontaneous personality marked her as a bird of different plumage from the Broome County variety. She herself was in love with everyone and everything, most of all with her young husband, and visions of settling down to an idyllic existence rose before her. Had such dreams proved substantial, the story of Myra Clark would never have been written. "Mrs. W. W. Whitney" would have been but another of the millions of women who then were making homes, making sacrifices, and incidentally making a nation. But Myra Clark was destined for another field than that bounded by Whitney babies and the intimate details of Binghamton gossip. To be sure, babies came to Myra, and came fast, but by the time young William, Jr., had arrived, she had already launched forth on her unique career.

Myra on the Levee

THERE was one loyal soul who never ceased to remember Daniel Clark—Josef David Degoutin Bellechasse.
The Colonel had settled down on a sugar plantation in
Cuba, but the recollections of the trust his dead friend had
placed in him and the strange disappearance of Clark's last
will had been present in his mind many times since the
stormy days of 1813. Often Bellechasse thought of the
child Myra, and at length after a number of years, feeling
that the growing girl should by this time be able to comprehend something of her past, wrote her a letter in care of
Dr. Hulings of Philadelphia.[1] The doctor, it will be remembered, had been the American vice-consul in New
Orleans before the cession and had been associated with
Daniel Clark as co-worker and friend for many years.
Bellechasse waited expectantly but received nothing in
reply. Later, the Colonel sent a communication to Myra,
this time in care of Samuel B. Davis and made sure that
his postal conveyance was thoroughly reliable. But again
the months sped by and no answer came to the old Creole

living out his days in Cuba. The Davises, of course, did not care for Myra to know of her origin, thinking then that it would be cruel to inform her that she was not their child. Not until she had become Mrs. William Whitney did she have a chance to learn the contents of the long-withheld letters which Bellechasse had written her. These with other bits of information and the story the Davises told her began to weave before her eyes a strange and entrancing pattern. What if, after all, she, Myra Davis Whitney, were really heiress to a great fortune in faraway Louisiana, land of her childhood? Suppose, instead of being a cast-off orphan—or worse—she was in truth the acknowledged daughter of a man of pride and position, that impulsive man whom she dimly remembered as one who would pick her up in his arms, kiss her, and fill her hands with pretty presents? And while she was but a child had she been put out of the way, defrauded of her very birthright? Could not something be done about it?

She would see.

So it came about that in the middle of the very next summer, a ship with Myra and her husband on board slipped past the grim walls of Morro Castle into Havana harbor. The Whitneys were en route to Louisiana, with the intention of first stopping in Cuba and locating Colonel Bellechasse, if he were still alive. It was very important, they knew, to see this stanch friend of Myra's father before they went further. They had little opportunity for arranging an interview with the Colonel, as letters for such purposes would have required weeks, but they hoped that the man they sought was yet living and as friendly as his messages made it appear. William

Whitney had gladly acquiesced in his young wife's plan of making a joint voyage of discovery and, as they fondly dreamed, of fortune. They were both very hopeful, very young.

On a large sugar plantation near Matanzas,[2] some days after this, visitors were announced as wishing to see Colonel Bellechasse, the owner of the place. To be more exact, there was one visitor, as the story goes, an apparently young woman, heavily veiled. The grizzled Spanish Colonel, somewhat stiff with age, but always the gentleman, bowed before the veiled lady and offered her a seat. They spoke in French, perhaps one reason why William Whitney was left out of it. Myra had been somewhat uncertain of this unknown foreigner—she certainly had reason to be suspicious of her "father's friends"—and decided that she would carefully study her host and his attitude before revealing her identity.

"I have learned," she began, "that Monsieur the Colonel lived for a long while in New Orleans."

Bellechasse made a gesture of assent.

"Then you knew Daniel Clark who was living there when you were?"

"Daniel Clark," rejoined the Colonel instantly, "was the best friend I ever had." His face expressed pleasure at the recollection.

For just a moment more the veiled lady hesitated. Then, with a quick movement as though she had come to a sudden decision, she asked significantly: "Did Daniel Clark leave with you certain papers indicating property which he wished you to keep for his daughter?"

The old officer stiffened to instant attention. Astonishment and suspicion were both written on his face. "Why does Madame ask?" Then a sudden gleam of some intuitive knowledge gave him the answer. He arose excitedly. "Are you Myra?"

The visitor threw back her veil dramatically. She was always a superb actress.

"I am Myra!"

Bellechasse was delighted. He had both the Whitneys come to his home where he entertained them as his house guests for several days. He put Myra in full possession of all the facts he knew concerning her father's life and estate. Old times in Louisiana were recalled and experiences with her father, of whose nobility and generosity the aged officer could hardly say enough. As to the will, the Colonel told Myra he had himself read it and had been prepared to carry its provisions into effect, and that it distinctly declared her to be his *legitimate daughter*. Bellechasse firmly believed that Richard Relf had destroyed that final will, and but for Relf's baseness, he asserted, Myra would long since have inherited vast property. In the course of their conversations, the Colonel brought out the very map Clark had given him, showing the location of the lots in the Faubourg St. Jean which he had commanded Bellechasse to keep for Myra.

These lots Myra felt should certainly be hers, and before the Whitneys left they secured them from the Colonel by a $20,000 purchase, the land being stipulated as Myra's "paraphernal property." This sale is a matter of record, though how much actual money changed hands cannot be stated. What Myra wanted, of course, was an unquestioned title to the property as coming through the Colonel. This apparently she received.

Armed with this undoubted inheritance from her father and vastly heartened by the words of the loyal old Colonel, the Whitneys took an affectionate leave of the one friend who had been true to the trust of Daniel Clark and so sailed on their way. They never saw Bellechasse again.

II

In a few days Myra Clark stood on the New Orleans levee. But what a change since she had last been there!

In 1812 she had left a growing little city with a few ships in the river, a few flatboats and barges tied up at the levee. Now she and her husband saw about them a southern metropolis, with the ships from the seven seas at the wharves.[3] Everything was larger, more impressive. The steamboat had arrived and with it the expansion of the whole region to the northward. The vast trans-Mississippi country, which Myra's father had helped secure, was now in process of opening, just as the trans-Allegheny country had been in the previous generation. The American people were not merely expanding. They had caught that sense of destiny, of a mission to conquer wildernesses and develop empires which marked the advance of the American frontier. Westward the star of empire was decidedly moving. The great valley to the north, spread out fanwise, was springing into life and the old Creole city at the handle of the fan was now receiving produce from the Northwest as well as from the Northeast. The port had developed; new business concerns were making money. Negro slaves brought higher prices on the block downtown. Travelers passed to and fro. The flotsam and jetsam of the Gulf, with roustabouts and river men, still hung about in the saloons and gambling hells on the river front. But a more suave type of crook, with ruffles on wrists and derringer in pocket, had made the city one of his ports of call between steamboat trips—a polite but steely individual who had learned that card games in the saloons of lazy, luxurious steamboats were quite profitable when wealthy cotton planters and the like could be induced to cut the pasteboards.

New Orleans then was entering its great boom period. It had grown fast enough as it was, but from 1830 to the Civil War the city enjoyed fabulous prosperity. Even the Creoles who had haughtily "riffused" to learn English caught the spirit of enterprise. There was an expectant atmosphere, almost a hurry about the formerly staid city. New buildings were going up, heavy drays were rolling over streets recently cobbled with the stones brought in as ballast in ships from foreign ports. Canal Street near the levee had become a stirring emporium of commerce, while the stately stacks of an occasional steamboat could be seen majestically moving along the river above the levee. But over against all this metropolitan impressiveness, one could note on either side of the old streets the same open ditches with the stagnant sewage and dirty water exactly as it had been in the days of Daniel Clark, and each summer there was a threat from "yellow jack" or cholera, those twin scourges of the tropics. Nevertheless, it was a prosperous and wealthy city to which the Whitneys had

come, and Myra knew that the property of her father
would be vastly increased in value by this time.

What she did not know, though she soon learned, was
that individuals as well as property had taken on importance with the years. The president of the Louisiana State
Bank turned out to be her father's quondam friend, the
Chevalier Francois Desuau Delacroix; while the cashier of
that same bank was her father's former partner, Richard
Relf. The collector of customs for the district of Mississippi
and the port of New Orleans was the Honorable Beverly
Chew, holding his original commission from President
James Monroe.[4] These old acquaintances had evidently
come up in the world since the days of 1813.

III

The young couple from the North found quarters, no
doubt at some leading hotel where all the "quality" of the
day were accustomed to stay during visits to the city. But
the Whitneys' presence then amid the passing throng of
strangers hardly created a stir, and they knew scarcely
anyone. As to Myra's story of her parentage, the few who
first heard it looked utterly incredulous and no doubt
slightly puzzled. It may well be imagined that even those
who might otherwise have wished her well would draw
away from her when they learned that this vivacious
woman actually believed herself to be the child of Daniel
Clark. Clark! The elegant bachelor merchant who had
been dead all these years secretly married to this lady's
mother? Social acquaintances who were prepared to like
the amazingly attractive Mrs. Whitney felt that the least

she said of all this in New Orleans the better for her. Few knew her and none really cared.

What the Whitneys did not know and what every Louisianian did was that no person of illegitimate birth could ever inherit property from parents, no matter what a written will might say. The ancient Code, making plain the rule of succession in every Latin country, so directed, and tragedy after tragedy in Louisiana had come about because of it. This gracious young person with her insouciant air, so charmingly unconscious of the law in this respect, claimed to be left property by a father whom everyone knew had never been married! What utter nonsense! Suppose she were Daniel Clark's child? Suppose he had made a will in her favor—what of it? She could not possibly claim any property from the Clark estate on this ground. And after all these years? If the young woman were wise she would be silent and let the veil of time hide the skeleton of the past.

So New Orleans might have reasoned.

But the Whitneys thought otherwise. They were young and impulsive and had absolutely no experience to guide them in the romantic undertaking on which they had embarked. William Whitney, however, did have a level head on his shoulders and began his moves in a systematic way. His canny Yankee blood doubtless is to be thanked for this. At any rate, the first thing he did was to go to the records of the Probate Court and there make a diligent search for all matters connected with the Clark estate. He noted particularly that the executors of the will of 1811 had made no report or return to the Court of Probates as to the manner in which they had administered the property. Louisiana law required this to be done, and the failure to comply gave Whitney another count in the indictment he was drawing up against his wife's despoilers.

Myra for her part was not idle. She had inquired about her mother's people and began to get in touch with the various members of the Carrière family. She soon found both her Aunt Sophie and her Aunt Rose and learned their story.

IV

Fortune had not been altogether kind to the beautiful Carrières. Madame Sophie Despau had had domestic difficulties culminating in a divorce, and Madame Rose Caillavet likewise had her troubles. The sisters had gradually withdrawn from public notice and were living in the subdued quiet of their little sphere, when the privacy of their retirement was interrupted by the astonishing appearance of Zulime's daughter. Madame Caillavet had a son-in-law, Señor Morejon, living in Cuba on a plantation next that of Bellechasse, and it was possibly through the Colonel that Myra learned the whereabouts of her aunts.

They received her kindly and Myra soon obtained from them information of the highest importance. Madame Despau told her that not only had Daniel Clark really married her mother but that *she had been present at the ceremony*. She said that this marriage had been performed by a Catholic priest in Philadelphia. Madame Caillavet confirmed her sister's account.

This was evidence of the most vital import. It confirmed the dying declaration of Clark as locked up in his will.

From that time on, the Whitneys were convinced that, with the will, Myra's father had kept other papers in the little black case and they were sure that these would have established Myra's full claim if they likewise had not been secretly destroyed.

They were now prepared to press for redress in an orderly way, but the year was slipping by fast and they saw that legal steps could scarcely be taken before the season closed. In view of this, the Whitneys decided to sail for their home, where they could spend the winter in preparing their case and collecting additional information which might help them prosecute it. Perhaps there was another reason for returning to Binghamton, for before many weeks had passed another claimant had been added to the number looking hopefully at the Clark estate. His name was William Wallace Whitney, Jr.

The winter in the North was spent in welcoming the Whitney heir and in correspondence with persons who the Whitneys felt might help them in pressing their claim at New Orleans. Two individuals especially had much to tell them. One was the Baron Boisfontaine, Mrs. Davis' brother, who was known to have been on the most intimate terms with Myra's father; the other was Mrs. Harriet Smythe of Opelousas, Louisiana, the former Harriet Harper of New Orleans, the niece of Colonel Davis. She it was who had nursed Myra in infancy. The Whitneys had no trouble in reaching these two relatives of the Davis family and from them received messages and eventually depositions which aided them greatly. So the winter passed.

V

Early in 1835 William Whitney and Myra with little
William were back in New Orleans. They felt that they
now had a collection of such evidence as could not be
denied, and without more ado Whitney took the first
formal step toward securing his wife's rights by filing his
claims and charges in the Court of Probates for the Parish
of Orleans. It was the beginning of a long and truceless
war.

Whitney's statement was accompanied by the amazing
allegation that Daniel Clark had made a later will than the
one probated and that this posterior will had been suppressed. The fraud, Mr. Whitney directly asserted, was to
be attributed to none other than Richard Relf, cashier of
the Louisiana State Bank.

Then indeed New Orleans heard his story.

Something of a sensation was created but the account
was generally received with heartless amusement border-
ing on disdain. The Creole city knew how to enjoy an impossible story of that sort but made an expressive grimace
at the droll effrontery of its claim to truth. Who was this
Whitney person? The child of the DesGrange woman?
The older inhabitants with rare gusto proceeded to recount
what they knew of Zulime. Daniel Clark married to *her!*
As for Mr. Relf destroying a will—preposterous! The city
shrugged its shoulders and prepared to dismiss the matter.
But Richard Relf did not.

If William Wallace Whitney of Binghamton, New
York, thought his assertions would stand unchallenged by
the man he denounced, he was in for a quick disillusion-

ment. It came in the form of officers of the law bearing a warrant for his arrest, and he was at once called to answer in court to a formal charge of libel against Mr. Relf. The New Yorker was hailed before a Judge Watts, who instantly made it clear that he was personally resentful of the affront which this unknown stranger had offered to one of the leading citizens of Louisiana. To make clear his resentment and to let the prisoner know the full extent of the crime he had committed, the Judge remanded Mr. Whitney to prison unless he could immediately raise $25,000 bail. As if that were not enough, the sheriff added $10,000 more for "security of the person." William Whitney was led at once to the common jail and locked up with criminals and felons, with the prospect of raising $35,000 or remaining there indefinitely. Horror was added by the fact that cholera was then raging in the city. It was in vain that "excessive bail" was urged in an effort to free Whitney. Judge Watts was obdurate. Louisiana would show these people how she dealt with calumniators!

This then was the end of their roseate trip from the lovely Susquehanna hills, a brutal farewell to idyllic dreams of fortune. Myra saw her husband locked in jail like any ruffian and heard her own name besmirched in the city of her birth. Her thoughts were bitter within her as she remained alone with her infant, while the man who had jeopardized everything for her sweltered in prison amid the noisome air of a tropical epidemic. And all he had done was defend his wife's name and demand her rights! New York was learning something about Louisiana.

But Louisiana was yet to learn something about the young mother who was then leaning over her infant son and bitterly bemoaning the imprisonment of her husband. During these dark days the iron first began to show itself in the character of Myra. The careless city which glibly dismissed her pretensions with scornful references to her past, the city that was so satisfied with its medieval code concerning inheritances, had yet to discover with what manner of woman it had to deal. The dreams of girlhood were now to be put away. Myra Clark knew that she had a mission in the world.

VI

The immediate thing, of course, was to get William Whitney out of jail. Accordingly, letters were dispatched to his family telling of his plight, and then legal machinery was set in motion. The man now being held under excessive bail in Louisiana was, it was remembered, a citizen of the great state of New York. If the local courts were tyrannical, perhaps those of the United States would be more just. The result was that a Federal writ was soon secured with the easy bond of $5,000 stipulated as security. This amount could be raised with comparative ease, and after three terrible weeks William Whitney heard the prison doors close behind him and returned to his wife and child. But Myra ever after vowed that his health had been irremediably impaired.

The imprisonment of Whitney had, however, served to advertise the cause of his wife, and during the time of his confinement and following it there came to Myra certain older persons who remembered some of the kindnesses of Daniel Clark. A few recalled the story of the lost will. Some were merely curious, but some few wished her

well. Prominent among the newcomers was Colonel
Richard Reynall Keene, the gentleman who had acted as
her father's second when Clark and Governor Claiborne
fought with pistols at the Iberville. Colonel Keene
definitely espoused Myra's cause and was soon engaged on
his own account in a libel suit with Relf over statements
regarding the lost will. The contest with Keene worried
Relf more than did the Whitney attack. For one thing the
immediate decision went against Relf, and while he
secured a new trial at once, his case was correspondingly
weakened in the public mind.

The prison experience, frightful as it was, taught the
Whitneys a valuable lesson, which Myra never forgot:
that state courts and Federal courts are different entities.
Before this, to her lay mind, a court had been a court; the
law was the law. Now she knew that there were two different legal jurisdictions in Louisiana. The one had been
oppressive, the other kind. She was soon to learn that there
was more than one kind of law—in Louisiana.

It is somewhat significant, therefore, that about this
time William Wallace Whitney and Myra Whitney, his
wife, filed a suit in the Circuit Court of the United States
for the Eastern District of Louisiana, to compel the executors of the will of her father, Relf and Chew, to render an
account of their trust and restore to Myra Whitney her
father's inheritance. They were appealing to the Federal
power.

The first legal skirmish was short and indecisive. When
the event came to trial in the Federal court, Relf and Chew
objected that as they were acting under a will which had
been regularly probated by a probate court, their actions

were not open to question by a Circuit Court of the United States. The point was well taken, and the judge informed the Whitneys that matters of probate were beyond the jurisdiction of his particular court; if Mrs. Whitney had any rights under a later will than the one which had been established, she must get that later will regularly probated before the Court of Probates of the city, as that court alone had charge of such matters. Until that was done, a United States court could do nothing.

But before anything definite could be attempted in the Probate Court, there came on in the same United States court the libel case, *Relf* v. *Whitney*. The Federal court did not lack jurisdiction here, as it had evidently taken over the suit of Relf against Whitney when it freed Whitney from the New Orleans jail and the contest now involved not property but persons. Relf made it clear that he was going to prosecute to the fullest extent of his power the man who had spread upon the public records of New Orleans the story that he, Richard Relf, cashier of the Louisiana State Bank, had destroyed the last will of Daniel Clark and fraudulently administered his estate. He sued Whitney for heavy damages.

Whitney decided to make his defense on the sole ground that he had alleged and published *nothing but the truth*. He put the whole case in issue, and welcomed a regular legal test. The decision would of course affect no property rights but would serve to let the world know the exact status of the contending parties. The whole city had again become interested, and the Whitneys themselves hopefully awaited the day of the trial.

On their side they had Bellechasse's testimony to the

effect that Daniel Clark had truly made another will, and that his friends had searched for it after his death; they had the record taken from Judge Pitot's court of 1813, whereby the Chevalier Delacroix had asked the notaries to appear and certify whether they knew of any record or duplicate of a last will by Daniel Clark; they had the testimony of Madame Despau as to an actual marriage between Clark and Myra's mother; they had Mrs. Smythe's testimony that she had read and handled Clark's last will affirming Myra's legitimacy. They had collected other bits of helpful information, and while it is not clear that the evidence mentioned had all been formally sworn, and it was certainly not well arranged, the young husband and wife felt that they had a clear case. They were convinced that the world would now believe them when it heard their story in open court.

But the world has heard impossible stories before and has sometimes failed to believe even the true. A United States court especially is not one in which to spring fairy tales. Although the hopeful Whitneys were convinced that they had enough to prove that Richard Relf was a purloiner of wills, one who had cheated a child of her rights, they were shockingly disillusioned. They had put in issue the truth. Very well, Richard Relf was going to let them have the truth and the whole truth. To the Federal court, to the whole city, he opened a hidden chapter in the life of Daniel Clark and told the story of another child of Clark and Zulime named Caroline.

Richard Relf publicly declared not only that Daniel Clark had never been married but that he had had a child by Myra's mother before Myra had been born. Relf was absolutely certain about this, and gave names, dates, and places.[5] That long-ago trip to Philadelphia back in 1801 or 1802, Relf declared, had been for the purpose of concealing the fact that Madame DesGrange was then *enceinte* by Daniel Clark and that she had shortly thereafter given birth to a girl under the care of the famous Dr. William Shippen of Philadelphia. Not only so, but the child, Caroline, had always been treated by Daniel Clark as his own and had been brought up under the care of his partner, Daniel W. Coxe of Philadelphia. She was at that very time alive and married to a man named John Barnes living near Philadelphia. Furthermore she was herself interested in the Clark estate. Mrs. Mary Clark, the mother of Daniel Clark, had early taken Caroline to live with her, and the old lady had willed to her before her death a fourth share of her own property, calling her a "natural child" of her son. If Mrs. Whitney thought there had ever been a marriage between her father and mother, how could she account for this frank recognition of illegitimacy with reference to Caroline Barnes? Relf had letters to prove the facts he alleged and referred to the aging Daniel Coxe of Philadelphia and to Caroline Barnes herself as persons who would vouch for the truth of these assertions.

It was a thunderbolt. The Whitneys were stunned. It proved to be far worse than any imprisonment could be—but Mr. Relf had not finished. He alleged further that Myra herself was illegitimate and had been admitted so by her guardian, Samuel B. Davis, in a suit filed by his son, Horatio Davis, in 1817 when the Davis family was attempting to get some alimony from the Clark estate for the benefit of Myra.[6] On this also Relf seemed sure of himself and gave a record of the suit in question. Again his shaft found its mark. The result was that the United States court found a verdict in his favor and declared William Whitney guilty of libeling Mr. Richard Relf. The court was kind, however, and to ameliorate the outcome for the unfortunate husband fixed the fine at one dollar. This was well meant, but the case had been lost.

VII

The Whitneys now tasted the contumelious scorn of their opposers in this hostile, foreign city. They decided to file, or had already filed, a suit in regular form before the Probate Court in order to attempt something there, but the days succeeding were rather dark for them. Others would have quietly crept away in shame, but Myra was made of sterner stuff. She knew, not merely with a woman's intuition, but from actual evidence, that she had right on her side. As to the Caroline story, that could wait for later investigation. Her aunt Sophie when questioned admitted something of the Caroline account but asserted that Caroline was a child of DesGrange. What Myra actually knew was that her father had truly made a last will and solemnly declared in this his last testament that she, Myra, was his *only,* his *legitimate,* daughter. That fact was her anchor in a sea of incredulity, contumely, and scorn. Upon it she would continue her fight.

But the Whitneys had now learned the might of the forces arrayed against them, and the temper and ability of their opponents. They had been too impulsive, too child-like. What they were undertaking was a monumental task, though to them only a matter of justice. But both realized that if anything else were to be done it would require time, money, excellent legal counsel, and the painstaking and careful arrangement of evidence. They must proceed slowly, study the legal aspects of the situation, learn the ways of courts and the stranger ways of the Louisiana Code, and obtain their just due, even if it took years to do it.

They had met very little friendliness and much hostility since they had been in New Orleans, and as time would be required for pushing the case further, a voyage back to their home was proposed and doubtless gladly planned. They felt, too, that they might secure from Colonel Davis and perhaps from others evidence with which to prosecute the case. So a continuance was arranged for before the Probate Court and the Whitneys went on board a boat bound for the North. They left the city in defeat.

But if New Orleans thought that it had seen the last of that young woman who had departed on the ship then moving down the river toward the Gulf, New Orleans was very much mistaken.

The Lines Are Drawn

To THEIR amazement, the Whitneys found that news of their case had preceded them. Scarcely had they landed when a copy of the Philadelphia *Pennsylvanian* was thrust into William Whitney's hands and he saw featured in it the romantic quest of his wife.[1] The New York *Evening Star* had also printed the tale, it was learned, and on all sides the young couple discovered an avid and admiring interest. Sympathy was overwhelmingly theirs, but unfortunately the newspaper account had reacted against one whom the Whitneys least wished to see injured, Colonel Samuel B. Davis. Myra's foster father was then in his second term as state legislator and about that time became a candidate for Congress. The story that he had been a party to keeping a young lady in ignorance of her rights was calculated to damage his influence greatly. The explosive Davis was becoming increasingly restive under the sudden publicity given his private home life, and Myra saw it. So William Whitney went at once to the rescue with an open letter to the *Pennsylvanian*. As the

Colonel was quite a local personage, the Philadelphia editor did his part handsomely by an introduction in which he contrived to blame the whole thing on the New York *Evening Star.*

Whitney's letter, while castigating the "monstrously illegal and fraudulent administration" of Daniel Clark's estate, bravely defended Davis as knowing nothing whatever of a lost will. The letter ended by promising that when the Court of Probates in New Orleans should finally act, "the whole judicial record of this case shall be spread before the world."

The public reaction to Whitney's letter was instantaneous and gave Myra her first taste of newspaper support. It was like wine to her. Publicity in that era was nothing like the huge, unashamed science it has since become, but its underlying principles have always been the same, and Myra Clark, whether she knew it or not, instinctively had every one of them at her finger tips.

II

Richard Relf of Louisiana had also seen a copy of the *Evening Star* and in brief order sent to the northern newspapers a long letter defending himself, claiming that Daniel Clark left no fortune, only a mountain of debt:

"As regards the so much commiserated lady, who from the manner she is spoken of, might be considered to be a legitimate daughter of Mr. Clark, from whom for some vile purpose, the name of her parent had been kept concealed, a matter for which her guardian alone is answerable, I have to inform you, that when an infant, but some years before Mr. Clark's death, she was taken into the family of Col. Samuel B. Davis, now residing in Philadelphia, and brought up by him bearing his name, and was led to consider him her parent until a short time previous to her marriage; nor did Col. Davis ever set up any claim for her upon Mr. Clark's estate, except for alimony which the court refused to grant. If she be the daughter of Mr. Clark, who was never married, and her reputed mother, she is the offspring of an adulterous bed. . . .

"Would to God that the millions you speak of had never existed, they might have spared me the years of toil and anguish I have gone through, and saved me from which I consider infinitely more injurious, the opprobrium with which it is attempted to tarnish my reputation.

"With respect to the will said to have been purloined, I shall only observe that all the persons who pretend to have any knowledge of it, unite in saying that it was scrupulously enjoined upon them by Mr. Clark, to keep it a secret both from Mr. Chew and myself; it is not therefore to be presumed that I knew of its existence. . . ." [2]

Mr. Relf's long-range broadside definitely transferred the case to the newspapers. It was now William Whitney's turn to respond, and he did so by putting all his documents into the hands of the *Evening Star* editor. The New York editor saw that he had a human-interest story that a newspaperman would go far to obtain. In consequence, he broke the whole thing open to the reading public in his issue of November 11, 1835. Naturally the story was long, but it set people to talking all the more. From that time on, there were many who followed the fortunes of Myra through all her vicissitudes.

Thus the winter passed. The Whitneys spent their time in making every preparation possible for a renewal of the conflict when spring should come. They knew now that their undertaking was one that would cost, and cost enormously, if it were carried through. Former experiences had taught that. But they were young, sanguine, and playing for a vast fortune. They could well afford to spend hundreds to gain hundreds of thousands. Assets were turned into cash for the legal war chest, and hope continued high. Their kinspeople proved sympathetic, and, while the canny New York mind perhaps had its doubts concerning the outcome of these vastly expensive journeys to New Orleans, the young couple found encouragement from those they loved. Old Joshua Whitney himself was a hard fighter, and while his ninth son lacked his burly strength of fiber, William Whitney had far more than his share of moral courage and considerable mental keenness. He went back to New Orleans, taking his wife and babies, utterly unafraid.

III

As the characters in the legal drama began to move to their appointed places, suddenly there appeared among them one who had played a stellar role in the original cast. Zulime came back from France and went straight to New Orleans!

The rather subdued Madame Gardette of 1835 was not

the flashing Zulime DesGrange of thirty years before. Although it was impossible for time to efface altogether the conquering gypsy beauty which had always proved so devastating to men, nevertheless it was undeniable that the years had stolen something of her exotic charm. In place of it, time had added a measure of timidity, suggested something even of suffering in her face. She had lived in Philadelphia with Dr. Gardette for a number of years, had borne him children, and then gone with him to France. Now he was dead, and the widowed Madame Gardette was returning to her own land, her own people. Her grown son, Dr. James Gardette, was in New Orleans, and she came to live with him. It was a curious twist of fate that brought the mother back at the very time when her long-lost daughter set foot in the same city to claim her inheritance.

And what of the first meeting of this oddly paired parent and child, living in different worlds, lost to each other until now? One does not look for the traditional rapturous embrace, or imagine the daughter throwing herself into the arms of this mother who had permitted her to be taken away as a child to face the world alone. But one cannot be sure. The blame of course was Zulime's, but Myra was too much like her father to harbor futile resentment. With her, one thing now had come to matter—her suit—and she saw in her mother a potent ally. She soon made her definitely one. Zulime may have forsaken Myra but Myra never forsook Zulime. They became friends, confidantes. Myra was one day to say that she would immediately abandon the fight were it not for her mother's good name at stake. Her mother's good name!

In a short while Myra became the mightiest champion Zulime ever had. In turn, Madame Gardette, living quietly on Burgundy Street with her son James, was a loyal, though somewhat reticent, supporter of her daughter's cause. Myra was in constant touch with her and learned many details connected with the points at issue. In 1836, soon after Myra's return from the North, she persuaded her mother to resign certain claims to the estate in her favor. In these claims Zulime held forth as the legal wife of Daniel Clark, and through an instrument prepared by Myra she definitely deeded them to her, May 7, 1836. This gave the daughter a clearer title, she felt, to her father's estate, certainly to Zulime's share of it.

IV

William Whitney and Myra had not been the only ones to prepare for a further struggle during the winter season. Richard Relf and those who had bought parcels of the Clark land from him were deeply interested in bolstering their legal breastworks, especially since the Keene libel case had gone against Relf. There was considerable writing around and consultation among the heirs and executors of the Clark estate. In a short while the surviving sisters of Daniel Clark found themselves drawn in, interested jointly with Relf and Chew in supporting the will of 1811.

It may be recalled that this will, the one probated, named Mrs. Mary Clark, the mother, as sole heir of the testator. It was in her name that Relf and Chew were supposed to administer the property. She, excellent old lady that she was, knew little of her brilliant son's property rights and seems to have been much more concerned over his moral lapses. She bitterly regretted the liaison with Zulime. She believed that the child, Caroline, who really had been born to Zulime, as Relf had said, was her son's child; but the old lady, as well as all the Clarks, kindly and considerately accepted her. As the girl grew, the grandmother especially became much attached to her.

In 1825 old Mrs. Clark died in Germantown, far from the coasts of Ireland. Her property she had disposed of by a short will entrusted to Dr. William Hulings. This will directed that her property was to be divided among her three daughters and Caroline, a fourth part to each. The daughters were Eleanor O'Beirne, Jane Green, and Sarah Campbell. Caroline took her share as the frankly recognized daughter of Daniel Clark, deceased. It was understood that the Mary Clark estate consisted principally of the New Orleans holdings of Daniel Clark.

Mrs. Clark in drawing up her will had been reminded of the girl Myra. But she preferred to say nothing whatever in her will concerning this Myra. The least said of her the better, she felt. But Dr. Hulings and Coxe insisted, for reasons known to themselves, and Mrs. Clark at length consented to put an item in her will directing that a small legacy be left to Myra, the "natural daughter" of her son, Daniel Clark.[3]

How close a contact there was between the Clark heirs and Relf and Chew is not known, but it was quite evident that they were all together involved in supporting the will of 1811. Hence when Myra came into court attempting to set aside this will, she found her own aunts, her father's sisters, at the head of the opposition.

The reader who looks for philosophy underneath law may now begin to see why that "medieval" Code of Louisiana set such store by family integrity and was so merciless regarding illegitimacy. As the growing litigation, seeking to unravel the tangled threads of this case, got under way, beneath the play and interplay of legal principles, one discovers the clash of personalities, the cleavage between blood kin. Almost the first battle was Myra against Caroline. They were sisters, or half sisters, if we take Myra's version, since she held that Caroline was the legitimate child of DesGrange. Caroline explained Myra as no Clark at all, but the daughter of Zulime by some other man. Myra paid no attention to this allegation, treating it as beneath contempt. But her opponents spread the tale far and wide: Zulime had imposed Myra on Clark as his child while in reality she was the child of another of her lovers.

Thus with Relf and Chew were arrayed the Clark heirs —O'Beirnes, Greens, Campbells, and Caroline Barnes—all interested in supporting the will of 1811 against their niece and sister, Myra, and doing it by disclaiming her entirely. There was also the aging Daniel Coxe of Philadelphia, whose testimony was strongly relied upon to prove the illegitimacy of Myra. And Coxe himself had benefited under the will of 1811.

On Myra's side were the Carrières—Madame Despau, Madame Caillavet, Zulime herself, and her son, Dr. James Gardette. The aunts were the chief witnesses as to the factum of a marriage in Philadelphia. With Myra also was the Davis connection—the Colonel and his wife in Delaware, the Boisfontaines in France, and Harriet Harper Smythe, now in Opelousas, Louisiana. One Davis, however, was against her. This was the Colonel's son, Horatio, who as a boy had sailed for school with Daniel Clark when he first went to Congress. Now Horatio Davis was an attorney in New Orleans. He was Myra's foster brother but was later to prove a thorn in her side.

Naturally the attorneys for Relf and Chew called attention to the fact that Myra's chief witnesses were her kinspeople, and that their testimony was to be discredited accordingly. Myra's attorneys countered by showing that Relf, Chew, the Clarks, and even Coxe were all interested financially in upholding the "fraudulent" will of earlier date. The Relf and Chew interests were not at this stage convinced that the Whitneys could give them serious trouble, but Richard Relf himself was undeniably worried over the sudden publicity and the attitude of the northern papers. Furthermore, he had left himself open to attack in the matter of making a legal return as to his trusteeship of Clark's property. The law said this should be done within one year. Twenty years had now passed, and the Probate Court records were bare of any return filed by Chew & Relf, executors for Daniel Clark. Whitney undeniably had a telling point against him there.

The battle was on.

V

The news that the pretended Myra Clark had come back to make more trouble for the people who had bought her father's land spread with rapidity. This time New Orleans was more irritated than amused. The Whitneys began to feel the power of the hostility that they had aroused. To attempt to take houses and lands from people who had bought in good faith, and to do it by a claim that was an assault upon the most sacred tie of life, was scarcely to be borne by the conservative populace of New Orleans. Hardly a person in the city believed Myra's pretensions, and that she should be back to press them after what had happened the year before was deemed effrontery. They called her names that may well be omitted here—and meant them.

But other matters were clamoring for public attention at the time. The Seminole trouble in Florida was dragging along. General Gaines of the United States army had hurried away to Tampa with two or three steamers of troops early in February, but not much had happened to satisfy the American people that Oceola would get no more scalp locks. Gaines himself had been shuttled back, after getting a tooth shot out by the Indians, and was now on the Sabine preserving American neutrality in the Texas-Mexican fracas. New Orleans papers carried long accounts of the "Texian" troubles. The Alamo caused a surge of horror over the South, and then came the news of Houston's victory at San Jacinto. In May, New Orleans thronged to the levee to see a man lifted from a boat and taken to the Christy home on Girod Street. It was Sam Houston himself, supposedly about to die from a gangrenous foot.[4] But he did not die, and General Gaines over on the border soon found himself on the confines of a new republic, whose flag was a single star. New Orleans thrilled to it all, while in the North, on the far horizon of national life, a weazened, cynical wraith of a man lingered long enough to mutter sardonically: "I was twenty-five years too soon." [5]

It was Aaron Burr.

Then Mr. and Mrs. Whitney appeared before the judge of the Probate Court.

VI

His honor, the Judge, was no more rejoiced to see Mrs. Whitney than the rest of the city. He was in fact annoyed. The woman, he felt, had an utterly impossible case, affecting the real rights of many persons, among them certain individuals of consequence. For instance, there were Judge François Xavier Martin of the Supreme Court of Louisiana and Judge Matthews of the same tribunal. Both these eminent jurists had bought some of the Clark land from Richard Relf. Were they to be dispossessed now after all these years?

This question may have disturbed others but Judge Bermudez knew a simpler way out. Mrs. Whitney was there to probate a will? Where was the will?

The will, her counsel explained, was unfortunately lost. Its destruction was a part of Mrs. Whitney's contention. Her witnesses and their depositions would establish its contents.

But his honor ruled in effect: "Because of the peculiar laws in force in Louisiana the Court of Probates could not exercise the powers of jurisdiction of probating a will, unless the same were produced in open court."

It was in vain that testimony was adduced referring to the lost will. Judge Bermudez blandly ruled that if a will was to be probated, that will must be produced.

William Whitney then tried another tack. He asked the court for an order compelling Richard Relf to bring before the court itself all papers and letters of Daniel Clark that had remained, in order that these might be examined for any possible evidence.

At this the Judge showed unexpected asperity. He declared with feeling that he considered this an affront to the character of Mr. Richard Relf and flatly refused to enter any such order. Then the Whitneys saw what they faced. They could expect nothing whatever from the Probate Court. They lapsed into a contemptuous silence and ordered their counsel to make no further response. Judge Bermudez thereupon ordered a nonsuit entered.

They had finished with the Court of Probates forever. If they tried again it would be elsewhere.

Meanwhile little Rhoda Whitney had put in her appearance, a bright child named for old Mrs. Whitney up in Binghamton. But family matters seem to have weighed lightly on Myra. The vision of the fortune and the fulfillment of her father's last will were ever before her. She had become somewhat accustomed to what she termed the "law's delays"; she felt that victory would soon be hers and the family could live in luxury ever after. That their money was fast running out rested lightly upon her mind. So did Rhoda, and Julia also when she came along.

Yellow Jack Serves a Summons

CENTURIES ago there were wrought out two different systems of jurisprudence in widely separated parts of the earth, and these two systems were destined in the ongoing of time to meet in a peculiar way in one American state —Louisiana. One of them originated in Rome as that queen city of antiquity moved forward in her self-appointed task of giving law to the nations. Gathering together all that ever had been of law or custom, all that the wise men and jurists of Greece had to offer, everything that had the force of reason or right in life, she organized and articulated it in that thorough fashion peculiarly her own and then imposed it upon the world by the might of her legions. Justinian at length assembled the jurists of his day and by their aid promulgated that vast compilation known as the Justinian Code. It became the law of the lands where the Roman eagles were carried, and they were carried over the whole known earth.

With the dissolution of the empire, the Code continued, giving law to the new nations as they arose. The Latin

countries of southern Europe, closest in blood and tradition
to the Imperial City State, naturally kept it very much as
it had been, and their people carried the Code with them
wherever they went. It crossed the sea in the ships of
Columbus; it sailed around the Cape with Da Gama; it
was the law of the lawless conquistadors on the pampas of
the Argentine or in the halls of the Incas. The more pacific
French explorers acted in accordance with its tenets and
founded their colonies on its principles. In every Latin-
American country of the present day, as well as in the
nations of southern Europe, the Civil Code is the basis of
jurisprudence.

Noteworthy among the provisions of the Code are
those affecting marriage and the home. Its directions concerning property and inheritance are motivated by the intent to secure at all hazards the supremacy of the legal
family. So strongly are its provisions framed here that the
Code refuses to allow any parent to leave property to an
illegitimate child. It cannot be done, as Mazureau of New
Orleans once told Daniel Clark. On the other hand, every
father is compelled to leave his property to his lawful wife
or children. He cannot alienate it from them. They are his
"forced heirs" in spite of his or anyone else's wish. Disin-
heritance is not a Latin proceeding.

This Code was, and is, the fundamental law of the state
of Louisiana.[1] Jurists of that commonwealth call their system the Civil Code, or more simply, THE CODE. That, together with the legislative and other statutes and later re-
visions, etc., enacted pursuant thereto, is the law of the
state.

II

But centuries ago while Rome was evolving her iron law, another system of jurisprudence was slowly taking shape among a different people. Among the fens and moors of ancient England, among the south folk and the north folk, as the ages rolled on, there began to shape itself a great body of custom at last possessing the force of law. The rude pronouncements of tribal chiefs added to it, and each primitive assize lent it strength. Ancient sages repeated its unwritten provisions, and while eventually the Roman legions with their inflexible Code overran the land and stamped the impress of Rome even on the customs of the people, nevertheless an underlying spirit and ethos survived. History finally shows the Latin Codex in the hands of the conquering Norman bending to the will of the Saxon soul that was in Britain. The law survived. Kings and chancellors finally gathered together and organized its principles, until out of the heart of old England, vast, amorphous, unwritten, came The Common Law, mighty bulwark of Anglo-Saxon liberty. It was set before King John by the Barons of Runnymede; it came across the Atlantic in the ships of English explorers and rounded the Horn with Sir Francis Drake. It was at Plymouth with the Mayflower and Captain John Smith mentioned its provisions in no uncertain terms at Jamestown. It went into the American wilderness with the pioneer and was the guide of primitive hustings courts in backwoods communities. Finally, it was recognized by and in the Constitution of the United States and forms today the basis of its law. So when William Charles Coles Claiborne came riding into the Tchoupitoulas gate of New Orleans to take over the province for the United States, resting, as it were, upon the pennon of his little troop of horse, was the Common Law of England and America.

Accompanying the Common Law and in a measure correlative with it goes another system which is not so much law perhaps as a method of applying law. There is a flexibility, a difference in individual cases, for which the law fails to allow. So, by a process long and involved and too tortuous to outline here, the English people evolved a system called *chancery* or *equity,* wherein by a separate court the rigors of the law may be modified and the situation at hand justly or equitably decided. Thus the court of chancery as well as the court of law has come to be an inherent fixture among the Anglo-Saxon people. It is, in brief, the effort of English individualism to express itself and to acknowledge the fact that a regulation which may be out of place for one may be good for another. The law may say: "An eye for an eye and a tooth for a tooth"; but equity says, "Whose eye for whose eye? And whose tooth?" Naturally, chancery practice depends tremendously on the chancellor.

To summarize then: When Louisiana was admitted to the Union it continued to use the Civil Code for its own internal government and affairs, or as much of it as was not in conflict with the Constitution of the United States and the Federal statutes. The provisions of the Code as they affected property rights and succession were of course retained and today are enforced in its courts. The Common Law does not apply in Louisiana *except in United States courts,* where also chancery practice must be carried out.

But to this day there is no distinction made in Louisiana between law and equity in the courts of that commonwealth.

The reader will now begin to comprehend the lesson that the Whitneys learned early in their Louisiana experience, that state courts and Federal courts are different entities. Holding citizenship as they did in another state, they had the advantage of being able to choose their forum, or so it appeared to them. By this time also they had discovered the temper of the local courts. In every way, New Orleans had made its hostile animus clear to the visitors from the North. Besides the undeniable bias of the local judges, there was always held before them a veritable bar sinister. Myra, in the ugly language of the Code, was an "adulterine bastard," and it is doubtful whether by the Code she could be recognized as a person at all. She was "Mrs. Whitney" in the North, but in the New Orleans courts she was nobody. It appeared that in Louisiana one had to have one's rights in order to get them.

III

Early in the year, even before the disappointing scene in the Probate Court, the Whitneys had instructed their lawyer to enter a suit in chancery in the District Court of the United States for the Eastern District of Louisiana. They were asking the judge of that court to exercise his chancery jurisdiction in behalf of Mrs. Whitney, a citizen of another state who needed relief in the matter of Louisiana property left her by will. This time, besides naming their usual opponents, Richard Relf and Beverly Chew, the

Whitneys cited twenty-five other persons who were holding the Clark property.

When this step became known there broke out a mighty
expostulation in excited French. Most of this the alarmed
defendants poured into the ear of their banker friend,
Richard Relf. But that gentleman assured them all that, as
he had sold them the property in the first place, he would
see that no cloud rested on their titles, provided they followed his instructions. This they promised to do. Then
Relf got in touch with L. C. Duncan and John Slidell,
lawyers.

When the day came for Relf and his codefendants to
respond to the allegations made by Mrs. Whitney, he and
the twenty-five whom Myra had named came into the
court. The Honorable Samuel H. Harper was upon the
bench, no doubt observing with amazement the unusual
number included under one bill. Myra's counsel was present and it was expected that the case would quickly develop
the issue. But the court had scarcely opened when eleven
of the defendants averred that French was their maternal
language, and that they had been called into court by papers which were in English. The content of these legal
papers they said they did not know, or could scarcely understand. They prayed the court for oyer, or a view of all
documents bearing on the case *in French*.[2] Each defendant
asked the same as a matter of justice.

This was a shrewd trick designed to annoy, if not block,
the case altogether. It was before the time of multigraphing
machines or typewriters, and the translation of so many
papers, with the necessary printing in the French language
was, they knew, a well-nigh insurmountable obstacle be-

fore the complainants. The Whitney counsel objected bitterly. But Judge Harper, whatever his motives, ordered it done. The Whitneys were to furnish every defendant with a French copy of every paper.

This was in February. Before the May session of the court when the case was to be continued, Judge Harper suddenly died. To take his place a Judge Lawrence came on the bench. The Whitneys had remained in the city all this time hopefully awaiting the occasion.

The French-speaking defendants who had been so anxious for oyer of all bills against them never bothered to be present or to respond in any way when the May term of court came. Perhaps they had found that they need have no special worry with Judge Lawrence presiding, for he refused to take any notice of the case at all. The Whitneys pressed for an attachment for answer against Relf and the others, but the judge ignored the request. Apparently he called for order in his court, refused to notice the Whitneys or their counsel, and adjourned the session as far as they were concerned!

We have noticed that chancery practice depends largely on the chancellor.

IV

In the face of all these rebuffs and in view of the heavy expense, there is a natural wonder at the determination of the Whitneys to press their unpopular case. They had known little of law or of courts of equity a few months before. Now, these were becoming almost part of their normal life. William Whitney would do anything for Myra; and Myra had become devoted to her own cause with a passion that began to appear all-embracing. She had found, too, that outside of Louisiana she had many friends and was receiving from the North messages of encouragement. She was not in the least ashamed of her story and delighted in telling it. Already she had in mind the ultimate appeal to the greatest tribunal in the nation. She was pressing a case then in the United States court in Louisiana and knew that from that judicial chamber the leap was not far to the Supreme Court sitting under the dome of the Capitol in Washington.

Meanwhile the United States "District Court" was made the United States "Circuit Court," and all pending cases were transferred to that. The Whitney case was nothing if not pending, and so it came about that at the very first session of the new Circuit Court, there the Whitneys sat with their counsel, ready to renew the motion for an attachment.

But Judge Lawrence was on the bench again and alone. He had already refused to notice the motion made by these people and this time even refused to have any notice of such a motion entered on the records of his court. This was extremely highhanded. Myra's counsel insisted that, as he had made such a motion and as this had been overruled, a record of that fact should go into the minutes of the court's session. Judge Lawrence peremptorily refused and, noticing that the clerk of the court on his own responsibility had made a minute of what was done, ordered him to erase it at once.[3] He would permit no mention of the Whitneys at all. Evidently his Honor would have been glad to erase them as well as their case.

This was going far, but the Judge went further. He

entered a ruling in his Federal court that "henceforth in Louisiana the mode of proceedings in all Civil cases (those of Admiralty alone excepted) should be conformable to the Code of Practice of Louisiana and all the acts of the Legislature of that State." This was reversing the sovereignty of the United States with a vengeance and gave Myra the opening she wanted. She acted instantly and appealed to the Supreme Court of the United States. She intended to compel this defiant judge to proceed according to the practice that Congress said should prevail in every United States court.

Meanwhile the American vice-consul at Matanzas, one George Traub, got an order directing him to proceed to the sugar plantation of J. D. D. Bellechasse and ask him certain questions and cross-questions which were enclosed. Mr. Traub must seal his answers and forward them through regular diplomatic channels to the United States court in New Orleans. About this time a notary in Philadelphia went to see Colonel Samuel B. Davis and he too was asked to respond under oath to the same questions and certain other cross-questions. In various places, the legal machinery of the United States government was moving to get at the truth of this curious story of Louisiana.

But as the heat of August settled upon the lower Mississippi Valley, out of the miasmic marshes and disease-infected ports of the tropics there came into New Orleans a silent but dreadful visitor—YELLOW FEVER. The malady struck with a swiftness that demoralized the entire state. In a few days several hundred victims were down, with the fever rapidly spreading. The bells began to toll; they soon seemed to be eternally tolling, while the barred shutters and the early morning funerals by the score began to throw over the city an atmosphere of doom. Law courts were closed and nearly all business was paralyzed. The very air seemed to be laden with death and there was scarcely a family which did not have sick to nurse or dead to bewail. Ten thousand people had the fever within the short space of eight weeks, and, of these, five thousand died. This was almost one tenth of the population of the city and an unparalleled calamity.[4]

August went into September with the pall that the epidemic had cast upon the public mind impossible to break. The Whitneys had passed through the worst of it. They were greatly concerned for the children and took every measure that the blindly directed science of that day ordered. At one time great lines of blazing tar barrels were out in the streets, put there by public order to prevent the "spread of the infection." At other times cannon were fired in salvos to "disturb the air" and so bring relief. All efforts were of no avail. The early morning funerals increased in number, rumbling away with their dead to St. Louis cemetery as day followed day. September wore on and the virulence of the epidemic grew less and less. Then toward the middle of the month William Whitney complained of feeling ill and went to bed. On his face Yellow Jack had written the telltale marks.

Myra secured the services of a much-harassed physician. The doctor came and ordered the patient to be bled. Myra herself, so the story goes, got the necessary basin and held it while the doctor opened her husband's arm.[5] This was done three successive times, but the young man from New York state grew appreciably weaker. The familiar symptoms of the disease ran their horrid course until the dark, blotched skin betokened the end. This came on September 13, 1837. He had been ill but three days.

Myra, heartbroken, laid him to rest in New Orleans. The fever yet raged and there were the children to look after. The next year she had his body conveyed back and laid to rest among his own Chenango hills, far from the inhospitable marshes of New Orleans.

Throughout the whole murky, muddy case, nothing can be said to the discredit of William Wallace Whitney. He remains a knight unselfish and without fear.

The Supreme Court

ON A January morning almost two years later, an unusual group of persons might have been seen walking through the cavernous underground halls of the Capitol in Washington. Their destination seemed to be a common one, the room beyond the labyrinthine maze of short, thick columns where the Supreme Court of the United States was preparing to sit.

It was a miserable location for such an august tribunal,[1] but it was the best the nation at that time felt could be done for its highest court. The quarters assigned the court were a dim north room with few ornaments about it, though a rich carpet and silk draperies aided to some degree in effacing its bare austerity. Behind a low mahogany railing was a row of high-backed seats for the honorable Justices, with a neat desk in front of each for judicial elbows or for papers and briefs. The Justices, having no private room of their own, were forced to don their black gowns in front of everyone, and this public robing and disrobing detracted greatly from the dignity of their office. But when they were robed and seated, whatever may have been the unworthy surroundings, no one in 1839 would have found any lack of dignity in the Court itself.

The long tenure of John Marshall had come to an end and that of Roger Brooke Taney had begun. The mists of the Court's earlier adumbration were rapidly passing, and, thanks to its own intrinsic merit and struggle for life, it had made both President and Congress respect it as a coordinate branch of government. By the end of Marshall's term, it had begun to tower into the nation's sky. "There is no branch of our government that has had a harder fight to establish itself than the Supreme Court," stated Charles Warren. "And there is no branch that today enjoys greater respect." [2]

A pre-eminent group of Justices was sitting behind the mahogany railing on that January day in 1839.[3] Near the center sat the firm, broad-browed Joseph Story of Massachusetts, old in years, but well-nigh omniscient in legal lore—great constitutionalist, great Federalist, great authority on equity. Even the jurists of Britain looked to him with respect.

Present also was the huge, dignified John McLean of Ohio, whose tremendous aquiline nose and fearless gray eyes impressed one with the poise and majestic strength one imagines to have radiated from the old Roman conquerors. But despite the beetling brows and regal air of the big McLean, he was gentle in disposition and as regular at his Methodist "class meeting" as the Chief Justice was at attending mass.

The next Justice must hold our attention somewhat longer. James M. Wayne [4] of Savannah was used to commanding attention, especially in the social circle. An appointee of Andrew Jackson, Wayne had but recently come into the Court. To many onlookers, the Georgian was easily the most interesting figure on the bench. Stout, but graceful in figure, with clustering, wavy hair just tinged with gray, with a courteous manner and a tone of refinement in his voice, he created an impression of virile strength that both men and women, especially women, much admired.

Almost the very antithesis to Wayne was another Jackson appointee, the powerful, blocky John Catron of Tennessee, a hard-riding, practical circuit judge who had been elevated to the Supreme bench by the man whom he had supported in Tennessee politics. Catron, however, was no creature of Jackson. Sound, practical common sense was his prevailing trait. With it he had bludgeoned his way to the top, and he used it there.

Henry Baldwin of Pennsylvania and candid John McKinley of Alabama made up the other members of the Court, as Justice Thompson of New York was absent on account of illness in his home. In the center sat the thin, ascetic Taney, in his black robe looking like an unworldly ecclesiastic. The Court was already learning that Roger Brooke Taney, though but recently appointed, was no unworthy successor of John Marshall.

II

It will not be supposed that the collective mind of such a group of men could possibly be unbalanced by any story, no matter how strange or romantic. Technically they were assembled to hear counsel for a Mrs. Whitney of New Orleans ask them to issue a mandamus wherewith to compel a Louisiana Federal judge to proceed according to the rules of chancery. Actually Myra had staked her hopes on giving the highest court in the country a chance to view and review the manner in which her life had been thwarted since childhood. To her the occasion represented the ultimate in her hopes. She believed so profoundly in the truth of her cause that she was convinced that anyone who heard must likewise believe, and that any who believed would surely help. How this was to come about she scarcely knew. Before the Court she was asking a mandamus; actually she wanted relief and the championship of these august Judges.

The crier intoned the time-honored "Oyez." Her counsel stood, a man by the name of Walter Jones. "If your Honors please. . . ."

He was a small, plain, insignificant-looking man, this Walter Jones,[5] eccentric to a marked degree. But in spite of his nondescript appearance and the high falsetto in which he spoke, the Justices listened to him with attention. The plainness of his face was belied by a pair of eyes that "for piercing intelligence and shrewdness of expression, I have never seen surpassed," one observer remarked. In a brief military career he had earned the title of "General," and as General Walter Jones he was well known to all the Court. Charles Sumner once said of him that he was "unsurpassed if not unequalled by any lawyer in the country." Such was the man then standing up for Myra's interests before the Supreme Court. She was fortunate to have his services.

Indeed she was fortunate to have a case here at all after the dismal days of '37. The tolling of the bells in New Orleans as the yellow fever epidemic spent its force came near sounding the end of her hopes as they did that of her early happiness. The months succeeding the death of William Whitney were among the darkest of her life. She found at once that battling the world without a husband was a vastly more difficult undertaking than when she had a masculine arm on which to lean. For the first time financial worry raised its ugly head. The Whitneys had put almost their entire fortune into this Louisiana lottery of theirs. William Whitney's death left his widow with but a small residue of a once comfortable living. Was it not time for her to cease the bitter struggle against the hostile city where she had lost her husband and gained nothing but scorn? Why not go to quiet Binghamton and with the help of the generous, openhanded Whitneys bring up her children, now three clamorous little stairsteps calling always for food and attention?

Such a temptation may have come to Myra but she brushed it aside. Her cause was never more sacred to her than after William Whitney died. She rightly considered him a sacrifice for her "rights," as she was beginning to term her whole case. What William Whitney had died for was worth living and fighting for.

To Binghamton, however, she did go sometime during the next year and, at the end of the long, dreary journey, saw the body of her husband finally laid to rest.

Then she talked business with the Whitney clan. She meant to carry on and needed money.

No doubt the sensible Whitneys thought the whole

thing had gone far enough and may have told each other so in the privacy of the family counsels. But Myra was Myra, and she was also the wife of their dead William and the mother of his children. If not then, certainly later, the Whitneys did back her generously. She literally "talked the money out of their pockets," it was said. And so General Walter Jones was standing at the bar of the Supreme Court in Washington.

III

Lawyers in such a place and presence take an honorable pride in being at the peak of their own professional powers, and General Jones, for all his apparent carelessness, was no exception. He had a story to tell the honorable Justices, a story such as the highest court had never heard before, and he intended to make it a good one. As the end of his efforts he wanted an order to compel a judge in Louisiana to put chancery practice into the Federal court there. But the astute Jones knew that the documented history of a child cheated of her name and fortune would make a magnificent steppingstone for his call for a mandamus.

The little lawyer gave the Court the whole history beginning with Daniel Clark and ending with the ruling of Judge Lawrence in refusing to allow chancery practice in the United States Circuit Court of Louisiana. He cited the congressional act of 1822 whereby it was expressly declared that chancery practice should prevail in United States courts everywhere, and he concluded by asking the Court to see that it did prevail in Louisiana.

The shrewd little General felt that he had a clear case and had presented it well. He sat down.

The Court considered.

Three months later the long-awaited decision was handed down. Justice Story wrote it for the Court, perhaps because he was considered the country's greatest authority on equity.

He paid no attention to the romance involved in the story of the fair litigant. To him the question was simply: Ought the Court to issue a mandamus in this particular case? He asserted ponderously:

"That it is the duty of the Circuit Court to proceed in this suit according to the rules prescribed by the Supreme Court for proceedings in equity cases . . . can admit of little doubt. [Score one for Myra.] That the proceedings of the district judge and orders made by him . . . are not in conformity with those rules and with chancery practice, can admit of as little doubt. [Score two for Myra.] But the question . . . is . . . whether the case before us is one in which a *mandamus* ought to issue. And we are of the opinion that it is not such a case. [Defeat for Myra.] The district judge is proceeding in the case, no matter how irregular that proceeding may be deemed. And the appropriate redress, if any, is to be obtained by an appeal after the final decree shall be had in the cause. A writ of *mandamus* is not the proper remedy. . . . The motion for the *mandamus* is hereby denied." [6]

The crux of the matter lies in the words, "the district judge is *proceeding*." Their Honors thought that Myra had gone off on a collateral issue and started something new when she should have waited until the whole case was over and then appealed on the ground of its irregularity. The Court was not going to force the Louisiana judge to act in a certain way, but they meant to reverse him if he did not.

It was good law, sound law, and bound to be the law when the bespectacled Story handed it out, but it did not help Myra. She would have to spend more money waiting for the case to drag on toward an indefinite end and then appeal.

The district Judge was "proceeding."

The General

MEANWHILE heavy legal skirmishing had been taking place on the New Orleans front. The Clark property in the Faubourg St. Jean, or St. John, as it was now called, had come to be of enormous value with boom times on the river and the rapid spread of the city. Myra claimed this land not only because of the lost will but by virtue of the fact that she had purchased it from Bellechasse in Matanzas. As her campaign progressed and she added to her threat in the Federal court an actual move to hold and keep the St. John land, the Clark heirs, her aunt, cousin, and sister, aroused themselves. Caroline Barnes acting with her husband, Dr. John Barnes, and of course Relf and Chew, in turn went into court and had the sheriff, one Frederick Buisson, take possession of the squares in dispute. Whereupon Myra, who believed in returning blow for blow, sued the sheriff. The situation was becoming complicated.[1]

But it appeared to be a forlorn situation for the widowed Mrs. Whitney as the year 1839 dragged on. Her foes were powerful and well entrenched, her friends negligible. And then, when her sky was darkest, there bowed low before her a distinguished, if somewhat elderly, officer and gentleman, Major General Edmund Pendleton Gaines [2] of the United States army.

The General was a widower, queer and courtly. Over six feet tall, thin and erect, with sloe-black eyes which were in decided contrast to his snow-white hair, he possessed a leisurely southern drawl rather surprising for such an aggressive, military figure. He combined undoubted ability and bravery with a quixotic eccentricity that broke out in most unmilitary ways. He gave attention to petty foibles of dress and ballroom decorum that his great rival, General Winfield Scott, and his hard-fighting staff, found excruciatingly funny, and after the manner of the Napoleonic school prided himself as much on his ability to hold a lady's fan correctly as to lead a charge. The General had done both in his time. The ladies liked him immensely, and while men sometimes smiled at his oddities, the smile was a tolerant one. Under all his apparent foppery the old soldier was as brave as a lion and the whole country knew it.

He had been born in Virginia of a distinguished family and now at sixty-two years of age was rounding out an honorable military career. He was the wearer of a congressional medal struck in his honor for his gallant defense of Fort Erie against the British in 1814; and the three powerful states of New York, Virginia, and Tennessee had each rewarded him by a resolution and a handsome sword for his valor and victory on that occasion. At this time General Gaines was one of the two high-ranking officers of the army, the commander of the Department of the West. His headquarters were in New Orleans, from which place he kept watch on the border, drew plans for forts and stockades he thought the government should build, and sent forth a perfect bombardment of pamphlets appealing to the youth of the nation for "preparedness," as we should call it today. He had heard of Myra and her suit and remembered that he had known and liked Daniel Clark. An introduction was sought and arranged. The General was completely charmed by the vivacious young widow almost thirty years younger than he, and in a short while he became quite attentive. People said that he was old enough to be her father, but Myra was invariably gracious to everyone. It was not long before the courtly hero of Erie laid his heart and hand before her. Myra "considered."

The disparity in age was something, but Mrs. Whitney with her slender means, her children, and her expensive and growing litigation realized that the conquest of a well-to-do general of the United States army was not to be scorned. Furthermore, she had come to be genuinely fond of the elderly officer whose direct simplicity and unimpeachable integrity were doubly attractive to one whose whole life had been shadowed by duplicity. She knew that she could rely absolutely on the kindness, protection, and love of Edmund P. Gaines—and there were the children. It was the old story of June and October, but a rather forlorn June and a hale and sunny October. She accepted him.

Before the ceremony, a naïve marriage contract was drawn up and signed by the two parties. The General, who called himself the "party of the first part," listed on paper

all the assets that he was "bringing into marriage." These
were mostly lands located near Memphis, Tennessee, and
in East Florida, all valued at $107,000. Myra, the "party
of the second part," put her assets down as the Faubourg
St. John lots, valued at $100,000, and also her rights and
claims to the estate of her deceased father, Daniel Clark.
She added:

". . . that the said party of the second part, in consideration of the party of the first part being obliged to have
considerable trouble and expense in attending to her law
suits . . . hereby makes a donation to him *inter vivos,*
out of her property to be recovered from the said succession,
the sum of one hundred thousand dollars; provided the
same should produce an amount sufficient to render said
donation legal. . . ." [3]

All of which was duly drawn up, signed and attested
before W. Y. Lewis, notary public.

The marriage took place at the home of one of Myra's
friends, and there by a simple ceremony she became for the
second time a bride. Henceforth she was known as Myra
Clark Gaines.

By this marriage she stepped at once into a social position previously denied her. Louisiana society, like its civil
law, had refused to recognize her as a person. Now perforce
it must. The more-than-doubtful Mrs. Whitney, who
could be called unprintable names with impunity, was
now living in a handsome suite at the St. Charles Hotel,
the wife of the General who commanded every post on the
river. New Orleans of course had not changed its attitude,
and its inner circles were stonily locked against her. But
now she was definitely a "somebody."

II

The odd marriage contract signed by Notary Lewis had more than hinted that the party of the first part was going to have "considerable trouble" in attending to the lawsuits of the party of the second part. He was. Just how considerable, time alone was to tell, but be it said to his credit that the elderly bridegroom was not at all slack in attending to them.

A few days after the marriage, the lagging suit before the Federal court was revived by a new petition and a request asking that it now be conducted in the name of "E. P. Gaines and Wife." The Memphis lands and other collateral of the General were perhaps drawn upon to furnish the sinews for the legal war, and things began to happen. Relf and Chew awoke to the fact that their feminine antagonist had suddenly become far more powerful. The sword of Fort Erie was now in the scales of justice on the side of Myra, and it weighed something.

The immediate problem before the Gaines', and indeed the pivotal matter of the whole suit, lay in the attempt to establish the legitimacy of Myra. She had, in her petition to the Circuit Court, claimed the property of Daniel Clark on two counts: first, through the destroyed will, in which lay her weakest claim; and, second, as the legitimate daughter and therefore the forced heir of her father. If she could establish the latter status, will or no will, she would be entitled to four fifths of his property. In the event that she was Daniel Clark's legitimate daughter, it would be impossible for him to have willed all his property to his mother or to anyone else. Could Myra prove her legitimacy?

At first glance it looked, and yet looks, impossible by reason of the double marriage of Zulime. It was a matter of record that Zulime Carrière had married Geronimo Des-Grange in 1794. The Cathedral books showed it; all New Orleans knew it. It was a matter of record also that Zulime had married Monsieur James Gardette in 1808 in Phila-delphia. Zulime herself was even then living in Burgundy Street as "Madame Gardette." When, sarcastically asked Myra's opponents, had her mother ever married Daniel Clark? Or how could she marry him legally when she was the wife of DesGrange and never divorced? And, trium-phantly concluded her detractors, then she had married Gardette while she was the wife of Daniel Clark! It was too much. Did anyone think that a man of the personal force and public standing of Daniel Clark would stand idly by and see his wife taken from him by an unknown Philadelphia dentist? Absurd! Clark had two children by this DesGrange woman, certainly; and one of them, Mrs. Barnes, admitted her unfortunate status; only this Myra, this woman whom old General Gaines had married, "had by a perverted imagination attempted to work out a marriage of Zulime DesGrange to Daniel Clark." It was utterly preposterous! Logic and law both said—and, for that matter, may yet say—that her legitimacy was impos-sible. But neither logic nor law was Myra Clark Gaines.

The immediate bastion to be stormed was the position that Zulime and DesGrange had been legally married. If the Gaines' could show the DesGrange marriage illegal, they would open the way for the valid marriage of Clark

and Zulime that Myra's witnesses alleged. Myra decided
to cut in ahead of the Relf-Chew-Clark combine, and
prove the bigamy of DesGrange when he first married her
mother. Could she do it?

The case was not so hopeless as logic and law would have
us believe. For one thing Zulime was living then in New
Orleans, in constant touch with Myra. On the presumption that she really had been married to Daniel Clark, she
certainly could furnish her daughter an account of it. Myra
had not taken her mother's deposition as she had that of
her aunts and many others, but Zulime was undoubtedly
helping her by private advice. That is evident at all points,
and perhaps from her own lips or from the others, the old,
forgotten ecclesiastical trial of DesGrange for bigamy was
recalled. It was remembered that just before the Spanish
control ended, when the Church yet had power over
offenses against the marriage state, DesGrange had been
accused and some sort of trial or public hearing held. What
was it? What had been decided about it forty years before?

It was supremely important to find out. General Gaines
himself commissioned one C. W. Dreschler to make a
search. But unfortunately the Spanish officials had carried
away most of their archives before Claiborne took over the
government, and therefore little could be discovered.
Dreschler then looked into the old copies of the *Moniteur
de la Louisiane*. The files of 1803, volume 3, were missing.
He finally reported that he had secured a piece out of a
"printed publication" which read as follows:

"Zulime Carrière, at the early age of sixteen, married
in New Orleans, in the year 1796, one Jerome DeGrange,
a younger member of a noble French family. About the

year 1800, Zulime was informed that Mr. DeGrange had a former wife then living. DeGrange was charged by Zulime's family with his baseness, in thus marrying her while his first wife was living, and although he at first denied the charge, he subsequently admitted it. Zulime left him on the instant, and he fled the country. About 1803, DeGrange's first wife came to New Orleans, from France, and her husband happened to come to New Orleans at the same time, she prosecuted him for the offence of bigamy, and had him arrested, by the order of the Governor, and thrown into prison. DeGrange effected his escape, and never afterwards returned."

That was all. A piece out of a "printed publication," with no date, no name. Was it evidence? Would it be admitted into court? The Gaines' intended to see.

III

The display of other evidence and its interpretation is reserved until later, but altogether the Gaines' felt that they had testimony which now, before an unbiased court, would establish their contention that Daniel Clark had legally and wholeheartedly married Zulime.

An unbiased court, to Myra, meant a Federal court, and the further removed from New Orleans the better. If she could only get her case itself, not its technical side nor the collateral issues arising from it, before the Supreme Court in Washington!

Her opponents now decided to take a leaf out of her own book and bring suit against this woman who was continually suing them. The Barnes' and Clarks were worried over her attempts to get the St. John land, and finding certain records of sales Myra had made, determined to sue her for damages over her "possession" of a certain square of the land in question.

The Barnes' claimed that the land involved was worth $20,000 in rentals, and asserted that Myra was benefiting by this. They asked judgment for that amount and further prayed that they be allowed henceforth to have clear title to the whole property in dispute. Significantly they entered their suit in the district, or state, court, where everything was in their favor, not in the Federal court. For the first time Myra found herself the defendant, not the plaintiff, in a suit with a $20,000 penalty if she lost.[4]

She did not like the looks of this at all. The whole city was bitterly hostile and had perhaps become even more aroused since her marriage to the General. She realized that there was little chance of getting any favors from a jury drawn from among the very people whose land she was claiming. Her allegations were so sweeping that the very possibility of her claims having truth in them almost automatically set the conservative element against her. The land involved had been sold and resold, in separate lots and conveyances, until hundreds of people had an actual interest in the outcome of the case. It was scarcely possible to find a native Orleanian who did not take her claims as a personal affront. So, under the circumstances, the best she felt she could do was to make application to have the case held up awaiting the decision of the Federal court where the same matter was pending. She hoped that the Louisiana tribunal would consent to await the verdict in the United States Court, where *she* was the claimant and the Barnes' were defendants.

Her application was denied. Twenty thousand dollars in damages and the loss of any pretense of title to the St. John land threatened her when Judge Buchanan mounted to the bench and called the case of *Caroline Barnes et al.* v. *Myra Clark Gaines*.

Courtroom attendants had now become accustomed to the slight, graceful figure of Mrs. Whitney, but at the beginning of this case in the District Court they were treated to something new. One may imagine the stir about the court door on the day of trial as the imposing figure of General Gaines was seen entering with the lady defendant. He was dressed in full uniform, wearing all his decorations, and with old-school courtliness escorted his wife to her seat. Then he sat by her, erect, respectful, alert. It was noticed that he wore his sword.

The case, instead of going to trial at once on the matter of Myra's legitimacy and the lost will, took from the outset another tack. The Gaines' counsel objected to the case being brought at all, on the ground that the defendant (Myra) had never had possession of the land in dispute and therefore could not be sued for rents and damages. She had not even been admitted a title to it; the land was in litigation at that very time and Mrs. Gaines certainly could not be sued for "possessing" it.

The Barnes' counsel countered by calling the jury's attention to some papers they had unearthed showing that "Myra Whitney and William Whitney" had sold certain squares of this land to one T. B. Harper. In this the "vendee" had, unfortunately for her counsel's arguments, "acknowledged possession thereof." Furthermore, it was on record that Myra had sued Sheriff Buisson for this land in 1838, alleging that she was "in the real and actual possession of the same as owner."

The question for the jury turned not upon Mrs. Gaines' legitimacy but: What is "possession"? And how does it bear on this case?

No agreement could be reached and Judge Buchanan discharged this jury and empaneled another. But before the second jury could hear the case, Myra was heartened by learning that one of her opponents had given up. Daniel Clark's sister, Jane Campbell, found her part in the litigation too costly and the facts brought to light too embarrassing; she asked leave to take herself out of the case, leaving to the other three Clark heirs her share. Aunt Jane had had enough.

IV

Once more Judge Buchanan called *Barnes* v. *Gaines* and again before him sat the defendant, and by her side the white-haired General in full uniform.

An incident soon occurred that showed the temper of the sword of Erie. During the course of the trial, Myra's counsel fell into a wrangle with the judge and in a temperamental flurry rushed from the courtroom. Myra was left without a lawyer. Thereupon the elderly General remembered that he had once read law and even been admitted to the bar in Tennessee in the days of his youth. He rose to address the court. Claiming at first the right to represent his wife's interest, he soon showed that he had another object in mind. "Unfortunately," he said, "I have studied law in a State where a different system of jurisprudence prevails, and I feel somewhat at a loss before the courts of a civil law State. May I request that the lady defendant who is better acquainted with the remarkable facts of her history than anyone else shall be allowed to address the jury."

The Judge nodded. Then the General, "with grand dignity," as the account has it, led his wife forward. Myra was prepared for such a chance, had perhaps prompted the General's speech. She soon was reading document after document to substantiate her story. Judge Buchanan grew more and more restive as she went on, and at length interrupted, stating that the defendant was "not presenting evidence." But Myra read on regardless. She invariably grew excited over the tale of her own wrongs. Again the Judge broke in and this time peremptorily ordered her to be seated. Then the Irish and Latin blood in Myra flamed up and she came back at the Judge, accusing him also of having an interest against her.

It became his Honor's turn to grow angry, and with considerable heat Buchanan notified General Gaines that he was "expected to control his wife in court"—as though anyone could control Myra. Then the General arose, tall, imposing.

"May it please your Honor, for everything that lady shall say or do I hold myself personally responsible in every manner and form known to the laws of my country, *or the laws of honor.*" Gracefully he laid his hand on the hilt of his sword.

The uniform, the gesture, the reply, aroused the Irish

MAJOR GENERAL EDMUND PENDLETON GAINES
From an engraving

fire in the Judge to a higher pitch. "General Gaines," he
cried, "this court will not be overawed by the military
authorities."

"Rest assured, your Honor," replied the General, "that
when an attempt of that sort is made, the sword which I
wear in conformity to the regulations of the service, and
out of respect to this honorable court, will be unsheathed
to defend the rights and dignity of your Honor and all the
civil tribunals of my country." [5]

Peace was restored at this but the Judge felt that he
should note Myra's charge that he was interested. He
therefore said he should reduce it to an "exception of recusation," and require the evidence to be produced to
sustain it. Now it had happened that in one of the court
appearances in New Orleans before this time, Buchanan
had made a motion for a brother lawyer who was against
Myra. This was all she could adduce at that moment to
sustain her charge of prejudice. It was deemed insufficient
to justify recusation on the part of the judge. The truth
was, as Myra knew with woman's intuition, that
Buchanan like everyone else was against her. But intuitive
knowledge is not court evidence. The trial proceeded.

And Myra won! The jury found in her favor and the
$20,000 suit was dismissed, though the Barnes-Clark
counsel at once moved for a new trial. But Buchanan,
prejudiced as he really was, felt compelled to refuse this
motion. He held that since two juries already had the case,
and "very extraordinary efforts had been made to influence
public opinion through the newspapers," it would be
difficult to find an unbiased jury. He would not order a
new trial, though he publicly announced that he thought

the verdict of the jury was "contrary to both law and to evidence."

The Barnes' of course appealed and the issue was put in line to go up to the Supreme Court of Louisiana. On that high tribunal, sitting as though waiting for this particular case, was the blind, crabbed Chief Justice, François Xavier Martin,[6] great jurist, great historian, great miser. Old Judge Martin had himself bought some of the Clark land from Relf and Chew, and New Orleans believed that what Judge Martin had bought, Judge Martin would keep.

The Exciting Forties

IN Washington the hospitable Tylers had introduced
the delightful custom of having the band play upon the
White House lawn on pleasant Saturday afternoons
through the spring and summer, and official Washington
made an occasion of it. Persons of national prominence
moved about with republican simplicity amid the strolling
crowds. Daniel Webster enjoyed these concerts and Mrs.
Wharton remembered seeing him there *"en plein air,* in
blue swallow-tailed coat with brass buttons, open vest and
expansive white ruffled shirt front, in company with
General Walter Jones." [1]

On one of these informal occasions during the early
forties, regular habitués noted with interest an oddly
assorted couple who seemed to be there for the first time.
The officer in uniform, it was learned, was old General
Gaines, while bobbing about on his arm, "like a silk
reticule," [2] one woman remarked, could be seen a lady
whose youth was patent in every step and glance. The
General had brought Myra to Washington.

One of the social dowagers of the day looked her over

and took her measure: "Mrs. Gaines is of medium height," she wrote, "slender but well rounded and symmetrical in form. Her brown hair is thick and clustered with short curls. Her eyes are dark and brilliant, her complexion fair and clear. Her features are regular and she is beautiful beyond criticism. Full of life and animation, fresh in feeling and impulse, with a store of information and a mind well cultivated, possessing rich humor and spirit with manners cordial, piquant, and winning, she is a universal favorite in society, and has a court of gentlemen about her whenever she moves." [3]

It was true. Myra became a social sensation from her first arrival in the capital. She lacked the rich and sensuous beauty of Zulime, but the Irish verve of Daniel Clark had full sway in her dynamic little person. The agelong Latin trick of using the hands and shoulders as she talked was most compelling. Women admired her even more than men. In that day of repressed femininity she typified a life to which many secretly aspired—the incarnation of embattled womanhood, undismayed amid difficulties. Men saw her as a brave, pretty woman fighting against odds, and were for her, every one. As for the genial, white-haired General, he was thoroughly devoted to the courageous Myra and was never prouder than when he could present her to some old friend as his wife. On her part she was fond of her fatherly husband and showed such solicitude for his well-being that someone was heard to remark that she had only two ideas in life, "her case and her husband."

Meeting official Washington proved helpful to her in other ways. Contacts were formed with the great of the nation, and as the General's official visits called for occasional returns to the capital, Myra was enabled to keep and enlarge this circle of friends. At one of the presidential receptions which she attended, it was noticed that two of the Justices of the Supreme Court stood near by, the handsome James M. Wayne of Savannah, and the quiet, gentlemanly John McKinley of Alabama. These judges had already passed upon her suit in its technical aspects. She hoped that the day would come when they would review it as to matters of fact. She was sure that if the supreme tribunal gave a decision in her favor, it would smash all opposition in New Orleans.

Occasionally at social functions in Washington, General Gaines and Myra met another officer with his lady. Then General Winfield Scott and Myra's husband bowed stiffly to each other and passed on. A lady of the capital, observing at a presidential reception the coolness between the two men, got off a ponderous pun which was thought clever at the time: "The one dislikes what most men pursue—Gaines; the other, though a descendant of a Caledonian, hates the Scott." [4]

Myra herself shot forth a barb at Scott. After taking a good look at the big, plume-capped and gold-braided commander of the Department of the East, she caustically observed that "nobody could be much whose mouth could be covered with a *button*." [5] It was true. Scott's mouth was ridiculously small for such a mountain of a man and his obvious "fuss and feathers" accentuated it. Myra's remark was bandied about, and one may even find it today in bulky histories of the Mexican War. But under their glittering epaulettes, the two officers maintained a truce after years of bitter rivalry.

II

The litigation in Louisiana continued to pile up and the case was punctuated by two heavy explosions early in the forties. Of these more will be said later, but at this time, engrossed in the social and official whirl, Myra was glad to travel about with her General, enjoy Washington, and visit her old home. No matter where she was, however, she kept in view her "rights," and was always in touch with the home base.

What she did with her children during these days is somewhat uncertain. William was turning out to be a regular boy, and Rhoda a child very much like her mother. Julia, unfortunately, seems not to have survived childhood. Myra took care of the children in her own fashion, but, after all, it was not as a mother that she became famous.

The General during this time had full opportunity to present his favorite theme of preparedness. He eventually decided that he could do this better by lecturing in some of the larger cities of the East where he might urge the young men of the nation to be trained to arms. The long line of the Mexican border was then stretching from Oklahoma to the far Northwest. England was in conflict with the United States over opposing claims to the Oregon country, foreshadowing "Fifty-four Forty or Fight." The General prepared a huge map and arranged his lecture tour.

Myra forthwith determined to accompany him and, not liking to be left out of the picture, begged to be allowed to lecture also! So decided, so done. The old General could

never say no to her in anything. Amazingly enough Myra
chose for her theme, "The Horrors of War." How she
reconciled this with the General's accompanying call for a
militaristic citizenship no one has been able to discover, but
lecture she did. At Wilmington, Delaware, she astonished
her old friends by appearing on the platform and making
a public speech. One wonders if Colonel Samuel B. Davis
was present to hear his foster daughter, who had by this
time taken such strange wings and flown into the nation's
sky. The era was one that frowned upon a woman who
lectured or spoke in public. Ladies were expected to remain
in the cloistered seclusion which Anglo-Saxon chivalry
decreed for them, but Myra made her own rules. Her
public appearances added interest to her suit.

In New York at "the Tabernacle," the Gaines' double
lecture drew a great crowd.[6] Myra sat on the third seat immediately in front of the platform while the General was
speaking. He had on his dress uniform and with his sword
pointed gracefully to the embouchure of the Mississippi
on the great map hanging behind him. His speech was
well received, but the New York audience was waiting
for the lady. "When he had concluded Dr. Griscon
advanced to Mrs. Gaines' seat and conducted her to the
platform amid immense cheering. She was dressed in a
black velvet palaisse and wore earrings and diamonds in
her hair, with a rich silk hat, ornamented with a waving
plume of bird of paradise feathers. She held in her hand a
small manuscript from which she read her lecture."

The General stood behind her all the time. He was not
one to be seated while a lady was standing.

III

The early forties saw the case taken back to the Supreme Court of the United States. Again it was the conduct of Judge Lawrence that served to bring the highest tribunal's attention to it. At this time, each Supreme Court Justice was assigned a large circuit of Federal courts over which he presided, and Justice McKinley had Louisiana as part of his circuit. Before him and Judge Lawrence sitting as a court, came the "Gaines Case," as it was beginning to be called. Judge Lawrence was still proving obdurate on the matter of using the Federal Chancery Court to establish rights under an unprobated will. Justice McKinley disagreed with him in this particular, and, reaching no agreement, the two jurists decided to refer the matters at issue to the Supreme Court upon a "difference of opinion." [7] So again into the little low chamber under the dome of the Capitol came the honorable Justices to hear the case.

Again Myra's versatile little lawyer, General Walter Jones, pressed for the rights of "Edmund P. Gaines and Myra Clark, late Whitney, complainants." But this time he was not unanswered. Relf and Chew had secured the ablest man they could find in the learned Richard Smith Coxe [8] of Washington.

A forensic contest at once took place between these two lawyers as the technical aspects of the case were thrashed out. But the Court vigorously reaffirmed its former mind. Chancery practice not only must prevail in Louisiana, but must prevail in this particular case. The old annoying demand for oyer of all documents in French was overruled, and the case put upon the rule docket. The Court then delivered a stinging stricture on Judge Lawrence:

"It is a matter of extreme regret that it appears to be the settled determination of the District Judge not to suffer chancery practice to prevail in the circuit court in Louisiana in equity causes. . . . This court, as has been heretofore decided, has not the power to compel that court to proceed according to established rules; all that we can do is to prevent proceedings otherwise, by reversing them when brought here on appeal." [9]

It was a victory, but a victory only in the sense that it was not a defeat. Myra could go on suing. It was also certain that she would have the right of appeal on the merits of the case itself *if* and *when* the lower court should finally decide against her.

This second decision of the Supreme Court added bitterness to the attitude of the Orleanians. A slow hate had gradually formed against this woman who so persistently sought their lots and homes. Threats were muttered. Louisiana was not fond of Federal jurisdiction.

Then the State Supreme Court received the Barnes appeal and gave the decision that New Orleans knew ought to be given. Old François Xavier Martin recused himself and stepped off the bench when the cause came on, as everyone knew that he had profited by sales from Relf and Chew. But he left four state Justices behind him who felt as he did and who had bought no Clark land. They made short work of Myra's contention that she had never possessed the St. John land.

They held that she had "possessed" the land by virtue of her claims, and in the very next sentence swept away all

her claims. They reviewed the case, cited Clark's will of
1811, as well as that of Mrs. Mary Clark, and concluded
stonily: "The defendants appear to be strangers to the
estate of Daniel Clark."

"It is therefore ordered and decreed, that the judgment
of the district court be annulled and reversed; and that the
plaintiffs, Caroline Barnes, wife of John Barnes, Jane
Green and Eleanor Maniff [the daughter of Eleanor
O'Beirne, now dead] be and are hereby declared . . .
owners of three undivided fourth parts of the property
described in this petition . . . and that the said defendants pay the costs in both courts." [10]

With this verdict New Orleans found no fault at all.
The city was not sure about the law but was certain on the
facts. The "Gaines woman" was a stranger to the estate of
Daniel Clark.

IV

And now events began to move with startling rapidity,
if litigation can ever be called rapid. Relf and Chew determined to press the advantage they had gained in the state
court and to finish the suit once and for all in the Federal.
It may be recalled that Myra as complainant had named a
number of other persons as well as Relf and Chew in her
bill. This gave the opposing lawyers what they considered
a splendid opportunity to plead *multifariousness,* i.e., that
the suit in question was binding together situations that
should be treated separately. Mrs. Gaines, they said. was
undertaking to sue different persons for different things all
in one bill. To meet this they decided to demur.

A demurrer in legal phraseology is an admission that
even though matters be as represented there is no cause for

court action. It is a sort of legal "what-does-it-matter?" by which a contest is avoided and a suit nullified. In this particular case the defendants planned to admit Myra's entire contention for the sake of argument, but to insist that the whole affair was one to be settled by a court of probates and not by a court of the United States. Furthermore, they continued to contend that the case belonged to law and not to chancery.

Myra and her General did not want to meet the case on a demurrer but hoped to have it tried on its own merits. So they published an offer agreeing to "make a liberal reduction in favor of all the purchasers . . . who will, without further delay, come to trial at the present term of the Circuit Court of the United States."

In response to this a certain Charles Patterson, who had bought some of the Clark land, "came to trial." His action in doing so was looked upon with suspicion by the other defendants, some of whom even whispered that he was in league with the Gaines'.

Meanwhile, the demurrers were making their way before the Circuit Court of the United States for the Eastern District of Louisiana. In the presence of that tribunal, when argument was advanced, a sharp division of opinion again occurred. Once more the judges divided, and the upshot was that they sent another difference of opinion up to Washington for decision by the Supreme Court.

V

This was in 1843. As that year came to a close, all signs pointed to the fact that at last the colossal interests involved in the suit would be passed upon by the Justices in Washington. The certificate of difference of opinion was on its way there, and so was the appeal of Mr. Patterson, the man who did not demur with the others but decided to fight the case on its merits.

Relf and Chew had long since ceased to treat Myra's pretensions with scorn. To them, it was unthinkable that she should have gone as far as she had, but there she was, brilliant and indomitable, with powerful counsel preparing again to push her claims before the supreme tribunal of the nation. Signs are not lacking that her opponents were already immeasurably wearied by the whole affair. They had everything to lose, nothing to gain. But there was no chance to retreat even had they wished to do so. Furthermore, whatever may have been the real feelings of Richard Relf, the vast army of her opponents sincerely believed that Myra Clark Gaines was a fraud and an impostor. They now meant to prove it. Three of the best lawyers available, with Richard Smith Coxe at the head, were secured to appear before the Supreme Court and overthrow her claims.

Another lawyer had been added to the Gaines' counsel in the meanwhile, Francis Scott Key,[11] of "Star-Spangled Banner" fame. Mr. Key was fated to earn immortality by his song, but during his lifetime his associates knew him as a lawyer of no mean ability, one who took rank with the foremost. He made a strong addition to the Gaines' side. Chief Justice Taney, it may be added, was his brother-in-law.

Of course, little General Jones still stood forth as Myra's undefeated champion; but in order to match the triumvirate that Relf and Chew had retained, Myra and the

General decided to secure still another lawyer and so sent to Maryland for the Honorable Reverdy Johnson [12] of Baltimore to act in that capacity. Johnson was then climbing rapidly into that "rank and reputation unsurpassed at the American bar" which his admirers were long to claim for him. He combined vigorous aggressiveness with a statesmanlike poise and was competent anywhere. Maryland was soon to elect him senator and the President one day to make him the Solicitor-General of the United States.

So the two sides lined up. The nation was not uninterested. There was a vacancy on the Supreme bench then, and the New York *Globe* suggested that the President should hurry to fill it as the "important Gaines will case" was soon to be heard. The New York *Herald*'s Washington reporter echoed this interest, calling it "the great New Orleans Gaines will case, in which some $15 or $20,000,000 (I know not how many) are involved." [13]

But for the third time the Supreme Court heard the case not on its merits but on technical matters involved. The cause soon turned into a lawyers' battle. The lawyers on both sides were intrigued by the implications of the case, and the legal ability of the great advocates who faced each other there in January, 1844, had full sway. The trial might be likened to an artillery duel, with big guns. That a woman's character and fortune were at stake was not so much in evidence as the heavy legal firing. At the end Myra's counsel swept everything before them [14] and the court decided every point in their favor. The demurrers fell; the suit could go on. Myra and the General began to glimpse victory ahead.

And then firing of a more ominous sort was heard down on the Rio Grande, and the General had other matters to look after. War was about to break with Mexico.

VI

The General, all this time, amid the piling up of litigation, was still the commander of the Department of the West. He was too good a soldier and too enthusiastic an exponent of preparedness to be caught entirely off guard in the eddy of troubled international waters that accompanied the annexation of Texas. Keenly he noted the increasing tension on the Mexican border, now no longer at the Sabine, but somewhere southwest of San Antonio. The government in Washington was striving to gain its ends by peaceful means, but the General got ready for trouble.

Then Zachary Taylor, down on the lower Rio Grande, fought two sharp little battles with a Mexican army, both sides blazing away in the chaparral, amid much glory and perspiration and quite a bit of bloodshed. President Polk may have wished to minimize this incident, but General Gaines, now in New Orleans, took a serious view of the situation. If Washington would not act, the commander of the West decided that he would and at once called on Louisiana for volunteers. There was no telegraph with which to ask Washington for orders—Morse was then tinkering with his underground wire between Washington and Baltimore—and the General may be excused for feeling that the time had come for action, not diplomacy. His proclamation caused great excitement. In spite of a

belated warning from William L. Marcy, the Secretary of
War, General Gaines went ahead and called on Mississippi, Alabama, and Missouri for more men. Volunteers
hastened to respond. Companies were formed through the
South and West everywhere. Gay uniforms were bought
and there was feverish drilling on public squares in the
cities and on the commons in the little towns. Before long
a roistering aggregation of "Zouaves," "Rifles," "South-
rons," and "Volunteers" in varied assortment of uniform
and equipment came rolling down the river by steamboat
or marching overland to fight the Mexicans.[15]

The General in New Orleans was in his glory, and
signed volunteers up as fast as they arrived, for three or
six months' enlistment; then he sent them on to Zachary
Taylor camped somewhere near the mouth of the Rio
Grande. Taylor did not know what to do with the troops
when they got there and they were left to camp as best
they could on the hot, sandy stretches of the Texas coast
and grumble for a chance to fight. When Washington
heard all this there was a storm.

Whatever may have been the original policy which
President Polk had meant to carry out with regard to
Mexico, the action of General Gaines definitely blasted it.
A peremptory order came at once from Marcy relieving
the General of his command and ordering him to report
immediately before a court of inquiry at Fortress Monroe
and answer to the charge of having exceeded all possible
authority. The General was not any too well liked by
Secretary Marcy, since he had in an official report once
said rather pertly concerning Marcy's orders: "I carelessly
submit to them as they seem to be a source of pleasure to

the War Department and certainly inflict no injury on me." But this time he did not so "carelessly submit," as the order to face a court of inquiry seemed to mean the end of his active life. His military career had always been his pride. There was something pathetic in the attitude of the old soldier when he found that he really was to be broken for what he had done. As he and Myra were making their preparations to leave New Orleans it chanced that the officers of the "Louisville Legion," about to embark for the Brazos, met the General. Wistfully he said in his stilted way, "Gentlemen, we are in diametrically opposite positions, glorious to you but painful in the extreme to me. You go to meet the foe. I for the first time in my life am compelled under the hard obligations of duty and under superior orders to turn my back on him."

But the General was by no means subdued. Although relieved of his command, when he got to Mobile he signed up a number of other officers for war with Mexico. This added wrath to the chagrin that President Polk and his cabinet already felt. General Winfield Scott made no secret of the fact that he believed General Gaines was crazy. Scott said so again and again in his official documents and Gaines' quixotic actions seemed to lend color to the charge.

However, at Fortress Monroe there was a turn in his favor. The General conducted his own defense [16] with vehemence and insisted that since General Taylor had been given the right to raise volunteers, he, a Major General, who outranked Taylor, ought certainly to have that right also. The younger officers on the court of inquiry saw that whatever might be the political implications of his activities, the General's intentions had been of the best. President Polk himself had come to feel so, and the upshot was that Gaines was not ordered to go before a court-martial. "General Gaines is now a very old man," Polk confided to his naïve diary (August 15, 1846) "& although guilty of acts which cannot be justified . . . yet I determined in lenity to him to yield to the recommendation of the Court of Inquiry and take no further proceedings against him." [17]

VII

As a sop to his pride, it was decided to place the General in charge of the Department of the East, where it was felt he could do no harm. This saved his dignity, but it was in reality a hard blow. He was compelled to sit idly on the eastern seaboard while his rival, General Scott, and his friend, General Taylor, earned immortal fame by their fighting in Mexico.

Myra, of course, went with the General and, while the military fortunes of her husband had suffered a reverse, her own war of litigation was decidedly favored by the shift at this time from New Orleans to New York and Washington. The Patterson suit was now pending before the Supreme Court, and the General's wife lost no opportunity to make contacts with personal helpers, to encourage her lawyers, and to gather additional testimony. She was in touch with her now aged guardian, Samuel B. Davis, who was spending the quiet evening of a stormy life in beloved

Delamore Place. Occasionally, perhaps, she saw the Whitneys at Binghamton. Throughout her long life Myra never lost touch with the family of her first husband.

If the General's fortunes were down, Myra's were not. Her star of popularity was in the ascendant, and at the stiff social functions in Washington or New York, she continued to occupy a regnant position. She knew all the great and near great, including the members of the Supreme Court, who by this time, it may be guessed, had come to know *her*. The General was busy with affairs connected with the war, directing operations from his headquarters in New York. Perhaps occasionally he was called to Washington, and no doubt there were the usual parades and inspections according to the immemorial rites of the military.

Early in 1847, the General got in trouble again with the President by publishing a personal letter written to him by his comrade, General Zachary Taylor, then campaigning down in Mexico. "Old Rough and Ready" held ideas similar to those of Gaines regarding the attitude of the administration toward the war, and expressed them. General Gaines gave his letter to the New York *Herald,* and it was copied with avidity by Washington papers.

Polk and his cabinet were vastly disturbed. It was "highly improper" and "its publication was prejudicial to the success of our military operations in Mexico." [18]

But the General thought it would help those operations by getting some action from Washington. Besides, Polk's government had been highly prejudicial to *him*.

By the end of that year the war was drawing to a close. Winfield Scott in all his plumage and panoply had already reined up his horse in the Grand Plaza of Mexico City and dramatically proclaimed the "conquest of Mexico." But before the peace commissioners came together, the Supreme Court in Washington met to decide the Patterson appeal coming up from New Orleans and pressed by Edmund P. Gaines *et ux*. Myra's war, it appeared, would have neither truce nor end.

Book 3

The Case

Myra's Witnesses

THE reader may be somewhat curious by this time as to the exact nature of the evidence upon which Myra Clark Gaines was relying in order to establish her claims. It will be necessary now to spread this forth as a coherent whole,[1] as Messrs. Johnson and Jones were about to do before the Supreme Court. Over against what Myra presented let the powerful testimony and argument of her opposers also be viewed, and then let the merit of her claims be determined on an impartial basis. Most certainly there were two sides.

Fortunately for those interested, the courts may be depended on to settle the complicated legal principles in the case. But on the matters of fact involved, especially those upon which the whole case hangs—whether Daniel Clark really married Zulime Carrière, and whether he left a will in favor of Myra, his daughter—upon these questions the reader may consider himself to be as competent a judge as any of the black-robed justices who have filed into the Supreme Court room in Washington. Was there a marriage? Was there a will?

To display the case as a whole it is necessary to deviate somewhat from the chronological order in which testimony and argument were introduced. Some of Myra's evidence was gathered early. Boisfontaine, for instance, died in 1836 shortly after he made his deposition. Some of it had not been brought to light by 1847 when the Patterson appeal was heard. The case itself grew, as did its record, as time progressed. Nevertheless the absolutely contradictory nature of the opposing claims was well established by the middle forties.

The bulk of the testimony was taken by deposition, properly authenticated. This has been condensed wherever possible.

II

Testimony of Mrs. Harriet Smythe

The witness, being duly sworn, in answer to interrogatories and cross interrogatories, testified:

My name is Harriet Smythe; my age is fifty years; my present residence is Opelousas. From 1804, till some time in 1814, I resided in New Orleans. Prior to removing to New Orleans I married William Harper, of Philadelphia, who died in 1828. In 1834, I married George Morris Smythe, M.D.

I became acquainted with the late Mr. Clark shortly after my arrival in New Orleans in 1804. I enjoyed his confidence. Mr. Clark and my husband were intimate friends.

Mr. Clark left to my knowledge, but one child only, a daughter named Myra Clark, whom I suckled in her infancy and who is now Mrs. Myra Clark Whitney.* I was residing with my late husband in the family of his uncle, Colonel S. B. Davis, when the infant Myra was brought into the family of Colonel and Madame Davis. I had at that time an infant of my own. I was solicited by them to suckle the infant they had brought, which I refused to do unless they first disclosed to me the name of her parents; both Colonel and Madame Davis then told me she was the child of Daniel Clark, and that he, Mr. Clark, was particularly anxious that the child should be under the care of Madame Davis. Mr. Clark afterward assured me she was his child, and always told me she was his only child. She was always called Myra Clark by the whole family. I never knew her by any other name till her marriage.

I always understood from Mr. Daniel Clark himself that he destined his daughter Myra to be the sole heiress of his large fortune, and on the occasion of his duel with Gov. Claiborne, in, I think, 1807, he told me after that affair that he had previously, by way of precaution, secured to his daughter Myra the amplest provision, in case he should have fallen, and that he had also left documents so arranged as to manifest everything of interest to her.

In 1813, some few months before Mr. Clark's death, he told me he felt he ought no longer to defer securing his estate to his daughter Myra by a last will. Near this period he stopped one day at my house, and said to me he was on his way to the plantation of Chevalier Delacroix, for the purpose of requesting him to be named in his will one of

* Mrs. Smythe's deposition was taken in 1835.

his executors, and tutor to his daughter Myra. On his return he told me, with much apparent gratification, that Delacroix had consented to serve, and that Judge Pitot and Col. Bellechasse had consented to be the other executors. . . .

In his conversations respecting his being engaged in making his last will, he talked a good deal about the plan of education to be laid down, in his will, for his daughter Myra. He expressed the most extravagant pride and ambition of her; he would frequently use the emphatic language, that he was making her a bill of rights; he mentioned, at these times, that this will would contain a complete inventory of all his estates, and explanations of all his business, so as both to render the administration on his estate plain and easy to his friends, Chevalier Delacroix, Judge Pitot, and Col. Bellechasse. About four weeks before his death, Mr. Clark brought this will to my house; as he came in, he said: "Now my will is finished; my estate is secured to Myra beyond human contingency; now, if I die tomorrow, she will go forth to society, to my relations, to my mother, acknowledged by me, in my last will, as my legitimate daughter. Here is the charter of her rights; it is now completely finished, and I have brought it to you to read."

He left it in my possession until the next day. I read it, deliberately, from beginning to end. In this will Mr. Clark acknowledged Myra Clark as his legitimate daughter, and only heir, designating her as then living in the family of S. B. Davis. Mr. Clark, in this will, bequeathed all his estate to the said Myra, but directed that an annuity of $2,000 should be paid to his mother during her (his

mother's) life, and an annuity of $500 should be paid to
Caroline DesGrange, till she arrived at majority, when the
annuity was to cease, and $5,000 were to be paid her as a
legacy. He directed that, one year after his estate was
settled, $5,000 should be paid as a legacy, to a son of Judge
Pitot, of New Orleans, and that one year after his estate
was settled, $5,000 should be paid as a legacy, to a son of
Mr. DuBuys, of New Orleans. He provided for the
freedom and maintenance of his slave, Lubin; he appointed
Mr. Desuau Delacroix tutor to his daughter Myra; he
gave very extensive instructions in regard to her education.
This will contained an inventory of his estate, and explanations of his business relations; he appointed Mr. Desuau
Delacroix, James Pitot, and J. D. D. Bellechasse executors; the whole of this will was in Mr. Clark's handwriting; it was dated in July, 1813, and was signed by him; I
was well acquainted with said Clark's handwriting.

The last time Mr. Clark spoke to me about his daughter
and his last will, was on the day he came out for the last
time (as far as I know) from his house, which was the last
time I saw him. He came to my house about noon, complained of feeling unwell, asked leave to have prepared for
him a bowl of tea; he made his visit of about two hours'
duration, talking the whole time of his daughter, Myra,
and his last will; he said a burthen of solicitude was removed from his mind, from the time he had secured to her
his estate beyond accident, by finishing his last will; he
dwelt upon the moral benefit to her, in society, from being
acknowledged by him, in his last will, as his legitimate
daughter; he said it would be the greatest boon from his
God to live to bring her up. After Mr. Clark's death, Col.

Bellechasse stopped at my house, and told me Mr. Clark's last will was suppressed, and that the old provisional will of 1811 was brought forward; he repeated what Mr. Baron and Lubin said (as he said) about the matter. Knowing well the unbounded confidence reposed in Lubin by Mr. Clark, I sent for him; he came and related to me what he said occurred. Soon after said Clark's death, I understood that the notaries of New Orleans were summoned in court, on the petition of Mr. Desuau Delacroix, to swear whether they had a duplicate of Mr. Clark's last will. The late John Poultney came with several friends to examine an iron chest of Mr. Clark's, that stood in my house, in faint hope, as they said, of finding a duplicate of Mr. Clark's last will, that is the will of 1813.

The mysterious disappearance of Mr. Clark's last will produced great excitement among Mr. Clark's friends. A short time after the death of Mr. Clark, I heard, with surprise, that the Chevalier Delacroix, the tutor of Myra, in the last will, in whom Mr. Clark had so confidently trusted, became very friendly with Mr. Relf, and received from him a large number of Mr. Clark's negroes, and other favors. Thus were the fond hopes of Mr. Clark ended.

I do not know whether Mr. Clark was married or not; that is to say, I was not present at his marriage and therefore do not know whether he was married; it was asserted that he was married to the mother of Myra; whether the unblemished character which she had borne, forbade the idea that she could form any connection except under the sanction of marriage, contributed to form this opinion, I cannot say.

I never heard Daniel Clark acknowledge any other child than the said Myra, whom he called his legitimate daughter; he told me she was his only child; that the mother of Myra had another daughter named Caroline, six or seven years older than Myra, who was the child of Mr. DesGrange. I never heard Mr. Clark say that he had any natural children. I never heard him say there was any stain upon the birth of his daughter Myra.

My feelings toward Daniel Clark's daughter are those of disinterested friendship; I am not connected with her by ties either of affinity or consanguinity and have nothing to gain or lose by the result of this suit.

Testimony of Boisfontaine

My name is Pierre Baron Boisfontaine; my age is about fifty-eight; I have been some time in Madisonville (Louisiana); the place of my family abode is near New Orleans, opposite side of the river; I was eight years in the British army; I was several years agent for Mr. Clark's plantations; since his death have been engaged in various objects; I now possess a house and lots, and derive my revenue from my slaves, cows, etc. I am in no manner connected with, or related to, any of the parties of this suit; I have no interest in this suit.

I knew Daniel Clark between nine and ten years; I knew him as the father of Myra Clark; she was born in my house, and was put by Mr. Clark, when a few days old, with my sister and brother-in-law, Samuel B. Davis. I was Mr. Clark's agent for his various plantations. He respected our misfortunes, knowing that our family was rich and of the highest standing in St. Domingo before the revolution. The mother of Myra Clark was a lady of the Carrière family. Not being present at any marriage, I can only declare it as my belief, Mr. Clark was her husband. To answer this question in detail as is demanded, it is necessary that I state what was communicated to me. It was represented to me that this lady married Mr. Des-Grange in good faith; but it was found out some time afterwards that he already had a living wife, when Lady Nee Carrière separated from him. Mr. Clark, some time after this, married her at the north. When the time arrived for it to be made public, interested persons had produced a false state of things between them; and this lady being in Philadelphia and Mr. Clark not there, was persuaded by a lawyer employed, that her marriage with Mr. Clark was invalid; which believing, she married Monsieur Gardette. Some time afterwards, Mr. Clark lamented to me that this barrier to making his marriage public had been created. From the above I believe there was a marriage.

Mr. Clark left at his death a daughter named Myra, whom he acknowledged as his own before and after her birth, and as long as he lived. In my presence he spoke of the necessary preparation for her birth; in my presence proposed to my sister and brother-in-law, Mr. S. B. Davis, that they should take care of her after her birth. After her birth, he acknowledged her to me as his own, constantly, and at various places. He was very fond of her, and seemed to take pleasure in talking to me about her. When he communicated to me that he was making his last will, he told me he should acknowledge her in it as his legitimate daughter. The day before he died, he spoke to me about her with great affection, and as being left his estate in his last will. The day he died, he spoke of her with the interest of a dying parent, as heir of his estate in his last will. She is still living, and is now the wife of William Wallace Whitney.

I was present at Mr. Clark's house about fifteen days before his death, when he took from a small black case, a sealed packet, and handed it to Chevalier Delacroix, and said, "My last will is finished; it is in this sealed packet with valuable papers; as you consented, I have made you in it, tutor to my daughter. If any misfortune happens to me, will you do for her all you promised me; will you take her at once from Mr. Davis? I have given her all my estate in my will, an annuity to my mother, and some legacies to friends; you, Pitot and Bellechasse, are the executors." About ten days before this, Mr. Clark, talking of Myra, said that his will was done. Previous to this, he often told me, commencing about four months before his death, that he was making his last will. In these conversations, he told me that in his will he should acknowledge his daughter Myra as his legitimate daughter, and give her all his property. He told me that Chevalier Delacroix had consented to be her tutor in his will, and had promised if he died before doing it, to go at once to the north, and take her from Mr. Davis; that she was to be educated in Europe.

Two or three days before his death, I came to see Mr. Clark on plantation business; he told me that he felt quite ill. I asked him if I should remain with him; he answered that he wished me to. I went to the plantation to set things in order, that I might stay with Mr. Clark, and returned the same day to Mr. Clark and stayed with him constantly till he died. The day before he died, Mr. Clark, speaking of his daughter Myra, told me that his last will was in his office-room below, in the little black case; that he could die contented, as he had insured his estate to her in the will. He mentioned his pleasure that he had made his mother comfortable by an annuity in it, and remembered some friends by legacies. He told me how well satisfied he was that Chevalier Delacroix, Judge Pitot, and Bellechasse were executors in it, and Chevalier Delacroix, Myra's tutor. About two hours before his death, Mr. Clark showed strong feelings for said Myra, and told me that he wished his will to be taken to Chevalier Delacroix, and just afterwards Mr. Clark told Lubin, his confidential servant, to be sure, as soon as he died, to carry his little black case to Chevalier Delacroix. After this, and in a very short time before Mr. Clark died, I saw Mr. Relf take a bundle of keys from Mr. Clark's armoire, one of which, I believe, opened the little black case; I had seen Mr. Clark open it very often. After taking these keys from the armoire, Mr. Relf went below. When I went below I did not see Mr. Relf, and the office-room door was shut. Lubin told me that when Mr. Relf went down with the keys from the armoire, he followed, saw him then, on getting down, go into the office-room, and that Mr. Relf, on going into the office-room, locked the office-room door. Almost Mr. Clark's last words were that his last will must be taken care of on said Myra's account.

When, after Mr. Clark's death, the disappearance of his last will was the subject of conversation, I related what Mr. Clark told me about his last will in his last sickness. Judge Pitot and John Lynd told me that they read it not many days before Mr. Clark's last sickness; that its contents corresponded with what Mr. Clark had told me about it. Judge Pitot and John Lynd are dead. The wife of William Harper told me she read it. Colonel Bellechasse told me that Mr. Clark showed it to him not many days before his last sickness; that it was then finished. Colonel Bellechasse and the lady, who was Madame Harper, are living.

Mr. Clark was a very fond parent; he sustained the house of Mr. Davis and Mr. Harper, because my sister had her in care, and Mrs. Harper suckled her. He sustained Harper as long as he lived, and conferred great benefits on my brother-in-law. He spoke of her (Myra's) mother with great respect, and frequently told me, after her marriage with Mr. Gardette, that he would have made his marriage with her public if that barrier had not been made, and frequently lamented to me that this barrier had been made, but that she was blameless. He said he never would give Myra a stepmother. While I was with him at his death-sickness, and even at the moment he expired, he was in perfect possession of his senses; and no parent could have manifested greater affection than he did for her in that period. She, the said Myra, is the only child Mr. Clark ever acknowledged to me to be his. She was born in July, 1805.

III

Testimony of Colonel Bellechasse

My name is Josef Deville Dagoutin Bellechasse. I was born in Louisiana, in 1760, and followed the profession of arms there, until it was transferred to the United States; after the transfer to the United States I held various important civil and military offices under the American government, and managed my own affairs, which were extensive and related principally to real estate. I continued to live in Louisiana until 1814, and then established myself in this island (Cuba), where I reside, on my sugar estate, and enjoy the rank of lieutenant-colonel, in the service of Her Majesty, the Queen of Spain. . . .

My friendship and intimacy with Daniel Clark began towards the end of the last century, and lasted with uninterrupted harmony and confidence till his death, which happened in August, 1813. I was intimate and intimately connected with him under a variety of circumstances. For several years previous to the transfer of Louisiana to the United States, I had been in the habits of the greatest intimacy with said Clark; this was commenced, I suppose, by our liking each other, and was cemented and made permanent by proving ourselves worthy of confidence and friendship. Our business and political connexion only drew closer the cords of friendship. Such was my respect for him, said Clark, that when, in November, 1803, I was solicited by the French colonial prefect, Mons. Laussat, to accept the command of the militia of the province of Louisiana, then about to be delivered to him by Spain, and not knowing with what view the prefect was actuated, resisted his offer, and communicated the same to the said Daniel Clark, then United States consul at New Orleans, who disapproved of my refusal, and earnestly recommended that if it was not too late, I should accept the proffered command; in consequence of which I informed the prefect that I would take the command of the militia, which was given me as soon as Spain surrendered the country.

So, also, when the American commissioners arrived in New Orleans, and possession of that city was given to them, I yielded to the wishes of said Clark in accepting the command of the militia then again offered me. I was one of those intimate friends, whom, in 1806, said Clark assembled at his house, and after informing them of the imputed intentions of Colonel Burr, advised to exert their influence with the inhabitants of the country to support the United States government, and notwithstanding the incapacity of the Governor, to rally round him and afford him every aid, and to prevent, if possible, a meeting of the legislature. I was a member of the Legislative Council of Louisiana, and I was a member of the convention that assembled in 1812, and framed the Constitution of that State. Said Daniel Clark was the head of that political party to which I belonged.

I knew, from what Clark told me in repeated conversations, that he had a daughter named Myra, now the wife of W. W. Whitney, and that he treated her with the utmost paternal affection. Clark carried me with him on divers occasions to see Myra, and in my presence he manifested for her the most ardent love. Said Daniel Clark always gave me to understand, as well by reason of his extraordinary affection for said Myra, as by his positive declaration to that effect, that she would be the heiress of his fortune.

In 1811, said Clark made known to me that on account of a special emergency that called him to the north, he had made a will, (to the best of my recollection, in the month of May, in that year), which he merely designed as a provisional will, in which Richard Relf and Beverly Chew were named as executors, and that although he did not mention his said daughter Myra in that will, yet by confidential modes he amply provided for her; and that will said Clark told me he had deposited in the hands of said Relf.

In the year 1813, said Clark told me he was thinking of reducing to order his affairs that were various and complicated, and of making his last will, so as not to leave any longer exposed to risk the standing and fortune of his child, and that he wished me to consent to become one of the executors. I did so consent. Said Clark spoke of Judge Pitot and Chevalier Delacroix, as persons whom he contemplated to have associated with him; with much reflection and deliberation said Clark spoke of his being occupied in preparing his last will. On these occasions, in the most impressive and emphatic manner, he spoke of the said Myra as the object of his last will, and that he should in it declare her to be his legitimate child and heiress of all his estate. A very short time before the sickness that ended in his death, he, Clark, conversed with us about his said daughter Myra, in the paternal and affectionate terms as theretofore; he told me that he had completed and finished his last will. He, Clark, therefore took from a small black case his said last will and gave it open to me and Judge Pitot to look at and examine. It was wholly written in the handwriting of said Daniel Clark, and it was dated and signed by the said Clark in his own handwriting. Pitot, Delacroix, and myself were the ex-

ecutors named in it, and in it the said Myra was declared
to be his legitimate daughter, and the heiress of all his
estate.

Some short time afterwards I called to see him, Clark,
and learned then from said Relf that the said Clark was
sick in bed, too sick to be seen by me; however, I, indignant at an attempt to prevent me from seeing my
friend, pressed forward into his room. He, said Clark, took
me by the hand and with affectionate reprehension said:
"How is it, Bellechasse, that you have not come to see me
before since my sickness? I told Relf to send for you." My
answer was that I had received no message or account
whatever of his sickness from Relf. Fearful of oppressing
him, I retired, and told Relf that I would remain to attend
occasionally to Clark; Relf said there was no occasion for
it, that the doctor or doctors had ordered that he, Clark,
should be kept as quiet as possible, and not be allowed to
talk. I expressed apprehension for the situation of Clark,
but Relf expressed a different opinion; and on his, Relf's
promising to send for me if there should appear to be any
danger, I departed. On the next day, without receiving
any message from Relf, I went and found Clark dead. I
continued my way till I reached Pitot's, whom I found
much afflicted by the death of Clark, and very indignant
at the conduct of Relf, as well for having always prevented
the assistance of Clark's other friends, as for not having
notified them, (particularly him, Pitot, who lived near
Clark,) of his approaching dissolution; that by their
presence the fraudulent suppression of the last will of
Clark might have been prevented. Pitot, as well as others,
always spoke with the utmost indignation of the fraud-

ulent suppression or destruction of the said last will of 1813.

In the autumn of 1831, I saw in a newspaper a letter of said Relf. In that letter, said Relf declared that said Myra, if she is the child of said Clark, is the offspring of an adulterous bed. Knowing that this was a calumny, I, the contemporary of Clark, and acquainted with the facts, wrote to Mr. Whitney that this statement of said Relf was untrue. Mr. Whitney did not think proper to publish this letter, which I regret, as I feel that justice had not been rendered the grave of my departed friend, against whom, if living, no one could have uttered such a calumny. Dead, Mr. Relf is the last person who should asperse his ashes; for though he had withdrawn his confidence from him, still Mr. Relf had received from him, not only the greatest pecuniary favors, but taking him out of obscurity and indigence, Clark, with the nobleness of soul which distinquished his character, extended to him his kindness. I was the more shocked with this statement of Relf, because Relf knew to the contrary. I think it my duty now to declare, what I know to be a fact, that DesGrange was condemned for bigamy in marrying Miss Carrière, (subsequently the mother of Myra,) several years prior to the birth of said Myra. The prosecution and condemnation of said Des-Grange for said crime of bigamy took place at New Orleans towards the close of the Spanish domination in Louisiana; his first and lawful wife, whom he had married previous to his coming to Louisiana, (as it was proved,) coming to New Orleans in pursuit of him. When said DesGrange practiced the infamous deception of marrying Miss

Carrière, it was the current opinion in New Orleans that he was a bachelor or single man.

I cannot swear that Clark was married to Miss Carrière, the mother of his child, although many persons affirmed that such was the fact; but I am well assured that, if he was not married to her, he was never married to any other woman.

From said Daniel Clark himself, in repeated conversations, and from his last will of eighteen hundred and thirteen, I know that he, said Clark, left to his daughter Myra all his estate, which consisted of plantations, of land of immense value, of numerous slaves, of many debts that were due to him, and other various classes of property, which altogether made him a man of great wealth.

I never heard said Daniel Clark speak of having any other child besides the said Myra. I never heard him say she was a natural child. I never heard him speak of any stain upon her, or her birth, but, on the contrary, he styled her, in his will of 1813, his legitimate daughter. He told me that she was his only child.

The last will of Clark, viz., his will of 1813, was legal in form, because it was written wholly in his (Clark's) handwriting, and was dated and signed by him. It was legal in its provisions, because Clark had the power, even supposing his child not born in marriage, of giving her all the rights of a child born in marriage by declaring her in his last will his legitimate daughter. Few men were equal to Clark in talents and intelligence. He was well instructed in the principal matters that appertain to a gentleman and the proprietor of vast possessions; and the future happiness, fortune, and standing of his child were the objects dearest to his heart, and he satisfied himself that there was no obstacle to his bestowing his fortune upon her. Pitot, the judge of the court of probates at New Orleans, was one of the executors in Clark's last will, viz., that of 1813. Pitot examined the said will after it was finished, and he should have known whether the said last will of Clark's was legal in form and in its provisions. I am not related to or connected with the complainants or with either of them. I have no interest in the event of this suit. My only desire is that the issue be conformable with justice.

IV

Testimony of Colonel Davis

My name is Samuel B. Davis, Gentleman; residence, Philadelphia; aged sixty-eight. I have no interest whatever in the event of said suit—that is, in a pecuniary point of view. I am in no degree whatever related to or connected with the claimants.

I was very intimate with the said Daniel Clark. The circumstances that led to it were these: I commanded the ship *General Washington,* of sixteen guns, and came to New Orleans consigned to Mr. Clark, in the year 1799. At this time our commerce had been interrupted, and we were then in an open state of warfare with France, in the service of which nation I had been several years, where I had acquired some reputation as an officer. I had resigned my commission in the service as *lieutenant de vaissau,* and had lately returned to my country very poor, and this was my first command. Louisiana was then under the Spanish government. The kind reception which I met with from him (Clark) naturally gained my confidence, and my confidence was confirmed by the interest which he took in everything that related to me. My intimacy continued with Mr. Clark uninterrupted till 1809, or 1810, when from some cause, of which I have been ignorant, our mutual confidence was suspended.

At the time of Mr. Clark's death he left a daughter named Myra, who was then living in my family. Before her birth Mr. Clark acknowledged her to me as his own child, and came to me requesting me to make preparations for her birth. After her birth he placed her in charge of my family. He always claimed and acknowledged her to me as his own child, manifested the fondest paternal affection for her. In Mr. Clark's papers respecting her he called her Myra Clark.

Some short time before I left New Orleans, Mr. Clark induced me to retain in my hands two thousand three hundred and sixty dollars, the interest of which was to go towards the education of his daughter Myra, for which I gave him my note. This note was sued for shortly after Mr. Clark's death by Chew and Relf, and recovered, with interest, while I was at the north in the army, and the child lost the use of it.

Mr. Clark always did manifest the warmest affection and deepest interest towards his daughter Myra. He has repeatedly told me that he intended to leave her his property, and I never doubted that he was entirely sincere. I have heard Mr. Clark repeatedly say that she was his heir.

I have no knowledge of any written will. At the time of

Mr. Clark's death I was absent at the north, and had been absent from Louisiana for more than a year. I have perfect knowledge that the property owned by him, commonly known as the Bayou Road property had been secured to her (Myra) by a sale to Mr. Delacroix and D. D. Bellechasse, in separate portions, wherein he confided in blind confidence to their honor. This same property he had previously transferred to me in a bona fide sale in the same blind confidence, but in consequence of a coolness before mentioned, I gave it up.

I never heard of any will until after his death. Mr. Clark came as always to my house to see his child. She was always the subject of his conversation when he visited my house and he manifested if possible, more interest in his child in proportion as she grew older. His language was always the same but expressed with more enthusiasm as she became more interesting. At his last interview with his child, it was impossible for any father to have manifested more solicitude and affection than he did. In my last interview with Mr. Clark his conversation turned almost exclusively on the subject of his child. It was then I received instructions relative to her education, about which he seemed very solicitous; and alluded to the place that he wished her to take in society when arrived at the years of maturity.

I was not present at the birth of the child Myra but had the necessary arrangements made for her birth. I have maintained and educated the child Myra at my expense; she was born in New Orleans in June, 1804 or 1805. I did not see her mother before her birth, nor had she any communication with me; the terms on which Mr. Clark and myself were at that time, precluded the possibility of his speaking to me of his child in respect to the expense of her maintenance. I had been under so many obligations to him, and I believe he knew my character too well to suppose I would have tolerated such an allusion. Time rolled on, and the child grew, and as she grew she gained on our affections, and no conversation ever passed between me and Mr. Clark relative to the expense of her maintenance until we were about leaving that country for the north in 1812, when her education became an object of deep interest to him. Then he insisted on my retaining in my hands the two thousand three hundred and sixty dollars which I have already mentioned, the interest of which was to go towards her education; the requisite balance for her education was to have been made or remitted to me yearly. I never wrote to Mr. Clark on the subject of her expenses, nor ever should; his death put an end to our correspondence. Had he lived, I am sure he would have attended to it. I cannot say whether the child was ever christened or not at my house.

On one occasion Mr. Clark spoke to me of a child called Caroline, then living in New Jersey, but we had no conversation on her subject, if I remember rightly, but on one occasion.

Testimony of Madame Sophie Despau

I am seventy-one years of age. My present place of residence is Biloxi, Harrison County, Mississippi. I am acquainted with the complainant in this suit, Myra Clark

Gaines. I was present at her birth, and, with some intervals I have been well acquainted with her up to the present time.

I do know that the said Daniel Clark was married. He was married in the city of Philadelphia, by a Catholic priest, to my sister Zulime *née de* Carrière. I was present at this marriage. This, to the best of my recollection, was in the year eighteen hundred and three; although there are some associations in my memory which make me think it not improbable that the marriage may have taken place in the year eighteen hundred and two. My impression, how- ever, is that the marriage took place in eighteen hundred and three. It was, I remember, a short while previous to Mr. Clark's going to Europe. There was one child, and to the best of my knowledge and belief, only one child born to this marriage, to wit, Myra Clark, who married Wil- liam Wallace Whitney, now deceased, and who is now the wife of Gen. Edmund P. Gaines.

The circumstances attending the marriage of the said Daniel Clark with Zulime de Carrière were these: She had previously been married to a man named Jerome Des- Grange, with whom she lived several years until she heard that he had another living wife at the time of his marriage with her. This information, confirmed by the subsequent admissions of DesGrange himself, led to a separation when Zulime returned to her family. These circumstances were known to the public. While thus residing with her family, Mr. Clark made proposals of marriage with her. These proposals were made with the full knowledge of all her family. But it was considered essential, before any marriage could take place, that record proof of the invalidity of her marriage with DesGrange should be first obtained. To obtain this proof from the records of the Catholic church in New York, where DesGrange's prior marriage was celebrated, my sister and myself embarked for that city. It was agreed and understood that Mr. Clark should follow after us. On our arrival in New York we learned that the registry of marriage of which we were in search had, in some way, been destroyed. Mr. Clark arrived after us. We were told that a Mr. Gardette, then living in Philadelphia, was one of the witnesses to DesGrange's prior marriage. We proceeded to Philadelphia, and found Mr. Gardette, who told me that he was present at said prior marriage of DesGrange; that he afterwards knew DesGrange and his wife by this marriage; and that his wife had gone to France. Mr. Clark then said to my sister: "You have no longer any reason to refuse being married to me. It will, however, be necessary to keep our marriage secret until I have obtained judicial proof of the nullity of your marriage with DesGrange." They, the said Zulime and the said Clark, were then married.

Soon afterwards, our sister, Madame Caillavet, wrote to us from New Orleans that DesGrange's former wife (the one he had at the time of marrying Zulime) had arrived at New Orleans. We hastened our return to New Orleans where DesGrange was prosecuted for bigamy. Father Antoine, of the Catholic church in New Orleans, took part in the proceedings against him. Mr. DesGrange was condemned for bigamy in marrying the said Zulime, and was cast into prison, from whence he secretly escaped by connivance of the governor, as it was understood, and was taken down the Mississippi river by Mr. Le Breton

D'Orgenois, where he got a vessel, and escaped from the country. This happened not a great while before the cessation of the Spanish government in Louisiana.

Mr. Clark told us that before he could promulgate his marriage with my sister, it would be necessary that there should be brought by her action against the name of Des-Grange. The change of government, which took place about that time, created delay; but at length, in eighteen hundred and six, Messrs. James Brown and Elijah Fromentin, as the counsel of my sister, brought suit against the name of Jerome DesGrange, in, I think, the city court of New Orleans. The grounds of said suit were that Des-Grange had imposed himself upon her in marriage at a time when he had a lawful living wife. Judgment in said suit was rendered against DesGrange. But Mr. Clark still continued to defer promulgating his marriage with my sister, which very much fretted and irritated her feelings. Mr. Clark became a member of the United States Congress in eighteen hundred and six. While he was in Congress, my sister heard that he was courting a Miss Caton, of Baltimore. She was distressed, though she could not believe the report, knowing herself to be his wife. Still, his strange conduct in deferring to promulgate his marriage with her had alarmed her, and she and I sailed to Philadelphia to get proof of his marriage with my sister. We could find no record of the marriage, and were told that the priest who married her and Mr. Clark was gone to Ireland. My sister then sent for Mr. Daniel W. Coxe, and mentioned to him the rumor above stated. He answered that he knew it to be true that Mr. Clark was engaged to the lady in question. My sister replied that it could not be so. He then told her that she would not be able to establish her marriage with Mr. Clark if he were disposed to contest it. He advised her to take the advice of legal counsel, and said he would send one. A Mr. Smith came, and, after telling my sister that she could not legally establish her marriage with Mr. Clark pretended to read to her a letter in English, (a language then unknown to my sister,) from Mr. Clark to Mr. Coxe; the marriage between Mr. Clark and my sister was a private one. Besides myself, there was present at the marriage a Mr. Dosier, of New Orleans and an Irish gentleman, a friend of Mr. Clark's, from New York, whose name I do not now recollect.

By the marriage of my sister with Mr. DesGrange there were born two children, a boy and a girl. The boy died. The girl lived, and was named Caroline. She afterwards married a physician named Barnes. She was born in the year eighteen hundred and one. I was present at her birth, as well as that of her brother. It may, also, be proper to state that my sister afterwards, in the year eighteen hundred and eight, married, in Philadelphia, Dr. James Gardette, of that city.

I was present at Mr. Clark's marriage with my sister Zulime. The marriage was privately celebrated at a house in Philadelphia, rented by Mr. Clark for my sister, but I am unable to remember the name of the street on which it was situated or of the priest who officiated.

The great lapse of time which has taken place since these events renders it impossible for me to answer with the precision the question demands. As well as I can remember, it was in one of the early months of spring, in 1802 or 1803. Not a great while after the marriage Mr. Clark set out for Europe.

Mr. Clark did not give publicity to his marriage with my sister. He furnished her with a handsome house in New Orleans, in which she and I resided together, and where he frequently visited my sister, taking his tea with us almost every evening. This house was situated on a corner, and, I think, near what was then called the Bayou road; but I cannot recall the name of the street, or fix with certainty the precise locality. I do not know whether the marriage was generally known among Mr. Clark's friends at New Orleans or not; I always supposed it was known to but a few persons. Mr. Clark told us that he had informed Daniel W. Coxe, Samuel B. Davis, and Richard Relf of it. My sister and myself resided, as above stated, in the house provided by Mr. Clark until the rupture between her and him, a period, as well as I can remember, of between three and four years.

My sister has told me that in an interview with him in Philadelphia, after the marriage with Mr. Gardette, he expressed the deepest regret that that barrier had been placed between them, stating that he had become thoroughly satisfied that things he had heard in regard to her, and which had influenced him to postpone the promulgation of his marriage with her, were calumnies; that he acquitted her of all blame, and that but for the marriage with Gardette, he would then have claimed and recognized her before the world as his wife.

I am not prepared to state, of my own personal knowledge, what considerations may have governed my sister subsequently to her marriage with Mr. Gardette, as I was separated from her many years, and the subject being a painful one, has not often been the subject of conversation between us. I remember, however, having heard, either from her or from some one of the family to whom she had stated the facts, that she had solicited from Col. Davis the privilege of taking her daughter home to live with her, her then husband, Dr. Gardette, having given his free consent for her to do so. Col. Davis represented to her that Myra was happily ignorant of her parentage; that she believed herself to be Mr. and Mrs. Davis's daughter; that they both loved her as if she were their own child, and that he intended to leave her his fortune; that she was then happy in her ignorance of the painful circumstances connected with her history, and that she would be as well provided for as it was possible she could be by giving her up to her real mother. She yielded to these considerations for the benefit of the child.

I have already stated that the mother of Myra is my sister. She now resides in New Orleans, and is supported by her son, Dr. James Gardette. She has resided since 1806 in New Orleans, Philadelphia, and France.

V

Testimony of Madame Rose Caillavet

I am in the eighty-third year of my age; my residence is Biloxi, Mississippi. I am well-acquainted with Myra Clark Gaines. My personal acquaintance with her is of about fourteen years duration. My knowledge of her may be said to date from the period of her birth.

I did reside in the city of New Orleans about the year eighteen hundred, and for many years previous. My residence continued there until I went to France, about the year eighteen hundred and seven. I was well-acquainted with Daniel Clark, late of the city of New Orleans, deceased. My acquaintance with him commenced about the year seventeen hundred and ninety-seven. My intimacy with him, growing out of his marriage with my sister, continued during my residence in New Orleans.

I was not present at the marriage of Zulime de Carrière (who is my sister) with Mr. Clark, but it is within my knowledge, both from information derived from my sisters at the time, and from the statements of Mr. Clark, made to me during his lifetime, that a marriage was solemnized between them. It is to my personal knowledge that Mr. Clark, about the year eighteen hundred and two, or three, made proposals of marriage with my sister Zulime, with the knowledge of all our family. These proposals were discussed, and the preliminaries of the marriage arranged by my husband, at his house, in my presence. But my sister, having been previously married to one Jerome DesGrange, who was found to have had a lawful wife living at the time of his (DesGrange's) marriage with her, the marriage with Mr. Clark could not take place until proofs of the invalidity of her marriage with DesGrange were obtained. To procure these proofs from public records, my sister Zulime and Madame Despau went to the north of the United States, where DesGrange's prior marriage was said to have taken place. While there, my sister Zulime wrote to me that she and Mr. Clark were married. There was born of this marriage

one, and only one child, a female, named Myra, who was
put by Mr. Clark, while an infant, under the charge of
Mrs. Samuel B. Davis, in whose family she was brought
up and educated. Having suffered from the hired nurses,
she was nursed, through kindness, for some time after her
birth, by Mrs. Harriet Harper, wife of William Harper,
the nephew of Col. Sam'l B. Davis. Mr. Clark stated to
me, frequently, that Myra was his lawful and only child.
I have always understood that the marriage between my
sister and Mr. Clark was a private one, and that it was not
promulgated by Mr. Clark in his lifetime, unless he did so
in his last will, made a short time previous to his death. I
have heard that such a last will was made, but it was believed to have been suppressed or destroyed after his death.

I was acquainted with Mr. Jerome DesGrange, for the
first time, in New Orleans, about the year seventeen
hundred and ninety-five. He passed for an unmarried
man, and as such imposed himself on my sister Zulime.
Some years after this marriage it became known in New
Orleans that he had a prior lawful wife living. My sister
immediately separated from him, and came to reside with
her family. At a later period Mr. DesGrange was prosecuted, found guilty of bigamy, in having married my
sister Zulime, and cast into prison. He escaped from
prison, as it was reported at the time, by the Spanish
governor's connivance. I understood that Mr. Le Breton
D'Orgenois aided him to escape from the country. This
happened some time before the transfer of the government
of Louisiana to the Americans. The flight of DesGrange
from New Orleans is the last I know of him. I did not myself know the first wife of DesGrange, but it is within my

knowledge that she came to New Orleans, and, while there, fully established her pretentions as his lawful wife.

On the return of my sister, Zulime, to New Orleans, after her marriage with Mr. Clark at Philadelphia, she kept house with my sister, Madame Despau. The house was provided by Mr. Clark, who visited my sister frequently. He did not keep house with her. Their marriage being secret was a sufficient reason to the family for his not doing so, and for his not introducing her into society as his wife. I think this house was on Dauphine street, but I cannot state positively that in this particular my memory is correct.

Testimony of Madame Benguerel

My name is Louise V've Benguerel; aged about 57 years, gentlewoman; place of residence, Opelousas.

I am acquainted with Zulime nee Carrière, the mother of said Myra. I knew her in New Orleans a long while ago. Mr. Gerome DesGrange married the said Zulime, which marriage proved on his part bigamy: for after his marriage with the said Zulime, the lawful wife of said DesGrange, whom he had married previous to his marrying the said Zulime, came to New Orleans and the said DesGrange was then prosecuted and condemned for bigamy in marrying the said Zulime; and he was thrown into prison from which he escaped and fled from Louisiana.

My husband and myself were intimate with the said DesGrange and when we reproached him for his baseness in imposing upon the said Zulime, he endeavored to excuse himself by saying that at the time of marrying the said Zulime, he had abandoned his said lawful wife and never intended to see her again. I was very well acquainted with the said DesGrange and the said Zulime, and knew the said lawful wife of the said DesGrange whom he had married previous to imposing himself upon Zulime.

In addition to the foregoing depositions, Myra had testimony from Madame Davis and Madame Boisfontaine, echoing the facts stated by their husbands. She also had a powerful piece of evidence in the old court record showing that Delacroix, just after her father died, *had* declared to the judge of the court that he believed there was a later will made by Daniel Clark, and that he had actually secured a court order summoning all the notaries of the city to help find it. Delacroix was now vehemently against her —because, she said, he had received slaves from Relf and Chew—but his 1813 search for the lost will was a matter of record and could not be denied.

Does it appear that the above testimony makes an unbreakable case? Then view the equally powerful evidence against Myra's claims.

Evidence Against Myra

Testimony of Daniel W. Coxe *

MY NAME is Daniel W. Coxe; [1] my age is seventy-one years and a little upwards; I reside in the city of Philadelphia in the state of Pennsylvania. I have at present no particular occupation, having retired from the mercantile business.

I was acquainted with the late Daniel Clark, of New Orleans, from the time of my arrival in New Orleans, in the year one thousand seven hundred and ninety-one, until his death, in the year one thousand eight hundred and thirteen. Having been long associated with him in commerce, and in the purchase of real estate, my knowledge of him was intimate and our intercourse confidential.

Caroline Barnes, the wife of Dr. John Barnes, is the natural child of the said Daniel Clark, deceased, by Madame DesGrange, alias Zulime Carrière, of New Orleans. My knowledge that Caroline Barnes is the daughter of the said Daniel Clark is derived from the following cir-

* Coxe's testimony reproduced here was taken in 1841.

cumstances: In or about the year 1802, Madame Des-Grange brought me a letter from the said Daniel Clark, introducing her to me, and informing me in confidence that she was pregnant by him, and requesting me to place her under the care of a respectable physician, and to furnish her with money during her confinement and stay in Philadelphia. I accordingly employed the late Dr. William Shippen to attend her during her accouchement. He procured a nurse for her, and removed the child soon after its birth to the residence of the nurse. I paid Dr. Shippen's account. That child was Caroline Barnes, who before her marriage always went by the name of Caroline Clark.

I was not present at her birth. After the birth of the said Caroline, she was taken to the residence of her nurse, whose name, I think, was Stevens, and who lived, according to my recollection, in Eleventh street, between Race and Vine streets, in the city of Philadelphia. After her early years had passed, Daniel Clark, on his visits to Philadelphia, not being satisfied with the situation of the said Caroline, requested me to place her with some respectable person, where her health, morals, education could be attended to. I accordingly placed her under the care of Mr. and Mrs. James Alexander, of Trenton, New Jersey. Mr. and Mrs. Alexander had charge of her education until the said Daniel Clark and myself settled our accounts, in the year 1811. I defrayed the expenses of her board, education, apparel, etc., from that time until the death of Daniel Clark, in the year 1813. Her said expenses were paid sometimes by advances by me, and sometimes by remittances from New Orleans on his account.

After the death of said Daniel Clark, and the failure of

Messrs. Chew and Relf, his executors and surviving partners, an arrangement was made by Dr. Hulings and myself, by which a small annual allowance was made to
Caroline by her grandmother, Mrs. Mary Clark, and Caroline was placed with Mrs. Baizely, who kept a boarding
school in South Fourth street, in the city of Philadelphia,
under an agreement by which Caroline was to render services as a teacher, as a consideration for her board and education. She remained with Mrs. Baizely for several years,
and, as I believe, until the time of her marriage.

The first time Daniel Clark visited Philadelphia after
the birth of Caroline, was in the year 1802, and soon after
her birth. According to the best of my knowledge and belief, Daniel Clark did not visit Philadelphia during the
years 1803, 1804, or 1805. Being elected as a delegate to
Congress for the Territory of Orleans, for the session
which commenced in December, 1805 or 1806, he came
on to Washington and Philadelphia. During the period
he was in Congress he visited Philadelphia occasionally.
On these occasions he manifested parental concern and affection for her (Caroline). He was in the habit of caress-
ing her and making her presents, and also of making
presents to Mr. and Mrs. Alexander, with whom she
lived.

Daniel Clark was never married, to the best of my
knowledge and belief. He paid his addresses with a view
to marriage to Miss Louisa Caton, of Baltimore, grand-
daughter of the late Charles Carroll, of Carrollton, and
was partly engaged to her. The engagement was afterwards dissolved in consequence of demands on the part

of the lady's family of settlements and other stipulations, which convinced him that the match would be ineligible.

Daniel Clark had not, to my knowledge, any other child and children besides Caroline. Daniel Clark never acknowledged any such child to me. My intimacy with him would have justified, and would have been likely to induce such a disclosure to me, if there had been any such child or children. Such, at least, is my belief, though in some respects Mr. Clark was a man of very peculiar character. After the death of Daniel Clark, I was informed by Dr. Hulings and Samuel B. Davis, for the first time, that he had another daughter by Madame DesGrange, born in New Orleans, called Myra.

I did personally know Zulime nee Carrière, alias Madame DesGrange, alias Madame Gardette. To the best of my recollection and belief, she left Philadelphia for New Orleans, soon after her recovery from her confinement, consequent on the birth of Caroline, in the year 1802. I believe that she returned to Philadelphia in the autumn of 1807, when I saw her. She remained in Philadelphia until she married Mr. Gardette, in the year 1808, and she continued to reside in Philadelphia with Mr. Gardette until he went to France.

The said Zulime Carrière did know of Mr. Clark's addresses to Miss Caton, of Baltimore. In an interview between her and me, at her request at her lodgings, she complained to me of Clark's desertion of her, said she understood he was going to marry Miss Caton, of Baltimore, and intimated that she considered herself at liberty to marry another. While we were conversing, Mr. Gardette came in, and I took my leave. This was the only conversation I ever had with her on the subject. Soon after this, her marriage with Mr. Gardette was announced.

The said Zulime never informed me, either before or after the death of Daniel Clark, that she had been married to him. Nor did she ever inform me that the said Myra was her daughter, or the daughter of Mr. Clark. I have already stated that the said Zulime, after marriage with Gardette, did reside in Philadelphia. The said Myra did reside in Philadelphia during part of the time that Mrs. Gardette resided there. During the common residence of Mrs. Gardette and the said Myra in Philadelphia, no visits were interchanged between them, to my knowledge; nor was there any recognition, that I know of, by either of them. I have no knowledge on the subject.

While the defendant Myra resided in Philadelphia, she resided in the family of the said Samuel B. Davis. The said Samuel B. Davis was her reputed father; at least, such was the generally received opinion. I do not know who was her reputed mother, further than I have been informed by the said Samuel B. Davis and Dr. Hulings, who I believe received his information also from Davis, that Madame Des-Grange was her mother. Mary Clark named the said Myra, in her will, as the natural daughter of Daniel Clark, at the pressing instance of Dr. Hulings and myself, and we were induced to do so from the representations of Samuel B. Davis who represented the said Myra to us as the daughter of Daniel Clark. Mary Clark named her in her will, in the manner above stated, very reluctantly. Mary Clark and the Clark family made a difference in their treatment of the said Myra and Caroline, in having a very close and intimate intercourse with Caroline, and very little intercourse with Myra.

A close, constant, and occasionally a confidential correspondence was carried on between the said Daniel Clark and myself from the period of our first connexion in business up to the period of his death. In my letters to him, frequent reference was made to Caroline. These references, by Mr. Clark's particular request, were not made openly and directly, but by innuendo and disguisedly, to prevent other persons from understanding any allusions to her.

I am not interested directly or indirectly in the event of this suit, according to my understanding of the matters in controversy and the issue pending between the parties thereto.

I took from Messrs. Chew and Relf, in part payment of a debt due to me as per the settlement of our co-partnership accounts, the lands debited to me in their account current. I also took in part payment of a debt due from the estate of the said Daniel Clark to the late Edward Burd, my father-in-law, a tract of land at New Iberia, of about twelve arpents. As I understand the matters in controversy and the issues depending between the parties, I do not consider myself interested in the event of this suit.

II

Testimony of Francois Desuau Delacroix

I arrived in New Orleans in 1793, and am a little over seventy-three years of age; I am a planter. In 1806, or 1807, I was a member of the Legislature of the Territory of New Orleans. I was a Director of the Planters' Bank of Louisiana, President of the Louisiana State Bank, and President of the State Insurance Company. I have known Chew and Relf since I lived in New Orleans; I have always believed them honest; if not, Daniel Clark, who knew human nature as a perfect judge, would not have employed them as a commercial house. When I went to France in 1819, I designated Richard Relf as one of my alternative attorneys, in case of the death of the two others named, which I would not have done if I had not thought him honest. Daniel Clark was a man of honor and integrity, otherwise he would not have been a friend of mine. Clark was never married; if he had been, I should have known it from my intimacy with him. Mr. Clark told me he had a child with a married woman, an adulterous child; that child was placed by Daniel Clark in the house of Samuel Davis in Terre Boeuf; her name was Myra; she is the same who married Whitney; and subsequently married General Gaines. About two years before Clark's death, he placed in my hands two portions of land on the Bayou Road to be remitted to Myra in case of his death; which portions of land I remitted to Myra the first time she came here with Capt. Davis. I met Captain Davis at the Exchange, and asked him if he had brought Myra; he answered "yes." I then told him I desired to remit the two portions of land which were confided to me by Daniel Clark. The answer of Captain Davis was, "She will not receive that from you because she is entirely ignorant that she is the natural child of Daniel Clark." But a few days after this she accepted, and the business was settled before a notary.

I saw Daniel Clark the day before his death; he was lying on a mattress, on the floor of his parlor. When I entered, some persons who were present retired on the gallery. I came close to him, I put my knees on the mattress where he was lying. He took my hand and kissed it a hundred times, covered it with his tears. In that supreme instant he uttered not a word. In that sacred moment when the most profound secrets involuntarily escape, not a single word escaped him about his pretended marriage. I frequently visited Clark taking breakfast and dinner with him. I lived in the country. I never saw Madame Des-Grange in his house, never heard that Clark was married to her. Clark always spoke to me of Myra as his illegitimate daughter. Before his death Clark was much embarrassed. In 1810 he sent to me to get my endorsement on a note of $6,000, which I gave. A few months before his death, he said he was afraid he would fail, his circumstances were so embarrassing. This I kept a secret. Mr. Clark had a great mania to buy real estate. He was always tormented by the spirit of speculation. The reputation of Madame DesGrange was that of *"une femme gallante"* as we call it in French. I do not know how it is expressed in English.

I am not interested in this suit. Mrs. Gaines has sued me, but it is not this suit, which is against Chew & Relf. Whilst in France, my agent, Mr. Cavellier, employed P. A. Rost. Esq., to defend me in a suit in chancery. I do not know what Mr. Rost did in this case. I have never reflected on the consequences (to myself) which might result from the loss of this suit, so monstrous and iniquitous.

III

Testimony of Louis Bouligny

I am sixty-eight years old. I have resided in New Orleans, or its vicinity, for sixty-eight years. I do not know
the plaintiff, but have known Relf and Chew for a long
time. I was acquainted with Daniel Clark in 1791 or 1792.
In 1803 I became intimate with him; had business trans-
actions with him, and so continued, until his death. In
1803 we went together to Ouachita, where there was a
tract of land which I had sold to Clark. We laid on the
same bearskin during the night, and traveled on horseback
during the day. I used to take dinner with Clark, and he
with me, during several years. I used to go and sleep at
Clark's house, who was a bachelor, in order not to awake
my mother late in the night. Clark was generally reputed
to be a bachelor. He often gave *soirées* to which gentlemen
and ladies were invited. I never heard Clark was married; if
he had been from my intimacy with him, I should have
known it. I knew DesGrange by sight, danced with Madame DesGrange at the balls. The general reputation of
Madame DesGrange was bad. Public opinion had it that
Clark was the lover of Madame DesGrange. Clark never
spoke to me of Madame DesGrange, as either his wife or
lover. I only knew Madame DesGrange by sight; knew
nothing of her reputation. Clark could not have been married to a lady who did not enjoy a spotless reputation.

I danced with Madame DesGrange between 1798 and
1804; I saw her at every public hall, but not at society

balls; there was only one public ballroom in New Orleans at that period. Rumor said that the intimacy between Clark and Madame DesGrange began during the presence of her husband here—that is, in 1800, and continued for a long while. I never met Madame DesGrange at the *soirées* given by Clark, or at any other private parties or *soirées* given in Clark's circle of society.

IV

Testimony of Jean Canon

I am sixty-three years of age; was borne in New Orleans; knew Daniel Clark and Myra, his daughter by Madame DesGrange. Mrs. DesGrange did not suckle her child, as she wanted to get out of the way of DesGrange or his first wife. Clark spoke of Madame DesGrange as a beautiful woman, and very deservedly, for she really was a beautiful woman. Clark kept his amours secret, as he had several such connexions, and it would have given him trouble had his particular female friends known of them. I do not know whether Clark was married. I always forebore questioning him about Madame DesGrange, as I knew that Clark had an intrigue with her, but frequently in conversation, in speaking of beautiful women, Clark would ask me what I thought of Madame DesGrange. Clark courted a great many ladies in New Orleans; when Clark saw a pretty woman, he fell in love with her. I knew Jerome DesGrange; he kept an establishment in St. Anne street, and sold liquers; he was a stout, thick-set man, with a round, red face, and light or auburn hair.

V

Clark's Correspondence with Jane Green

The defendants brought forward an exchange of letters between Clark and his sister Jane, when she was living in Liverpool.

May 3rd, 1806

My dear Brother:

I scarcely know whether you will be obliged to me or not for the share I had in fitting up your truly elegant toilet, for the idea of its being intended for Mrs. D. Clark got strong possession of my mind, so much do I wish to see some one bear that name worthy of you, that nothing in my opinion would be too good to trust in it. I cannot think how the plan of such a thing could have entered your head for I assure you that it has been exhibited in London as a masterpiece of elegance and fashion. . . . You cannot think how uneasy I made myself when I heard you went to Vera Cruz. . . . Let me know if my suspicions are right about the destination of the toilet. . . .

Your affectionate sister,
Jane Green.

New Orleans, 14th, October 1806

My dear Sister:

I have received your letter and thank you kindly for the pains you took in filling the toilet. I assure you that it would have given me infinite pleasure to have offered it either to Mrs. Clark or to anyone likely to become Mrs.

Clark; but this will not be the case for some time to come, for as long as I have the misfortune to be hampered with business, so long will I remain single for fear of misfortune or accident.

Daniel Clark

Testimony of Madame Veuve Barbin De Bellevue, nee Trepagnier

I am thirty-six years of age. My mother resided on the Bayou Road, until 1813, near Clark's residence. Daniel Clark visited my mother's family every day. I was living with my mother then, being unmarried. Had two sisters— one younger and one older—then living with my mother. One of my sisters, (the elder) had been married and divorced. This was Heloise; the younger sister was Hortense. Clark paid his addresses to my sister, Heloise Lambert, with a view to marriage. He was engaged to her in 1813, up to the time of his death. . . .

Clark commenced his addresses to my sister about eight months before his death, when the engagement took place. He had been courting twelve months before his death. The marriage had been delayed for causes I do not remember; it was to have been celebrated within two months, when it was put an end to, by the death of Clark. In 1815, my sister was remarried to her former husband, Mr. Lambert, by a civil contract before a notary.

VI

Letter from Mazureau

The distinguished Etienne Mazureau,[2] a noted lawyer of New Orleans, was understood to have cognizance concerning certain matters connected with the case, and at Coxe's instigation wrote him the following letter which was duly put in the record:

New Orleans, May 1st, 1842

Sir:

In the conversation with you in February last, I mentioned in reply to your inquiries, that the late Daniel Clark once consulted me and the late Edward Livingston, Esq., —not "to ascertain whether he could make some provision by will for Myra, his supposed illegitimate daughter,"— but whether a certain will of which he showed me a rough sketch, would be valid in law in this then Territory. The will thus intended to be made, stated Myra to be his natural child, and instituted her his universal heir, leaving to his own mother, an annual rent of, I believe, $3000. Upon asking Mr. Clark what the name of the girl's mother was, he answered me: "You know the lady, it is Madame DesGrange."

"But that woman was married, and DesGrange alive when the girl was born. I recollect having heard a great deal of talk about it at the time, but never heard your name mentioned as connected with that love affair."

"Yes," said Clark, "she was married I know, and what matters it? The ruffian (who kept a confectionary shop here) had deceived that pretty woman; he was married when he courted her and became her husband, and, as it was reported, he ran away afterward from fear of being prosecuted. So you see, this marriage was null."

"That may be so, but until so declared by a competent tribunal, the marriage exists, and the child is of such a class of bastards as not to be capable by our laws of receiving by will, from her supposed father, anything beyond what may be necessary for her sustenance and education. Such are the positive provisions of our Code. The Spanish laws are somewhat more favorable. They permitted fathers to leave such a child, one fifth of the whole of his estate, but our Code has restricted that to mere alimony."

"What shall I do then?" asked Mr. Clark.

"Sir, if you have any friends in whom you can place confidence—you probably have some—convey them secretly some of your property, or give them money for the use of the child . . . when she becomes of age."

"That I'll do," said Clark and we separated.

I heard afterward from him and from Mr. Bellechasse, that he, Clark, had done what he told me he would do.

I may add here that the first husband of Myra wanted to retain me as his counsel to sustain her claim under the pretended will (which I sincerely think never was executed) as universal heir of Mr. Clark. I declined from motives above expressed; and as he confessed to me that the friends of Clark had conferred to her the property which he had entrusted to them for her use, I advised him to be contented with what he had.

The present husband of Myra came once to ask me whether I had any knowledge of a pretended will in favor of his lady by the late Mr. Clark; and in that case whether I had any objection to appear as one of her witnesses. My answer to him was this: "I have seen no such will, but he has consulted me upon a will of which he showed me a rough sketch."

"Well, that will answer our purpose," said the General.

"Very little, I believe, for if I were to give my testimony it would demolish all your pretensions."

"Never mind," said the General, "I will have you subpoenaed."

Upon this I stated to him all that had occurred between Clark and myself upon the subject, the opinion I had given him, and the determination he did say he had taken, etc. And he retired and I never was subpoenaed.

Before concluding, I must observe, that having been once of counsel for Mr. Relf in the case of libel brought by him against Myra's first husband in the Federal Court, I felt a natural delicacy and declined to appear as a witness for him in a suit that has since made so much noise.

As this is written in haste, I would not like it to meet the eye of the public, though every particle of it is most substantially true.

I remain, with great respect,
Your obedient servant,
Mazureau

Thus wrote privately the brilliant Creole jurist, of whom Charles Gayarré gives such an unforgettable picture as one who delighted to blast opposing witnesses, and especially to heap scorn upon the English system as compared with the Code in which he was such a master. Mazureau's honor was unimpeachable in New Orleans, but Myra's lawyers could point out that he had acted for Relf, and that he did *not* put himself under oath and testify to the above facts.

VII

The "Natural Child" Admission

A petition or suit for alimony was filed in 1817 by young Horatio Davis against Relf and Chew in behalf of Myra, and in this she was styled by her foster brother, Davis, a "natural child" of Daniel Clark. The suit was dropped, apparently on promise of Relf that something would be done about it, but the record with the damning "natural child" allegation remained. The defendants now brought it out against Myra.

They did more than that. They brought out Horatio Davis himself, who testified:

"I am the son of Samuel Boyer Davis and Mary Ann Rose Baron, his wife, now deceased. The infant Myra, was brought to my father's house some time in the year 1804. I have never had any reason to believe that any member of my family ever looked upon her in any other light than as the natural child of Mr. Clark. Myra was always treated by every member of the family as my sister. We seldom spoke of her relation to Mr. Clark; but when she was so spoken of, it was as his natural daughter."

This testimony was countered on Myra's side by the assertion of Colonel Samuel B. Davis that he had never authorized the use of such an expression as "natural child" in the 1817 suit. The elder Davis affirmed that this was done without his knowledge or consent. Horatio Davis bitterly complained that Myra's suit had driven a wedge between himself and his father. He attacked Myra openly in New Orleans newspapers for "arraying against each other the husband and only son of your benefactress [Mrs. Davis]."

VIII

*Averment of Caroline Barnes**

But even more damning was the sworn statement of Myra's own sister, Caroline:

In respect to the averments of Myra, that her mother was the lawful wife of Daniel Clark, and that Myra is the only legitimate child of that marriage, defendants answer and say that a more exaggerated fiction was never wrought up from a tissue of circumstance.

They are informed and believe that about the year 1796 Zulime de Carrière intermarried with one Jerome Des-Grange and lived with him for several years, till about the year 1801, when for some cause unknown to these defendants, they separated, having no children, as far as they are informed. After this time an illicit intimacy intervened between the said Daniel Clark and the said Mrs. DesGrange, of which the defendant Caroline, was the *acknowledged* issue, and the plaintiff Myra was the reputed issue, though this defendant Caroline has been frequently assured by her mother that she, Caroline, was the only child of Daniel Clark, and reports from others assuming to know, have verified the same fact that Daniel Clark was imposed upon and deceived into the belief that the said Myra was his child, when she was in truth the child of another man.

All these facts the complainants know or have been in-

---

* Caroline Barnes and John Barnes in the District Court suit in New Orleans.

formed of and the defendants would most gladly have suffered to remain in oblivion had not a perverted imagination
attempted to work out a marriage of Mrs. DesGrange to
Daniel Clark, and from thence the legitimacy of the complainant Myra, to the subversion of this defendant Caroline, and with an accumulation of dishonor and reproach
upon both her parents greatly beyond that which a regard
for truth and the necessity of the occasion required. Defendants deny that they ever heard the name Caroline Des-
Grange applied to the said Caroline Clark, until it was so
applied by the complainants, but that on the contrary the
said Caroline Clark Barnes from her earliest infancy has
always been regarded as the daughter of Daniel Clark and
never bore any other name than Caroline Clark.

Daniel Clark was *never married* to the said Mrs. Des-
Grange or anyone else and this defendant Caroline has
heard from her mother her repeated expression of sorrow
and regret that she had not succeeded in becoming the wife
of the said Daniel Clark. Said defendants further allege
that the defendant, Caroline Clark Barnes, is the daughter
of the said Daniel Clark by the said Zulime Carrière, and
that during the time the said Caroline was at the boarding
school of Mrs. Baizley in Philadelphia, and also after her
marriage, the said Zulime nee Carrière frequently visited
her and repeatedly assured her that she, Caroline, was the
only daughter of the said Daniel Clark and therefore the
said defendants assert and maintain that if the said alleged
marriage between said Daniel Clark and said Zulime did
take place as the complainants have averred, in that case
Caroline Barnes would be and must be regarded as the
legitimate child of that marriage; and therefore would be

entitled to all the rights and privileges of legitimate legal heirship.

John Barnes,
Caroline Clark Barnes.

The Patterson Appeal

*S*O STOOD the opposing testimony and conflicting claims when the Patterson appeal came before the Supreme Court in 1847. Patterson, it may be remembered, had not demurred to the bill of Myra but through counsel had answered it. The particular property owned by him was a valuable tract situated on Phillipa Street, New Orleans, between Perdido and Poydras. Patterson contended that it had been legally sold to him by Relf and Chew. The Gaines' claimed it, not under the will of 1813 (Myra could not establish that), but on Myra's forced heirship. The lower court had of course decided against Myra and she appealed to Washington.[1]

Myra's counsel, General Walter Jones, was now well on in years, but as he had added greatly to his reputation by his previous victories, he was willing to try for another. His former partner, Reverdy Johnson, had now become United States senator from Maryland, but this position did not take him out of the case, and he ranged his powerful talents along with those of General Jones when the appeal was argued.

The fame and importance of the contest might have been expected to secure a full bench to hear the argument, but it turned out that Justice Catron was sick and Justice McLean for some reason did not sit. The Chief Justice stayed out of it, giving as his reason that "a near family relative was interested in the outcome." It will be remembered that Francis Scott Key, one of the Gaines attorneys, was Taney's brother-in-law. Key died in 1843 but his family and estate no doubt would have benefited by a Gaines victory. With Taney, McLean, and Catron out, there were left but six associate Justices—Wayne, McKinley, Woodberry, Nelson, Daniel, and Grier—to hear the appeal. Wayne of Georgia was the ranking member of the Court.

By the time the case opened, rumors regarding Patterson's lack of faith were rife in New Orleans. It was believed by many that he had been secretly bought by the General and Myra and that he was not really fighting them. Else, asked New Orleans, why had he not demurred with all the other defendants? Such views were expressed so repeatedly that Patterson's lawyers, W. L. Brent and Henry May, felt it necessary to take notice of them before the Supreme Court. They assured the Court that there was no collusive understanding at all between their client and Mrs. Gaines, only "an anxious desire on his part to meet the claims . . . fully and fairly on the merits."

Brent and May then plunged into the case, terming the story of Clark's last will "the delirious ravings of a man in extremis." Their long argument concluded with a scathing attack on Clark and Zulime:

"For Mrs. Gaines, personally, we feel every sympathy; but how often it is that the innocent offspring is made to suffer for the acts of the parent! And if ever parents deserve condemnation here or elsewhere, these parents have deserved it. A mother who, for the world's false esteem, would discard from her maternal breast two helpless infants, and never again look upon her own offspring—a mother who, upon the case made by her own daughter, stands convicted of adultery before her pretended marriage with Clark, and with bigamy afterward—such a mother is above the judgment of human tribunals. And what shall we say of the conduct of Daniel Clark, if Myra be his lawful child, and Madame DesGrange was his lawful wife? Courting another woman while his wife was living, and at his death forgetting that she had been his wife, although he, as pretended, pronounced her blameless, participating in the crime of separating two infants from their mother to save the paltry pride of that mother—such a man, if the claims of this lady be just, should be consigned to infamy in all human estimation. Even now, the web of destiny hangs around this unfortunate but innocent offspring, and the dreadful past cannot be recalled. After the lapse of forty years, the sun of truth shines upon this dark and adulterous intrigue, revealing all its deformity on the highest judicial records, and showing the vanity of Clark's later attempts to efface the stain, if it could be called a stain, which his own wild passions had placed upon his child at her birth."

So the opposition summed it up, putting in order the reasoning that had been alive on the streets of New Orleans for the past ten years. Senator Johnson and General

Jones answered, throwing against it their weightiest arguments. But a weightier argument yet was given by one not of Myra's counsel, Justice Wayne speaking for the Supreme Court itself.

II

James Moore Wayne [2] was the handsomest man on the Supreme bench, and a southern gentleman to his finger tips. What was more important he was a jurist who combined a wide range of learning and fluency of expression with a sunny catholicity of view. He was a native Georgian, born in Savannah, and had been put on the bench by Old Hickory after the Georgian had stood with the President in the Nullification fight. Wayne was a Jackson man and remained so. The wavy hair tinged with gray, so much admired by the ladies in the eighteen thirties, was now unquestionably whiter, the face more leonine, its lines deeper. His portrait preserves today a keen, aggressive, and scholarly appearance, reflecting, too, an unmistakable hint of hauteur as of one who knew that his word was law. He had met Myra before, and after the three times in which her case had been before him, had definitely arrived at certain conclusions. Now at the head of a somewhat abbreviated Court it was Justice Wayne's time to write a decision. He did so by reviewing the former appearances of the case, by restating the arguments of the opposing counsel "in the strongest way," and then by demolishing them altogether.

"Our conclusions relating to the marriage of the mother of Mrs. Gaines to her father, the lawfulness of the marriage, and that she is the legitimate offspring of that marriage," he affirmed, "differ from all that has been urged against them."

Then Justice Wayne delivering the Court's opinion went vigorously ahead, establishing Myra's claims, triumphantly vindicating her witnesses. The testimony of her foe, Delacroix, was especially discredited. "There is in it," said the Court, "that cold hardness of a man of the world, unmindful of the relations of former friendship whilst professing to regard them. . . . Such men will not swear to what is false, but they may speak what is not true, by an indifference to exactness in what they do say. . . . Besides . . . there is a pecuniary relation between himself and the estate of Daniel Clark, which, unexplained, does not leave a favorable impression of his impartiality in this affair."

The Court's opinion rolled on to this conclusion:

"We shall direct the decree of the court below to be reversed, and adjudge that a decree shall be made in the said court, in this suit, declaring that a lawful marriage was contracted in Philadelphia, Pennsylvania, between Daniel Clark and Zulime Carrière, and that Myra Clark, now Myra Gaines, is the lawful and only child of that marriage. That the said Myra is the forced heir of her father and is entitled to four-fifths of his estate."

Present in the little courtroom to hear this decision were Daniel Webster, Henry Clay, General Jones, and a great number of other prominent lawyers and congressional leaders.[3] Myra was seated in the midst of a galaxy of admiring ladies. General Gaines was in New York but was notified at once by telegraph and returned answer that he would be in Washington the next day.

It had taken twelve long years, but the victorious little woman who heard this judgment pronounced by the highest Court felt that it was worth it. True, she was actually given title to but four fifths of two small lots in New Orleans, but that title, coupled with the decision of the Court, was the key with which to unlock the doors that kept her from possessing all of her father's great estate. Above everything else was the priceless pronouncement that a "lawful marriage was contracted in Philadelphia, Pennsylvania, between Daniel Clark and Zulime Carrière" and that she, Myra, was the "lawful child of that marriage."

Sword at Rest

*T*HE Patterson decision was handed down early in 1848. The General had seen the Mexican War end with nothing for him to do but hold inspection along the seaboard and regret the hard fortune that kept him out of the conflict where many of the lads he had commanded were earning imperishable laurels for themselves and incidentally getting sound training for a much more bitter war when they should fight, not foreigners, but each other. The comparatively innocuous command of the Department of the East practically erased the General from the military slate, though perhaps it gave him more time to help his wife with her suit.

That lady, it appeared, was well on the way to a position where she would need little more help. Her hopes were high that she could now return to Louisiana and take her claim with little more opposition, inasmuch as the Supreme Court had so sweepingly upheld her contention. Both she and her husband were anxious to get back to the South, and the General was successful in securing a transfer

later on in the year. The war was over, and the President-
to-be, Zachary Taylor, was a trusted friend. Once again
the General was given the Department of the West.

But back in the Crescent City, expanding rapidly as the
Spanish West was broken open by the few brief columns
of United States regulars and the many long columns of
covered wagons, it was discovered at once that the war
for Myra's claims was by no means over. New Orleans was
boiling over the Patterson decision. It was unthinkable
that this woman should have secured such a judgment.
How had she done it? It was soon discovered.

Charles Patterson, the man who took the appeal to the
Supreme Court, admitted [1] that he had done so on the
Gaines' money! It was a collusive case after all.

On the witness stand Patterson subsequently narrated
the story of his secret understanding with the General. It
is rather naïve and not quite so black as painted. It had
originated in the days when the General had first married
Myra. At that time the defendants were blocking every
move with their demand for oyer of all documents in
French. The Judge was recalcitrant; the Gaines' were
getting nowhere. The idea of making it worth while for one
of the defendants to bring the case to trial on its own merits
then occurred. The General first went to see—of all persons!—the Louisiana Chief Justice himself, François
Xavier Martin, who spurned the offer at once. Then
Charles Patterson was approached and had proved recep-
tive.

"It was agreed by General Gaines and wife, with me,
that if I would go on trial on the merits of the case, they
would indemnify me against all fees and costs, and that

my property should not be taken in case they succeeded
in their suit," Patterson later explained.

Lawyers unanimously deprecate such an agreement,
but it is impossible to feel that the General and Myra
were not honest in their motive though blameworthy in
method. "I was particularly requested by the General and
Mrs. Gaines," Patterson added, "to use my best exertions
with the aid of the best counsel, to make every defence in
my power to this suit. . . . I consider the agreement of
the General and Mrs. Gaines as an act of liberality on their
part growing out of a desire to come to a speedy trial with
some one or more of the defendants of this case."

That clearly was what it was. When in the course of
the trial, the Patterson counsel wanted to introduce the
record of the Probate Court, and the Gaines' counsel objected, Patterson privately appealed to the General and
Myra. Forthwith they overruled their own lawyer. "They
replied to me to get all the evidence possible, the stronger
the better. General Gaines remarked that it would be more
glorious to have it as strong as possible. I then caused the
proceedings to be introduced."

But earnest contest or not, it was a collusive bargain and
Myra was never to hear the last of it. Those who were
touched to the quick were the lawyers involved. They
were placed in the unenviable light of having prosecuted
a fictitious controversy before the Supreme Court of the
United States.

Patterson's admission was the spark that set off the
mine. It fitted in with everything that Myra's bitter opponents had asserted, and came on top of a startling decision in her favor, a decision that they knew she meant to

plead as a *res adjudicata,* or a closed judgment against every transfer of property which had been made since the death of Daniel Clark.

Covert threats had been sounded before. Now Latin rage and the colder hate of the northern race united in a peculiar venom. Myra's life was threatened. Menacing crowds formed about her whenever she was recognized. On one occasion, the carriage in which she was riding was suddenly blocked and surrounded by a milling mob. Epithets were hurled and evil faces pressed close to the carriage windows. Myra imperiously ordered the trembling coachman to "whip the horses," and the plunging beasts bore her quickly out of danger.[2] As a souvenir of such experiences she long preserved a small silk bonnet with a hole clipped cleanly in it where a lurking marksman had shot too close to be comfortable. But neither mobs nor bullets bent her from her purpose.

II

Following the first burst of rage felt by the growing number of those whose property was menaced by Myra's claims, came a determined desire to fight the case through and have done with this woman's interminable suit. The collusive nature of the Patterson agreement reacted heavily against Myra, and the defendants were sure that in the cold light of a legal appraisal they really had nothing to fear. The Supreme Court had decided for this woman because she had no real opposition. This time Relf and Chew meant to see that she did. The time for delay, postponement, and demurring was over. They would bring the case to trial on its own merits.

Myra's opponents realized that their easiest battle would be in the United States Circuit Court, that is, the lower court. They knew now the temper of their antagonist and that even if she lost in Louisiana, Myra would certainly appeal again to the Supreme Court. So they took no chances and set about to secure the best counsel they could find. Two New Orleans lawyers by the name of Duncan impressed Relf and Chew as able to take care of the local end of their defense; but for Washington they wanted a greater man. So they secured the greatest lawyer of them all, Daniel Webster himself.

Webster was then far advanced in years. He had recently been appointed Secretary of State, and was enjoying to the full the prodigious reputation he had built up through his long career. But, as it appears, Webster took no very active part [3] in the Gaines case. Perhaps he contented himself with looking over interrogatories and cross-interrogatories, as the surviving witnesses were once more compelled to tell their stories. This examination, however, was no small task. One hundred and twenty-one cross-interrogatories were propounded to Samuel B. Davis alone when he was on the stand for the last time in 1849.

But Myra and the General were not to be left without counsel in the great battle then impending. General Jones and Reverdy Johnson had left them or were engaged elsewhere, but there were many lawyers who would be glad to enter the now famous case. The honor of breaking a lance against Daniel Webster would itself have tempted many a prominent lawyer to champion Myra's cause. She finally retained a promising young Mobile attorney by the name of John Archibald Campbell. Mr. Campbell was to prove not unworthy.

During 1849 while the suit was pending in the Circuit Court, there was great activity on both sides. Depositions were taken right and left from any who might be able to throw even the least light on the respective claims. Boisfontaine, Bellechasse, and Harriet Smythe were now dead but their carefully certified testimony was of course presented again. The much-deposing Madame Despau, now an aged woman, was for a fifth time compelled to submit to examination and cross-examination, and her octogenarian sister, Madame Caillavet, was likewise interrogated once again. Up in Philadelphia, Daniel Coxe, also in advanced years, for a last time told his story and reiterated his contention that Daniel Clark had never married.

But there was one person from whom no deposition nor averment would ever come again. The drab, crushed life of Caroline Barnes ended a short while after the Patterson case had been heard. Myra had outlived her unfortunate sister, to whom she was such a contrast. All the power and glory of Daniel Clark flowered again in Myra; but all his chivalry and elegance paled into insignificance in the colorless figure of the little schoolteacher and seamstress, doomed from birth to expiate through uneventful years the sins of her father. Like some timid creature of the earth she had lived secretively until her whole life had been exposed to the pitiless glare of publicity by the fight of Myra, and, made of fragile material, Caroline wilted away. For the first time death had stepped in and removed one of Myra's foes.

III

While former witnesses were dropping out, new ones were being discovered. Beverly Chew's sister, Caroline, the widow of Colonel John Stanard,[4] residing in Fredericksburg, Virginia, told of her girlhood visit to New Orleans, and how a few months before he died Daniel Clark gave her "every proof that a gentleman could give" that he was *not* married. So Clark had proposed to Caroline Chew also. Her niece, a Mrs. Wood of New York, nee Julia Brockle, who had been with Caroline Chew when the Relfs, Chews, and Clark had lived together in the most intimate relations in the days of 1813, also affirmed under oath that she was positive that Clark was never married.

But Myra herself suddenly found a new witness. A certain congressman from Illinois named Baker got word to Myra that Bishop Philander Chase [5] of Peoria, Illinois, presiding bishop of the Protestant Episcopal Church, knew some things about her childhood. It was found that as a young rector in New Orleans he had lived next door to Samuel B. Davis and had seen Daniel Clark caress Myra as his own child. Myra at once realized the value of Bishop Chase's name and influence on her side. His testimony proved quite helpful.

IV

The taking of depositions went on apace through the warm spring days of 1849. Myra and the General continued to live in their suite at the St. Charles, the General giving as much time as possible to Myra's cause. Early summer and the bright days of June appeared, and with them that dreaded scourge of the lower river, cholera. But New Orleans by this time had passed through too many dangers to be alarmed by an epidemic. Cholera was merely cholera. The city went ahead and the Gaines' like everyone else went on with their affairs. The General was superintending the taking of a deposition from one of Myra's many witnesses when the disease smote him.

They got the stricken man into bed at the St. Charles, but it was clear there was little hope. A young soldier came in to help his chief.

"Well, my young friend," murmured the General, "my time is approaching and I suppose I must go. I have nothing on my conscience and am not afraid to die. I am an old man and have probably lived long enough."

That night he looked into Myra's face for the last time. "My dear wife, farewell. You cannot imagine how much I love you." At three in the morning the old soldier ceased to breathe.[6]

When the New Orleans *Daily Picayune* of the following day (June 7) recorded "with infinite pain" the death of General Gaines, a spontaneous and surprising wave of real regret swept the volatile city. New Orleans remembered his long and honorable career in her midst and unreservedly turned out to do honor to the man who had been a public character ever since he had come in with Claiborne. Even the General's debacle in the Mexican War was championed by the *Weekly Delta,* the New Orleans paper commenting truculently: "Had his views been carried out, the war would have been terminated sooner than it did."

Meanwhile throngs pressed through the St. Charles where the body of the General lay in state, covered with the well-known blue uniform, the familiar stainless sword at rest at his side. Two days later in the ladies' parlor of the famous hostelry the funeral was held. The Reverend Theodore Clapp, foremost Protestant minister of the city and the General's pastor, was in charge. Dr. Clapp took advantage of the occasion and in a eulogy that the papers were glad to reproduce, the Presbyterian divine likened the dead officer to George Washington. About the hot, crowded parlors in that decorous stillness that death demands gleamed the glittering uniforms of army officers, while sober civilian cloth marked out many a civic dignitary.

The lengthy civil and military procession at length formed outside and was put in motion toward the Ponchartrain Railroad station. The cars made their brief run to the Lake, and the steamer *Oregon* bore all that was mortal of the hero of Fort Erie toward Mobile and his final resting place.

But not by a line in a newspaper, not by a sympathetic comment in the few memorial letters that were printed, not even by a mention in Dr. Clapp's prayer, was Myra Clark Gaines remembered. The city, as though by unanimous agreement, simply ignored her. Perhaps New Orleans sincerely felt that the less said of this woman's connection with General Gaines the better. Only in the Reverend Mr. Clapp's eulogy [7] is there anything that may have been a reference to the part Myra played. The minister said that the General had left a name to his family "worth more than all the silver and gold of the universe. Contrasted with such a character as our friend has left behind him, how insignificant are the boastful possessions of worldly ambition."

By which Mr. Clapp may have meant something—and then again he may not.

The Ecclesiastical Record

DEATH waits for nothing, but law also moves on regardless. The General died while the final battle of the long suit was impending. Myra Clark had fought too long to give up now, and through the closing months of 1849 she was busily engaged in the further preparation of her case. The reader has doubtless decided by this time that, while due acknowledgment should be made for the love and chivalry of Whitney and for the money and influence of General Gaines, the real driving force behind the whole case was Myra herself.

As the coming legal struggle was to emphasize a somewhat different aspect of the original contest—the validity of the first marriage of Zulime—it will be necessary now to add to the testimony heretofore presented certain new, or rearranged, evidence that was before the courts in 1850. Myra's opponents felt that in spite of the Supreme Court's pronouncement in the Patterson case, if they could establish the fact of a valid, unbroken marriage between DesGrange and Zulime, the alleged Clark-Zulime later marriage would fall of its own weight.

On Myra's side, her aunt, Madame Despau, had again and again insisted under oath that Jerome DesGrange had not only been guilty of bigamy but had been tried for this offense before an ecclesiastical court back in 1802, and that he had managed to escape and flee before judgment could be pronounced. Was there any further proof of such a trial?

Apparently not. But what Myra's agents could not discover, her opponents suddenly produced. Out of the archives of the Catholic Archbishopric of New Orleans suddenly came a paper purporting to be the record of a prosecution of one Geronimo DesGrange for bigamy under date of 1802. As this "ecclesiastical record" [1] or "ecclesiastical trial" is of great importance in the case, a few words must be given to it.

The document produced seemed to be in regular form and contained what purported to be a lengthy record of "Criminal Proceedings against Geronimo DesGrange for Bigamy." After the citation, it contained the testimony of one Donna Barbara Jeanbelle, the woman whom Des-Grange was said to have married in New York. She denied being married to DesGrange. Next appears the examination of a certain Maria Yllar Soumeylliat whom DesGrange was alleged to have married in France and who was then, according to this record, living at the Bernard Marigny home in New Orleans. She also denied a marriage. Then "appeared before his Excellency Maria Julia Carrière" who admitted being married to DesGrange and testified that although she had heard that her husband was married to two other women, "she has not believed it and the report has caused her no uneasiness, as she is satisfied that it is not true." Zulime's signature is affixed to this. Last of all comes the examination of DesGrange. The Frenchman denied being married to anyone but Zulime. He admitted that he had known "Barbara Jeanbelle d'Orsi" in New York before he ever came to New Orleans and that he had wanted to marry her but that her father had refused his suit, "as deponent was poor." The entire proceedings close with this decree:

"DECREE: Not being able to prove the public report which is contained in the original decree of these proceedings, and having no more proofs for the present, let all proceedings be suspended, with power to prosecute them hereafter if necessary, and let the person of Geronimo DesGrange be set at liberty, he paying the costs.

"*Signed*, Thomas Hassett."

"Don Thomas Hassett, Presbyter Canon of this Holy Cathedral Church, Vicar-General of this Province of Louisiana and the two Floridas, has approved and signed the preceding decree, in New Orleans, this 7th September, 1802.

"*Signed*, Francisco Bermudez"

Such in brief outline was the "ecclesiastical record," largely relied upon by the respondents to show that Des-Grange had indeed been under *report* of bigamy, but that an official pronouncement had cleared him, and that Zulime herself had sworn that she believed him innocent.

Myra met this whole paper with a flat charge of forgery. She insisted that its origin was quite recent, and that it had been planted by an interested hand in the files

of the archives of St. Louis Cathedral where the good
Bishop Blanc might conveniently discover it. Zulime told
Myra's lawyers [2] that her signature to this purported
record was most certainly forged, that she had never been
before an ecclesiastical tribunal in her life. The Right
Reverend Antoine Blanc was himself put under oath and,
while he told an unimpeachable story as to how he came
to discover the paper, he admitted that he had never found
any other record of the sort in the same armoire or in any
other repository of archives of the archbishopric. Experts
were called in to examine the signatures appearing in the
paper, especially that of Zulime, while some of the older
inhabitants were asked if they recalled any person by the
name of Madame Soumeylliat who had stayed at the
Marigny home. Old Bernard Marigny himself took the
stand and said he had never heard of such a person.

Was the "ecclesiastical record" evidence that would be
accepted as such by a United States Court? If so, how
much weight would it have? It contained material supporting allegations made by both sides.

II

The Alimony Record and Mutilated Record

Another paper strongly relied on by the respondents to
prove the falsity of the claim that Zulime could ever have
married Clark was what became known as the "Alimony
Record." This purported to be a suit by Zulime against
DesGrange in which as late as 1805 she acknowledged
him as her husband and prayed for alimony as wife.

Myra's lawyers answered the presentation of the

"Alimony Record" by saying that however Zulime's name had been used by her lawyers in 1806, what she had really been praying for was a *divorce*. To sustain their argument they introduced a record of another—or the same?—suit filed by Zulime near the same date in which they asserted she was definitely attempting to gain a divorce. *Unfortunately, however, the petition of this suit could not be found*. The petition, which was the key to the suit, had been torn out, apparently at a later date, and again fraud was charged. A transcript of the record of the suit, however, was put in for what it was worth. It became known as the "mutilated record."

The question was: What was Zulime praying for in 1806? A *divorce*, as Madame Despau and others had steadily testified? Or *alimony*, as the damages awarded seemed to indicate? Did this suit have any relationship with the other alleged suit for alimony?

Both sides had their answers and both used the "mutilated record" for what they could make of it. Myra had introduced it, and, on the whole, it helped her claim.

III

The Marriage Certificate

Another paper of great interest had turned up while the Patterson case was pending before the Supreme Court, though *after* this case had been decided in the lower, or Louisiana Circuit Court. Young James Gardette, Myra's half brother, suddenly came across an old Latin certificate among the papers of his father. To Myra and her lawyers it instantly became of great value, as the actual marriage

certificate of DesGrange and Barbara D'Orsi. It was signed
by William N. O'Brien, pastor of the Church of St. Peter,
New York. It affirmed:

". . . that on the sixth day of July, 1790 I joined to-
gether in matrimony Jacobum DesGrange and Barbara
M. Orci. Witnesses present were John O'Connell, Charles
Bernardi and Victoria Bernardi. . . . Given in New
York, this 11th of September, A.D. 1806.

"William N. O'Brien."

The long-sought proof of DesGrange's prior marriage!
Small wonder that the discovery of this paper caused a
sensation. It was the defendants' time to cry forgery. That
Myra's brother, James Gardette, Zulime's son, had
"found" it just when it was most needed brought a scornful rejoinder from her foes. Who was this Father O'Brien?
Doubtless another mysterious priest whose whereabouts,
like those of the fictitious one who married Zulime and
Clark, would never be ascertained.

But they were wrong there. Myra got in touch with
Ellen Guinan, a young Irishwoman in New York who was
said to be a niece of Father O'Brien, and then both sides
put in motion the now familiar machinery of question and
cross-question under commission from the court. The
Reverend John Power, the vicar-general of New York, was
himself put under oath:

". . . I believe the certificate [that of DesGrange's
marriage to Mrs. D'Orsi] to be in the handwriting of
O'Brien. It is identically the same handwriting with the
records of St. Peter's kept by O'Brien."

To this Ellen Guinan added:

"I have resided in New York since I was nine years old.

When I first came to New York, the pastor of the Catholic Church in New York was my uncle, William Vincent O'Brien; he was pastor for thirty years and died in 1814; I have seen him write and identify exhibit A [the Latin certificate] as in his handwriting. . . . I think I have heard my aunt, Louisia Jane O'Brien, speak of the marriage of such a person as DesGrange; she mentioned particularly the dress of the bride."

Such was the "Latin certificate." The lawyers on both sides were not to allow it to be forgotten when the case was called.

Colonel Preston for the Defense

O N WEDNESDAY, January 20, 1850, before the crowded bar of the Circuit Court of the United States for the Eastern District of Louisiana, came the "Great Gaines Case" as the New Orleans *Weekly Delta* termed it. Justice John McKinley of the Supreme Court and Judge McCaleb of New Orleans were on the bench. The courtroom was packed. The long suit was to be ended at last.

But not so rapidly. Testimony must first be read, and that, it appeared, was a lengthy process with twelve hundred printed pages containing the record. Four days were spent in getting this properly before the court. Not until the following Monday was there a chance for argument.

Myra's counsel had the right to open but Colonel Isaac Preston,[1] representing the defendants, asked as a personal favor that he be allowed to speak first in order to attend to other important business elsewhere. His request was granted by consent of the Gaines lawyers, and the colorful Preston rose and addressed the Court:

"In 1813, died in this city Daniel Clark, a man of considerable note in the early history of this State. He died leaving his estate to his mother, and constituting Chew and Relf his executors. The latter, in the settlement of his estate, sell the property of his succession, by public auction, to various parties, who, or their assignees, now hold said property. When these sales were made, Clark was universally understood and believed to be an unmarried man. There was no risk in buying his property. The purchasers remained in quiet possession until 1836, for a space of twenty-six years, when suddenly a lady appears in this city, and startles the whole community by claiming all this property, alleging that she is the child of Daniel Clark by lawful marriage with Zulime de Carrière. And what does all this monstrous pretension—this extraordinary discovery rest upon? It rests upon the testimony of one single witness, Madame Despau, sister of Zulime, whose credibility, as a witness, will presently be inquired into. But taking her story for truth, what does it amount to? Why, that Daniel Clark had made a secret, a clandestine marriage with Zulime Carrière—that the marriage was made in secret, and the secret was long kept by all parties. Now, I shall show, by competent law, that such a marriage was not only illegal, but criminal. Under the Spanish law, and indeed in all Catholic countries, marriage is a sacred, religious ceremony, the solemnization of which should be notorious and public, that all the world might know it and be bound by it; and in order, if there was any legal impediment, that parties might come forward and make it known.

"And on what evidence does the fact of this pretended

secret, fraudulent, and invalid marriage depend? On the testimony of an adulteress! An *adulteress,* for such Madame Despau is proved, on this record, to have been. I refer to the proceedings of her husband against her for forfeiture of her rights in the marital property, in which she is charged with leading a rambling life, 'living in open adultery.' "

That was the opening gun of Colonel Preston's long and at times vituperative argument. "We saw this property advertised as Daniel Clark's," he continued with growing vehemence; "we knew nothing of your intrigues, your secret arrangements, your adulteries, and other abominations. We went in open day to Masparo's coffee-house—a public auction mart—and bid for the property. We paid our money for it, and acts of sale were made out to us before notaries public. To disturb rights thus acquired would be iniquity, not equity. But oh! we are told of 'constructive frauds' and 'legal implications,' and all these foreign interpolations that have been forced into our jurisprudence."

Then Colonel Preston asked the judges to look more closely "at the facts in the case." He made quite a point of showing how Madame Despau had changed her testimony as to the date of the "pretended marriage." In her deposition used in the Patterson case ("that infamous suit of Patterson which I would to God I could blot from the record of this court, where it must ever remain the memento of a disgraceful and outrageous fraud"), Madame Despau swore that the marriage of Clark and Zulime took place in 1803. "But when," said Colonel

Preston, "by the examination of numerous letters of Clark it was discovered that he was not within a thousand miles of Philadelphia during the year 1803, they change their position. As soon as they ascertained the discovery we had made (which my colleagues were for keeping a secret, but I was for making it public) and the complainant was required to fix the date when the marriage occurred, she comes into court and fixes the time in the 'Autumn of 1801, or the spring of 1802.' And the discrepancy between the averments and depositions of Madame Despau is got over in her testimony, taken in 1849, by saying that 'from certain associations' she thinks it was in 1802. Well now let us see if it is at all probable that the marriage took place in 1802."

Forthwith, Colonel Preston traced the movements of Daniel Clark when he made the trip to Philadelphia and Europe in 1802. He declared that Clark was at that time so worried over his business, especially the frauds in cotton packing, that he was in no state of mind to contract a marriage, even if the lady in the case "had been a second Helen for whom a Troy might have been destroyed." "Read his letters," exclaimed Colonel Preston, "and observe the distressed, the agonized state of his mind! He could think of nothing but the wreck of his fortune, his hopes, his reputation. Would he, the proud and yet cautious merchant, who refused the hand of a lady that has since become a Duchess—"

"A Marchioness," Mr. Duncan interrupted.

"—a Marchioness, Duchess, countess or something of that sort, I am not familiar with the titles of nobility— would this ambitious Irishman, who refused the hand of a distinguished lady rather than embarrass himself, turn aside from the perplexing anxieties which filled his mind, and overcome the gloom that frowned like a dark cloud upon his hopes, to burden himself with the cast-off wife of a poor, miserable French syrup maker!"

"But where was the poor, virtuous, forsaken Zulime?" continued Colonel Preston sarcastically. He proceeded to say that she was in New Orleans at the time of the pretended marriage instituting an inquiry into the alleged bigamy of DesGrange but swearing before the vicar-general that she did not believe a word about DesGrange's having been previously married. "Both parties then," said the speaker, "were a thousand miles from Philadelphia at the time it is averred they were married."

The Latin parchment, which purported to be a certificate from Father O'Brien of New York, in which this priest declared he had married Jacobum DesGrange and Barbara M. Orci, next aroused Colonel Preston's wrathful scorn. "Where did this certificate come from?" he asked. "Spread out in Latin with all the flourishes and pompous phrases. It was found among the papers of Dr. Gardette, who had procured it in 1806, at the time when he was the husband of another lady. What had Dr. Gardette to do with the intrigues, the secret arrangements, etc., of Zulime and DesGrange? Gardette's wife dies and he straitway marries Zulime, in as much haste as the Queen of Denmark, who did not wait for the meats to get cold before she supplied the place of her lost spouse—he thus rushes into the arms of the impatient Zulime, who no sooner hears the idle rumor that Clark is courting someone else, than she determines to commit bigamy. Gardette and Zulime marry, and this paper sleeps among Gardette's papers until it is exhumed, forty years later, for purposes of this suit. But even this certificate refers to the marriage of one *Jacobum*, not *Hieronynum* DesGrange, and is not therefore good evidence of the fact which it was intended to prove. No! May it please your honors, this is all a trumped up story!"

Court at length had to be adjourned for the day with Colonel Preston still holding forth. The next morning he resumed his argument where he had left it.

"I have stated under the Spanish law, which existed at the time of this pretended marriage, Madame Despau being a convicted adulteress, could not be received as competent proof of this marriage. She was the companion of her sister, they lived together, they went to Philadelphia together, and there Zulime, hearing of Clark's attentions to Miss Caton, married Dr. Gardette, in the very face of her pretended marriage with Clark. Now all this time Madame Despau stands by, aiding and abetting her sister in the infamous crime of bigamy—"

Judge McKinley: "We are not governed by the Spanish law of evidence; the common law governs in all matters of evidence."

J. A. Campbell: "I desire to call Colonel Preston's attention to the fact that Madame Despau does not say she was present at the marriage of her sister to Dr. Gardette."

"And why did she say she was not present?" rejoined Preston. "For the very purpose of avoiding this conclusion, of weakening this argument—this presumption against her character which would flow from the fact of her presence at the marriage of Zulime. But if not actually present, she was cognizant of all the movements, the acts, and the intentions of her sister. Here then we find this witness, upon whose testimony this immense property is to be wrested from its present honest proprietors, an accomplice in the atrocious crime of bigamy. It requires no sentence of law to pronounce her infamous and unworthy of credit!"

The speaker next emphasized at great length the story that was generally current in New Orleans: that Myra was not really Clark's child at all but the child of Zulime by another man; that Zulime persuaded Clark that Myra was his child ("when the child Myra was born she was supplied with a potent wand to control the feeling and conduct of Clark"); that she hoped to lure Clark into marriage and so started the rumors of DesGrange's bigamy to drive her husband away; that DesGrange was the real victim of the whole plot. "Alas, poor DesGrange," exclaimed Colonel Preston allowing pathos to supplant indignation in his voice, "you were the injured party in this whole dark tragedy. You return home from your native land expecting to find a peaceful and happy home; but you no sooner arrive than the story of your wife's infamy reaches your ears. The town is full of the intrigue of your wife and Clark; your wife's affections are gone forever from you; infamy rests upon your name and family. Under such circumstances no wonder the unhappy man flies from home, and buries his sorrow either in the grave or in some remote land, for he has not been heard of since 1806. And thus was poor Jerome DesGrange made the victim of this infamous intrigue which begot this infamous suit."

The speaker then whirled around to face Myra in the presence of the Court. "These are the acts of your mother rising up against you," he declared. "But your father was an honorable, a high-minded man . . . let us see what was his conduct."

II

"Early in 1802, as the story goes, Clark married Zulime, and he leaves immediately for Europe. She returns to New Orleans. So does Clark; but they do not come together. Whilst living here, Clark resides in his palace on the Bayou road; Zulime lives with her sisters, in a house of their own, constituting a seraglio, at which Clark is a constant visitor. Clark never takes her to his house to introduce her to his friends—those friends who were as numerous and sturdy as the trees in the forest. But the strangest phase in this complicated intrigue is the conduct of Clark in permitting DesGrange and Zulime to live together as man and wife, after her marriage with him. Was Daniel Clark this sort of man? Was he, proud, high-spirited, and passionate, the sort of man who would 'keep a corner in the thing he loved for another man's use'? No. This bare suspicion contradicts the whole life and character of Daniel Clark.

"But Clark, if not the protector of his honor, and that of his wife, was at least generous. In 1805 when Zulime was in that situation 'in which ladies delight who love their lords' (for Myra says she was born in 1806), she was in want—she wants bread and meat. Does she appeal to her generous husband, the merchant prince? No; she sues the wretched, ruined DesGrange for alimony. Clark, the husband, was bound to authorize this suit—to spread on record that his beautiful wife, now *enceinte,* should ask for crumbs from DesGrange. Clark knew of this suit, for in those simple times, suits were to lawyers like angels' visits—few and far between. He thus spread on record the disgrace of himself, his wife, and hoped-for offspring, by asking bread from her seducer. Impossible!

"Another scene in the drama. He is the first representative in Congress from the splendid acquisition of Jefferson. His fame, his talents, his wealth, precede his advent to the capital. The beauty and wealth of the country throw themselves in the salons visited by the splendid bachelor. He addresses the beautiful Louisa Caton, famed to the present day in the annals of fashion and gallantry. The husband of Zulime is enamored and engaged to Miss Caton. The unanimous voice of the country proclaims the father of Myra incapable of this baseness. He afterwards addresses and is engaged to Mrs. Lambert, while a married man; and, baseness number two failing, the Lothario addresses Miss Chew, whose words were even now those of simplicity and truth.

"The closing scene approaches, as the darkness of eternity when the heart can conceal nothing, begins to gather around him. He is stretched on the pallet of death. The Chevalier Delacroix, to whom he has confided all that was dear to him in the world from which he was just departing, kneeled down by his side to receive his last wishes. He did not die with the lie in his mouth, that Myra was his legitimate daughter.

" *'Hic Jacet'* was inscribed on his tomb, as printed in this record. *Hic jacet,* innocent of all the plunder it is attempted to perpetrate in his name. The same *hic jacet* invites us all to beds of eternal bliss, if we have been just on earth. But if we become participators in schemes of perjury and plunder, it will be inscribed over our sleep of death.

"I beg this court then, to take this case and determine it upon the evidence developed in the record, without regard to the fictitious and fraudulent showing in the Patterson case.

"The judge who will expose and denounce that compound of falsehood and corruption, will deserve the highest niche in the temple of justice. His *hic jacet* will record the virtue, the justice, the wisdom, without which elevated station can confer neither honor, dignity, nor respect."

John A. Campbell for Mrs. Gaines

THE irate, but breezy Preston swept through his *hic jacet* peroration and then, presumably, left to attend to that private business for which he had asked the right to be heard first. The Honorable W. C. Wright immediately set forth the case for the plaintiff. He finished at some time on the following day. Then the new lawyer from Mobile stood before the court.

John A. Campbell [1] was at that time forty years of age. He had behind him years of careful study and that close application to the minutiae as well as to the guiding principles of law which has invariably marked the great masters of jurisprudence. His environment had encouraged his juristic training, for Mobile, like New Orleans, had grown rapidly, land titles were overlaid, lost, or obscure, and the Civil Code ruled there also in many matters of inheritance. It is safe to say that as a master of the Code, he was the peer of any lawyer present.

Campbell stood before the court having every particle of evidence in the long record and every involved principle of the law clearly in mind. A sense of unshakable integrity as well as philosophic profundity always characterized his personal presence, and when he spoke he appeared more the judge delivering an ultimate, irreversible finding, than a partisan advocate seeking to convince. That Campbell was convinced carried conviction of itself. Now, after an impressive salutation, he laid bare the whole case in his first five sentences, and then began, as a visitor there put it, "to thread the Cretan labyrinth of fact and testimony, holding on as he went, to the thread of justice."

"May it please the Court:

"Daniel Clark, a citizen of Louisiana, died in 1813, leaving a large estate, both real and personal, in that State. The Code of Louisiana casts the succession of four-fifths of that estate upon his legitimate children, in opposition to any voluntary disposition he may have made during his life.

"The Plaintiff in this case claims to be the only legitimate child of Daniel Clark.

"The first question that arises in the cause is, whether the plaintiff is the child of Daniel Clark; the next, whether she is legitimate? Upon the solution of these questions in her favor, her rights to the legal succession depend."

Campbell had no trouble in making clear the "filiation of the plaintiff," that she really was the child of Daniel Clark. He brushed aside as the "idlest bar-room and brothel gossip" the allegation that Clark was impotent. He showed how Clark and Zulime had lived together in a house provided by Clark from 1802 or 1803 to 1806 or

1807, how Clark always treated the child Myra as his own, and how even Coxe and Relf in their letters always spoke of Myra as the child of Clark. The recently obtained testimony of Bishop Philander Chase was impressively repeated here by Campbell: "Daniel Clark embraced her in the presence of his friends as his child in my sight."

"The evidence of legitimacy," proceeded Campbell, "is of a somewhat different character." He went on to declare that "all presumptions of the law favored legitimacy," and that the fact that Myra was looked upon as the heiress of her father's estate was of added force in arguing for her legal status. More than that, her father's own assertion in his last will declaring Myra to be his legitimate daughter was sufficient, Campbell said, to attest this fact. He cited the Roman law on this point: "We have determined to ordain . . . that if anyone having a son or daughter of a free woman with whom he might have been married, shall say in a written act . . . *or in his last will,* that this son or this daughter is his child, and that he does not call them 'natural children,' they shall be reputed legitimate; and no other proofs shall be demanded of them." "No witness who has testified in this case (save Delacroix)," asserted Campbell, "has testified that he ever heard Clark speak of the plaintiff as his 'natural child.' Bellechasse, Boisfontaine, and Mrs. Smyth, testify fully to the declarations in the will."

Campbell then took up the question of the actual marriage which he strongly asserted was a fact proved by the evidence. Against Preston's argument that Clark visited Philadelphia but once and at a time when Zulime could not possibly have been there, and that this was a

hasty trip under great stress of business worry, Mr. Campbell declared: "In some of the most material particulars
this is untrue. Clark left New Orleans for Philadelphia in
the latter part of October or early November of 1801. His
voyage was long, owing to a detention at Havana, and the
probability is that he reached Philadelphia in December
or early January of 1802. He remained in Philadelphia
until the 23rd of April, 1802, and then returned to New
Orleans. In June 1802 he left New Orleans and arrived in
Philadelphia in July or August. Zulime Carrière gives a
power of attorney on November 9, 1801, in New Orleans.
That power was used in January 1802. The proof is clear
that Clark left New Orleans about the time she did. The
conclusion therefore is, that there was no such difficulty in
the way of the formation of a marriage as Coxe intimates."

Myra's lawyer then went on to explain why the marriage of Clark and Zulime had to be kept secret in Louisiana
—because there had been no annulment of the DesGrange
marriage. "The necessity for obtaining the declaration of
nullity," observed Campbell, "seems to have been constantly impressed on the minds of both parties. Another
impression on the mind of Zulime, which seems to have
exerted the most powerful influence on her life, was the
belief that the validity of her marriage could only be
manifested by public and authentic registers of marriage."
He hammered this point home and explained that it was
the erroneous idea that a marriage to be a marriage had to
be publicly authenticated in writing which made both
Clark and Zulime act later on as though their own
marriage was invalid. He vehemently denied that any
subsequent conduct of Clark and Zulime—the one marry-

ing Gardette, the other courting Louisa Caton—could possibly break the marriage between them. "The marriage in Pennsylvania (of Clark and Zulime) was valid without any declaration of the nullity of the marriage between Zulime and DesGrange. That marriage could not lose its legal character. Lord Eldon has said: 'When once you have got clearly to the conclusion that a marriage has been had, that marriage must be sustained, let the consequences be what they may.' The French jurists are agreed to this principle."

Defending the evidence for the marriage, Campbell then entered the lists for Madame Despau. "In reference to her," said Campbell, "no witness could be better sustained. She has been followed from place to place, and her life examined for the last forty years, and with but a single result—a result which secures her from disparagement before this tribunal." To Colonel Preston's allegation that she was an adulteress, Campbell rejoined: "The defendants have sought to fortify themselves by a record of some proceedings between herself and her husband. It is certainly not necessary for me to state to this court that such a record is not admissible to impeach a witness; that such a judgment can have no effect upon the character of a witness in any court."

II

"But we are told," continued Campbell, "that there was an existing marriage, constituting an insurmountable barrier to the marriage from which the complainant sprung—that Zulime had another husband living." He admitted that Zulime "had been married to a man named

DesGrange" previous to her marriage with Clark, but declared that this marriage was void *ab initio* by virtue of DesGrange's previous marriage with Madame D'Orsi. He cited the mutilated record, which he called "the suit of 1806 against the name of DesGrange," as evidence. "Suppose DesGrange had died after his marriage with Zulime," he said. "Can there be a doubt that his property would have gone to his children by Barbara D'Orsi? A previous marriage makes a subsequent one void. It requires no sentence of invalidity, no decree of a court, because it never had any force or existence."

The ecclesiastical record, or trial of DesGrange for bigamy, was next examined. "Even if this record could be admitted as proof, the judgment by no means supports the conclusion of the defendants. It is a mere judgment of suspension of proof and further proceedings. 'It is ordered and adjudged that further proceeding be suspended, with power to prosecute hereafter.' This has none of the force of a final decree—and if it were such a judgment, it would not be proof in another suit."

In rapid succession Campbell disposed of the alimony record, and the record of Samuel B. Davis' suit of 1817 in which he, as Myra's curator, called her a "natural child." "Such proceedings would not be evidence against Davis, much less against the infant he pretended to represent," asserted Campbell. "Thus then, may it please the court, is every barrier to the marriage of Clark and Zulime removed."

"Colonel Preston has entertained the court with large drafts from the Spanish law to show that clandestine marriages were invalid. This is altogether an inaccurate view of the matter. Persons entering into clandestine marriages were subject to heavy penalties, but so far from such marriages being invalid, I shall show that Colonel Preston exposes himself to the anathemas of the Holy Church by even pretending that such marriages are invalid. But the marriage in this case, took place in Philadelphia and must be governed by the laws of Pennsylvania where it would have been valid though the ceremony was not performed by a court or in the presence of witnesses.

"Thus I have shown an unbroken chain of evidence, reaching from the birth of the child to the death of Clark to establish the legitimacy. Throw all other evidence aside, the birth, the acknowledgments, education—the will, so vilely suppressed, and the many other circumstances supporting the claims of the complainant—and put this case upon the testimony of Madames Despau and Caillavet, and it is sufficient to establish the legitimacy of the complainant. It would be sufficient if she had been picked up in the streets or thrown into the foundling asylum."

Campbell then went on to notice the "invective" in which he said the counsel for defense had indulged. "It has been the favorite theme of some of the counsel, that the vast difference in fortune and condition of Clark and Zulime forbade the marriage." Turning his attention to this argument, Myra's lawyer reviewed the circumstances when Clark and Zulime first met. He argued that at that early date there was no great difference in the two parties. Zulime was very beautiful; her family was well connected; "Madame Caillavet, one of her sisters and a witness in this case, has even now reached an advanced age and her reputation has never been sullied by a breath of scandal. Her history has defied even the inquisitive malice of Relf." That was, of course, to look back at the early days when Clark and Zulime first met. "But after this," admitted Mr. Campbell, "the relative positions of the parties were essentially changed. The cession takes place. Clark gains great distinction from his connection with that interesting event. He becomes a citizen of a republic. He rises to the distinguished post of first representative in Congress from the new state of Louisiana. In Washington he attracts much attention, mingles with the best society of the land, becomes a man of fashion, the intimate friend of Robert Goodloe Harper to whom he lends money. He is a quite different man from what he was in 1802. Now he makes difficulties in the way of acknowledging his marriage with Zulime. He looks higher, and poor Zulime has ceased to be a proper match for him. . . . She meanwhile has fallen in the scale of respectability. She has kept her marriage with Clark a secret, whilst continuing her connection with him and has consequently fallen into disrepute. Confining our view to that period, counsel may well say that there was considerable disparity between them. But if we look into the year 1802, is there any improbability founded upon the condition and relation of the parties, of the marriage of Clark and Zulime?"

So Campbell went on piling up his proofs, moving impressively ahead, clearing point after point, marshaling argument after argument. The plea set up by the defendants that they were bona fide purchasers of valuable property and should be protected in their titles was swiftly dismissed by Campbell as he drew near the end of his great speech. "A party cannot transmit a greater right than he possesses. The purchasers of the estate of Daniel Clark never dispossessed the heir of her legal rights, and those who hold under them have acquired no further title than their vendors possessed."

He then summed up his arguments, paid his respects to Richard Relf in a few scathing remarks, and concluded by saying: "And now we think a case of fraud is made out, which subsequent purchasers must inherit. They sit in the seat of their grantor; they are affected by all the previous frauds and misconduct of their vendors. They must restore the property of which this complainant has been so unlawfully dispossessed, and thus terminate the long period of privation, of suffering, of toil, and persecution to which she has been exposed in the wearisome and exhausting prosecution of her rights."

Judgment

CAMPBELL'S lengthy argument took a great part of the day on which he began to speak and all the next. In spite of the involved nature of his reasoning and the wealth of legal citations with which he garnished or buttressed it, a packed courtroom faced him throughout. A busy merchant who desired to be "on 'change" at a certain hour, "thought he would drop in for a moment, only a moment, to hear a few words of Campbell's argument and then form a hasty opinion of the gentleman. He did so—moments passed, hours, and still he moved not until the close. He has since declared that he could not tear himself away."

Campbell by this speech "all but immortalized himself," one of the New Orleans papers declared. He "reaped the field clean and garnered for himself a rich harvest." But had he reaped it clean for Myra?

Duncan and Miles Taylor of opposing counsel were there to see that he did not. They spoke for the next few days, Duncan beginning on Friday and closing on Tuesday, Taylor closing on Wednesday.

Then battered old John Grymes, wise in the ways of
the world and sin, closed for Myra in a speech that began
on Thursday, February 7, 1850, and ended on the following Saturday. Altogether the argument had lasted twelve
days.[1]

The Court took the case.

Speculation was rife as to what the long-awaited decision would be. Justice McKinley, having sat on the
Supreme bench during the Patterson case, was expected
to be inclined to the side of the complainant. But McCaleb,
the Louisianian, it was guessed, would prove adverse. At
length the day of judgment arrived, twelve days after the
argument had been concluded.

The courtroom was filled with "a large crowd of lawyers
and others" when the judges entered. Expectation was at
a high point. Then Justice McKinley arose.

But not to announce a decision. The Justice admitted at
once that he and Judge McCaleb had differed, but chiefly
over the binding force of the Patterson decision. He as a
member of the Supreme Court felt that this was binding
upon himself; but, Judge McCaleb, he said, felt in no way
bound by it. Under the circumstances, he, McKinley, had
decided to retire from the bench and allow the district
judge to decide the case. Justice McKinley added that
there was another reason also, which had influenced him to
withdraw: Judge McCaleb was better acquainted with the
local laws of Louisiana than he was, and he thought it better for the case to go up to the Supreme Court "with an
opinion written by a judge familiar with the peculiar jurisprudence of this state."

The decision then lay with McCaleb who without ado

overthrew all Myra's hopes. He affirmed that there was no marriage between Clark and Zulime; that, even admitting such a marriage, it was clandestine and created no civil rights in favor of the issue of it; that such marriage could not possibly have been legal without nullity of the Des-Grange marriage; that the defendants were purchasers in good faith; "and this action is barred by prescription." McCaleb ended bluntly:

"In every respect in which I have been enabled to consider this case, I am clearly of the opinion that there is no equity in complainant's bill, and that it must be dismissed with costs."

She had sued fourteen years to get this decision.

Everyone knew the case was going to Washington. Justice McKinley admitted it when he "retired" from the bench, and indeed did so in order to give the case a fairer hearing when it reached the capital. Courts, judges, justices, and everyone by this time realized that Myra would fight to the bitter end. She had enough material upon which to base an appeal, and the next step took the parties back to the Supreme Court at Washington.

II

The Court had changed but little since the Patterson decision had been handed down by Justice Wayne and his somewhat diminished group of associates. Only one new man, Benjamin R. Curtis, had come on the bench.

Myra's new champion, John A. Campbell, had so covered himself with glory in his handling of the case that she determined to send him to Washington for the last great battle. Her former lawyer, Reverdy Johnson, was likewise available. He had resigned from the Senate to accept the position of Attorney General under Zachary Taylor, but the death of Taylor in 1849 brought his resignation as a cabinet member. So he had gone back to Baltimore to practice law once more and was making a great reputation for himself in Washington as a constitutional lawyer. The doughty General Jones, now seventy-five years of age, was definitely out of it.

The defendants brought Greer B. Duncan from New Orleans to act with the great Webster, for whom this was destined to be almost a last case. They, too, were confident, since they came armed with Judge McCaleb's decision and the new testimony which they had unearthed. The case was called during the December term, 1851. Almost two years had rolled by since the New Orleans decision. But now time itself had ceased to be such a great matter with Myra Clark Gaines. Litigation had become her life; the courtroom scenes merely punctuated it.

"Oyez, oyez!" The case of *Myra Clark Gaines*, appellant, v. *Richard Relf and Beverly Chew,* executors of Daniel Clark, *et al.,* was called.

Court had scarcely opened when the attorneys for Charles Patterson in the previous case, asked leave of the Justices to make a statement. They stated that they had come to apologize to the Court for their connection with the former case, as they had no knowledge whatsoever of any collusive agreement made by their client with General and Mrs. Gaines. Their apology was received by the Court but the incident made a poor introduction for the complainant's appeal.

Once again the familiar arguments were heard, spun out with a wealth of detail and enforced with all the power of advocates who believed passionately in their cause. Duncan led the case for the defendants. Reverdy Johnson in his adroit, hard-hitting way again presented the Gaines claims. He was a great forensic lawyer, "cursed with neither nerves nor liver," and in addition to natural endowments his colleagues gave him credit for always making painstaking preparation before he appeared in court. But for all his ability, it was his colleague, the new man from the South, who dominated the attention of the hearers. Campbell had captured New Orleans; the Justices of the Supreme Court proved almost as impressed.

The lengthy record was read and examined again as one or another bit of evidence was brought to the fore, or as one argument or another was approved or rejected. Counsel for the appellees themselves made twenty-seven separate points in their argument, the whole thing revolving around the validity of the DesGrange marriage and the testimony of Madame Despau. But the longest argument must end and at last it was all over but the judgment of the Court. Chief Justice Taney again kept out of it and John McLean did not sit. So it fell to Justice John Catron to announce the decision.

III

John Catron [2] of Tennessee presented a decided contrast to the urbane Wayne, his brother on the bench. Catron's gestures were often awkward in their vehemence, not smoothly graceful as were Wayne's or Reverdy Johnson's. But this very unpolite directness made patent a character of dynamic force. John Catron neither trusted nor distrusted human nature. He simply understood it with an intuitive completeness that could only be given to one who was fundamentally a man of the people.

Now the Gaines case was in his hands, and he brought to bear upon its tangled mass of evidence and argument that canny insight into life which life itself had taught him. With his brother Justices he plunged into its long and involved record and weighed the argument pro and con. It soon became apparent that these distinguished Judges, like every other group, were hopelessly divided upon it. But at length a majority of five stood together—Catron, Baldwin, Grier, Curtis, and, surprisingly enough, John McKinley. They agreed upon a decision that Catron wrote and handed down. It is one of the longest on record and blasted, as by lightning, every single claim of Myra. Her witnesses were discredited, especially Mesdames Despau and Caillavet, the Court holding that they had sworn to a "plausible tale of fiction." The papers and documents which Myra had introduced were thrown out as inadmissible, while the ecclesiastical record and the alimony record put in by her opponents were taken as sound evidence. Not a scintilla of her contention was admitted, the Court even asserting that the deposition of Bellechasse had stated hearsay and rumor and was worth nothing. Only at the end of the long opinion did Justice Catron show that the Supreme Court was conscious of the ruin it was causing: "The harshness of judicial duty requires that we should deal with witnesses and evidences, and with men's rights, as we find them; and it is done so here. But we sincerely regret that it could not be satisfactorily done without making exposures that would most willingly have been avoided.

"It is ordered that the decree of the Circuit Court be affirmed, and the bill dismissed."

IV

It was over. The long suit begun with William Whitney back in the palmy days of youth had, after fifteen years, been definitely ended by the court of the last resort. Nothing was left for Myra except to pay the enormous costs of her lost case. But in her great disappointment she was cheered appreciably by a long blast of dissent that came from two of the Justices of the Court—her former champion, Justice Wayne, seconded by Justice Daniel. These had taken violent issue with the majority on both the facts and the law and so deeply did Wayne feel that he wrote out and placed in the record one of the longest dissenting opinions ever delivered by a Justice of the Supreme Court. The record says:

Wayne, J., delivered the following dissenting opinion:

"I dissent from the judgment just given, and will give my reasons for doing so as briefly as I can. . . .

"I think it has been proved that Myra Clark Gaines is the only child of her father, Daniel Clark, by his marriage with her mother, Zulime Carrière. That when the marriage took place, the parties were willing to contract, able to contract, and that they did contract in marriage in Pennsylvania according to the laws of that state, in the year eighteen hundred and two. I also think that there was nothing then or now in the laws of Louisiana which lessens in any way the validity of that marriage. The proofs of the declarations shall hereafter be pointed out, with the law in support of them."

Then for what appears in the record today as fifty-eight pages of closely printed matter James Moore Wayne vehemently championed each of Myra's contentions. The judicial calm with which he began soon turned into passionate pleading and the judge was lost in the advocate. The court's pronouncement on Myra's aunts aroused his bitter scorn: "By what principle is it, I ask . . . that the unsworn declarations of Clark, now repeated by Mr. Coxe, have been used to discredit Madame Despau's testimony? . . . Upon what rule of evidence . . . that the testimony of Mr. Coxe, standing as he does in the same legal relation as witness with Madame Despau, can be used to discredit both her and her sister, Madame Caillavet?"

The attack on the character of Madame Despau by other witnesses likewise incensed Wayne who declared that the method the majority of the Court had allowed "showed a disregard for all the rules. . . . I do not remember a more marked departure from them."

The several papers bearing on the case Justice Wayne reviewed with great minuteness, the ecclesiastical record especially, and he demonstrated point by point how each of these sustained the validity of Myra's claims.

"There was but one way to get rid of the force of the complainant's evidence in support of her legitimacy. It was to assail the integrity of her witnesses. The way in which that was attempted, I have shown in respect to Mesdames

From a photograph, courtesy of Mr. Alexander A. Lawrence

JUSTICE JAMES MOORE WAYNE

Despau and Caillavet. It has succeeded with the majority of the judges who have tried this cause with me. But I feel authorized to say, that in all of my experience in the profession, I have never heard of witnesses so assailed before and upon such illegal testimony; not insufficient, but inadmissibly introduced into this cause for that purpose. My brother Daniel thinks as I do, and will express himself accordingly. Besides, these witnesses have been said to be unworthy of credit, when in the most important particulars of their testimony, concerning Clark's marriage with the mother of the complainant, and of her legitimacy, they are confirmed by other disinterested witnesses to whom Clark admitted both; not once, but several times on different occasions. They have lived apart at remote distances for many years since the death of Clark, knowing nothing of his child, except as she was seen by them in her infancy, receiving publicly the caresses of her father and hearing from him his acknowledgment that she was his legitimate child. Boisfontaine tells us, that Clark frequently told him, after Zulime's marriage with Gardette, that he would have made his marriage with her public, if that barrier had not been made.

"Bellechasse's testimony confirms that of Boisfontaine. Mrs. Smyth, formerly Mrs. Harper, who nursed her, does the same. Each of them also speaks with positiveness concerning the will of 1813. With three such witnesses to sustain them, I believe that Mesdames Despau and Caillavet have spoken the truth concerning Clark's marriage with Zulime. If they did not, the testimony of Bellechasse, Boisfontaine, and Mrs. Smyth, is the most remarkable coincidence of truth with falsehood that has ever happened;

and it can only be resisted by imputing to all of them, a combination to perjure themselves for the same purpose. That, no one has said or can believe."

But after all, a dissent is but the wail of a defeated minority. The futility of it all seems to be in the mind of Justice Wayne as he drew near the end of his long plea. The impartiality of the judge once more supplants the fiery zeal of the advocate and, as the ultimate reaches and wider horizons of the case appeared, the suggestion of a Higher Equity came to the mind of the dissenting Justice:

"Those of us who have borne our part in the case will pass away. The case will live. Years hence, as well as now, the profession will look to it for what has been ruled upon its merits and also for the kind of testimony upon which these merits were decided. The majority of my brothers who give the judgment, stand, as they well may do, upon their responsibility. I have placed myself alongside of them, humbly submitting to have any error into which I may have fallen corrected by our contemporaries and by our professional posterity.

"The case itself presents thought for our philosophy, in its contemplation of all the business and domestic relations of life.

"It shows the hollowness of those friendships formed between persons in the greediness of gain, seeking its gratification in a disregard of all those laws by which commerce can only be honestly and respectably pursued.

"It shows how carelessness in business and secret partnerships to conduct it with others who are willing to run the risk of unlawful adventures, may give to the latter its spoils, and impoverish those whose capital alone gave consequence to the concern.

"It shows how a mistaken confidence given to others by a man who dies rich, may be the cause of diverting his estate into an imputed insolvency, depriving every member of his family of any part of their inheritance.

"It shows if the ruffian takes life for the purse which he robs, that a dying man's agonies soothed only by tears and prayers for the happiness of a child, may not arrest a fraudulent attempt to filch from her her name and fortune.

"We can learn from it, too, that there is a kindred between virtue and lasting respectability in life, and that transgressions of its proprieties or irregular yieldings to our passions in forming the most interesting relation between human creatures, are most likely to make them miserable and to bring ruin upon children.

"I do not know from my own reasoning that the sins of parents are visited upon children, but my reason does not tell me that it may not be so. But I do know, from one of those rays shot from Sinai, that it is said for the offense of idolatry, 'I, the Lord God, am a jealous God, and visit the sins of the fathers upon the children unto the third and fourth generation of them that hate me, and show mercy unto thousands of those who love me and keep my commandments.' It may be so for other offenses. If it be, let the victim submissively recognize him who inflicts the chastisement, and it may be the beginning of a communion with our Maker, to raise the hope of a richer inheritance than this world can give or take away." [3]

Book 4

Where There's a Will

The Lost Will

MELLOW notes of far-off steamboats making for the "bend"; heavy drays grinding over black cobbles; French chatter and English gruffness; Canal Street becoming commercial with new stores arising and old residences dwindling; the Jackson statue set up in the old Square; the Mistick Krewe of Comus organizing and taking over Mardi Gras; black slaves on the auction block, looked over coolly and appraisingly by canny gentlemen and cannier traders of meaner kind; steamboats putting in or pulling off with a vast stirring of water and cries of the roustabouts, perhaps the *Creole Belle* loaded to the guards with cheering excursionists off for a day; a carriage containing some of the "quality," silk-hatted gentleman and beribboned lady taking themselves very seriously—this was New Orleans in the fifties.[1]

Prosperity was now at its height in the dominant metropolis of the South. New Orleans had welded together its diverse municipalities, and the former faubourgs had coalesced to become the City. Population had doubled within the last ten years and new houses were in building everywhere. The great West was opening to the slow-moving wagon trains, as the eastern valley had opened fifty years before, and the call of gold had stirred to daring the adventurous spirit of the pioneers. As the whole Mississippi basin bloomed, the city bloomed with it; land was bought and sold with the avidity of gainful speculation, and even the devastating terror of the cholera in '53 failed to check the now manifest destiny of New Orleans.

The property of Myra Clark Gaines, or rather that for which she had so long contested, was of course being turned over again and again in the now redoubled building boom. Titles were given, and deeds once more exchanged for cash with no shadow longer resting upon the land that had once belonged to Daniel Clark. The Gaines case had been settled at Myra's expense, and the owners could garner their profits and continue with business or pleasure as usual. Only in the realm of national politics was there any shadow over what the future might bring. But, as the fifties fled by, that shadow grew larger and larger. Lines were being drawn between the South and the North; few realized it, but New Orleans with the rest of the country was far along toward the end of an era.

II

To some women life means men, to others admiration, or love, or home, or family, or career, but to Myra Clark Gaines life meant litigation. She had learned to accept it, then to use it, and finally to revel in it through the long years when she had fought for her rights, with the whole

MYRA CLARK GAINES

FROM AN ENGRAVING IN *The Court Circles of the Republic*
(MRS. E. F. ELLETTE)

country watching and thousands applauding her. It had put a queer virus in her veins, a virus that would not disappear even though the highest court in the land had said that there was "no equity in her bill." For fifteen years, a span that covered the full flower of her life, she had given her time and attention to contending through the law for her mother's good name and her father's fortune. Her vigor had been matched by her zeal, and when *finis* was written to all her hopes by the Supreme Court, she refused to see it. Her rights were her rights no matter what a court might say. If one set of judges was not for her, another might be. She had seen this happen before; it might again. Her whole life had been cast in the mold of legal striving, and she found it a joyous battle. Even when she was suitless—and it is doubtful if she ever was—she thought in terms of judgments and stipulations, of evidence and prayers. She came to know every item of the Code as it touched her case and was said to be a better lawyer than many who represented or opposed her.

The fact that she had lost and was branded before the country as a colossal fraud, as a woman whose very legitimacy was denied by the Supreme Court, seemed to have no effect upon her activities or her personal relationships. Those who believed in her continued to do so, and in the North particularly she found a degree of sympathy that amounted to wild enthusiasm. Daniel Webster himself said: "She had a band of sympathizers throughout the land that was more powerful than an army arrayed with banners." *Putnam's Magazine* featured her story and observed that "nobody could listen to her fifteen minutes without sharing in her enthusiasm and perfect conviction of ultimate success." In spite of the stain now authoritatively stamped on her birth, she continued to be received in the highest social circles. In 1853, she visited the White House when Franklin Pierce was President, and made a close personal friend of Mrs. McNeill Potter,[2] his niece. The two women kept up with each other and corresponded for the rest of their lives. General Gaines had a host of friends in military and political circles, and Myra was popular among them. New York city also became a frequent point of visitation and of course she was always sure of her welcome at Binghamton or Delamore Place.

Many who had played their part in the famous case passed away during these years. Boisfontaine and Bellechasse had long been dead. Harriet Harper also was dead and so now were Mesdames Caillavet and Despau, the much-abused aunts whose testimony the Supreme Court had said was "unworthy of credit." Beverly Chew had likewise gone the way of all the earth, leaving Richard Relf, well up in years, the only surviving executor of the 1811 will.

In 1853 Zulime dropped out and this time there was no coming back. Through the whole case her beauty runs like that of fabled Helen in the tale of ancient Ilium. Hers was the face that launched a thousand speeches if not a thousand ships, and even the black-robed Justices of the Supreme Court came to speak of her familiarly as "Zulime." She died as she had lived, in silence. What she knew she told no court. While the great contest raged, with property to the extent of millions and her own good name alike at stake, she, the one person who could have cleared the mystery, lived in mouselike seclusion on Burgundy Street. Myra never put her on the stand, and neither did the opposition. Perhaps Myra wished to spare her mother an ordeal such as her aunts had experienced; and presumably the opposition was afraid of her, feeling certain that her testimony would support that of Madame Despau. But not the least remarkable thing about the whole case is that the only living person who was a party to the much-debated marriage was never summoned by either side.

The lawyers who had been connected with the suit had also scattered. General Jones, an octogenarian, was living in retirement in the midst of his large family of daughters and their children. Isaac Preston, who had helped turn the tide against Myra in Louisiana, lost his life in 1851 in a steamboat explosion on Lake Ponchartrain. Reverdy Johnson was going deeper into national politics and enjoying an enormous practice before the bar of the Supreme Court. John A. Campbell had gone on the Supreme bench itself. When Justice John McKinley died there was some slight delay in finding his successor, whereupon the members of the Supreme Court decided to take a hand and suggest to the President for an appointment among them the Alabama lawyer who had so distinguished himself in the Gaines case. It was an unprecedented thing for the Court to do, but Justices Catron and Curtis walked over to the White House and presented to Franklin Pierce the letters recommendatory of the Court.[3] The President acquiesced and Campbell was placed on the bench where he soon made a great name for himself. Even Carson, the unemotional historian of the Supreme Court, refers to Campbell as "this great Judge." The Court soon had heavy work to do with the epochal Dred Scott case coming up in 1857, a divided court foreshadowing a divided nation.

Time had made changes in Myra's domestic life also. Rhoda had married a North Carolinian named Robert Strother; William Whitney was a stripling on the threshold of manhood, one not overeasy to manage if the stories told of him are true. Myra herself was growing older and the marks of the struggle were etched in telltale lines upon her face. *Harper's Magazine* ran a woodcut of Mrs. Gaines toward the end of the fifties, and, while some allowance must be made for the severity of the black and white cut, it is undeniable that the girlish bow of the lips, so noticeable in the eighteen thirties, had now straightened into a firm, almost hard, line. The face is that of a strong, determined woman who had learned how to give and to take the buffetings of life. Her enemies called her all manner of names, but no one ever applied the term *coward* to Myra Clark Gaines.

III

By this time the urge to litigate, to go into court, would appear to be pretty well blocked. The Probate Court had early finished with her; the Federal waited on the Probate in regard to setting up the alleged will; the state, in both the lower court and the Court of Appeals, was heavily adverse; and the Supreme Court of the United States had capped it all by affirming that she was not heir-at-law to Daniel Clark and there was "no equity in her bill." More, they made her pay for the declaration. Was any possible tribunal left? Apparently none. The Gaines case was *res adjudicata,* dead and done with as far as the courts were concerned.

But it was not a thing decided in the mind of the one person most interested. She had moved from forum to forum as the battle had gone against her. She would move to another. The only immediate one that seemed open early in the fifties was that of public opinion, and she kept on battling there.

In 1852 she secured from Justice Campbell, in Washington, an opinion designed to assist her in any further efforts she might make. This, together with a statement from Mr. Perin, a Louisiana lawyer whom she had retained, was published in a booklet, *The Present Position of Mrs. Gaines' Claim.* The little volume [4] is interesting chiefly as showing that she never for a second gave up hope. She had the born publicist's instinct for remaining in the spotlight, and her work had its effect.

She went to the North for a time and with friends and advisers in New York talked over her possibilities. A visit to Binghamton may have been a part of her program, and perhaps Delamore Place also. Samuel B. Davis died in 1854, but to the last he was heart and soul with his foster daughter. He had married again after the death of his first wife, and at his demise left a second growing family. The Colonel was the Colonel to the end, keen of mind despite impairment of sight and hearing. On the night he died, there was a loud, unexplained detonation somewhere within the precincts of Delamore Place,[5] and the frightened servants always believed that it had something to do with the passing of the stormy Colonel.

Money was now Mrs. Gaines' most needed weapon.

The General had left her well provided for, but the cost of the long suit had eaten away the Gaines fortune as it had the Whitney. But by persuasion and promise, by perseverance and tact, she managed to get enough to keep on. It is more than suspected that the Whitneys of Binghamton generously assisted her.

IV

The idea of the lost will had always been in her mind. Her very first claims in New Orleans, years before, had been based on this will's existence. The undiscovered will to her was as real as the one Relf and Chew had produced. When she had early learned that the Probate Court would not consider her claims unless the lost will was presented, and that the Federal Court could take no action until the Court of Probates did, she had then perforce taken the only available opportunity open—to push her claim as legitimate daughter and heir-at-law. Now that the Supreme Court had flatly and finally denied her status as the legitimate daughter of Clark, her busy mind again turned to the lost will. Was there hope in that quarter?

There had been none years before in the city Probate Court, but now with a new state constitution providing for an elective supreme judiciary able to hear appeals on matters of probate, there might be. Her plan was simple enough in conception, but for sheer audacity has scarcely been equaled in our nation's courts. She determined to write out the lost will of Daniel Clark and get it probated!

So conceived, so undertaken. She had of course considerable descriptive material or secondary evidence on which to build, and in regular legal phraseology, drawing upon all that her witnesses had sworn concerning the alleged will and describing and cataloging the vast property involved, Myra had her lawyers frame the instrument upon which she pinned a new hope.

On January 18, 1855, her petition was filed in the Second District Court of New Orleans, the court then commonly used in matters of probate. The petitioner claimed to be a "resident of the City of New Orleans and of the State of New York," told of her relation to Daniel Clark, and affirmed that on the thirteenth day of July, 1813, in New Orleans the said Daniel Clark made his last will "which was in substance and to the effect following":

"In the Name of God, Amen! I, Daniel Clark of New Orleans, do make this my last will and testament.

"*Imprimis,* I order that all my just debts be paid.

"Second: I do acknowledge that my beloved Myra, who is now living in the family of Samuel B. Davis, is my legitimate and only daughter; and that I leave and bequeath to her, the said Myra, all the estate, whether real or personal, of which I may die possessed, subject only to the payment of certain legacies hereinafter named.

"Third: It is my desire that my friend, Chevalier Francois Desuau Delacroix, shall have the charge of my said daughter, Myra, and I do appoint and constitute him tutor to her.

"Fourth: I give and bequeath unto my mother, Mary Clark, now or recently at Germantown in the State of Pennsylvania, an annuity of two thousand dollars, which is to be paid out of my estate during her life. I further give and bequeath an annuity of five hundred dollars to Caroline DesGrange until she arrives at the age of majority, after which I give and bequeath her a legacy of five thousand dollars.

"Fifth: I hereby nominate and appoint my friends, Francois Desuau Delacroix, James Pitot, and Joseph D. D. Bellechasse, my executors, with power to execute this my last will, and to settle everything relating to my estate." [6]

The record stated, "The petitioner further avers that the said will contained other legacies and dispositions . . . etc." A list of these was given.

On January 27, 1855, Judge J. N. Lea sitting in the Second District Court of the City of New Orleans received the Gaines petition and ordered the will "proved" before him. He had already summoned Richard Relf, to be on hand as the surviving executor of the will of 1811. The Judge opened the hearing with an air of meticulous and impartial exactness such as former Louisiana judges had not always shown. Judge Lea no doubt knew with whom he had to do, and wanted no appellate court later to find an error in his proceedings.

Mrs. Gaines had as usual retained a powerful array of lawyers to present the will. P. E. Bonford, Smiley and Perin, Edward W. Moise, and W. M. Randolph were together as able a group as the city might then furnish. Relf's lawyer, Mr. Duncan, represented him.

Her petition was met at once by three separate interventions filed by as many parties—that is, opposing petitions requesting the court to allow the petitioners to become parties to the proceeding. Relf, of course, was interested, and filed, and so did the blind, ninety-year-old Delacroix. The aged Chevalier was represented as saying that he was "indisposed to accept the executorship of the supposed will of Daniel Clark." Further, he asserted that he had "no knowledge, information or belief that the said deceased Daniel Clark ever made such a will as is set forth in the petition to this case" and that "if any such will was ever written, the said Clark never intended to publish it as his will, but must himself have destroyed it." As Delacroix was named in the supposed will, he wished to be allowed to become a party to the contest over its probate.

The City of New Orleans also came out with a frank opposition and filed a plea for intervention before Judge Lea. The City had always been interested, but rather through its individual citizens than as a unit. Now for the first time the corporation definitely stepped in as an entity. Twenty years before, New Orleans had bought $45,000 worth of the Clark land from a certain E. Blanc, who had previously acquired the property from Relf and Chew. Now in 1855, Judge Lea was told by the City's attorney that New Orleans was "in possession of a considerable part of the said purchase," and was therefore directly interested.

The Gaines battery of lawyers took exception to the interventions. Judge Lea adjourned court for three days that he might consider. Then he gave out a rather elaborate opinion refusing to let Richard Relf or the City intervene. Delacroix might do so. After this Lea heard the case.

The old records were once more broken open, and old witnesses recalled. M. Preval, who had affixed the procès verbal, repeated his oft-told story. Thomas Harper, a son of Mrs. Harriet Harper, was called to certify to his mother's signature. The elderly Louis Toutant Beauregard was put on the stand to testify to the character of Bellechasse. He told what he knew of both Clark and Bellechasse and spoke of them as honorable men. P. B. Boisfontaine, son of Pierre Boisfontaine, described the death of his father in 1836. Other witnesses were called, and the whole case was heard over again.

There was a stir in the court when the bent, tottering figure of Francois Delacroix [7] was seen entering upon the arm of his son. Those who witnessed it never forgot the ensuing drama. The feeble nonagenarian had been brought to support his previous testimony that he had no "knowledge, information or belief" concerning a lost will of Daniel Clark. But Myra was ready for him, and put in Delacroix's own testimony given to Judge Pitot in 1813, "that he has strong reasons to believe, and does verily believe that Daniel Clark had made a posterior will to that before the court." The record of this 1813 proceeding had been preserved through the years with its description of the summoning of the notaries in the futile search for the lost will. All was read in court, and Delacroix could not gainsay it.

It appears that he did not attempt to do so. Adjured by the Gaines counsel, the aged witness recalled for a last time the fateful summer of 1813. His mind appeared clearer than his speech, and with an effort he told again of the sealed packet that Clark had flung before him with *"pour être ouvert en cas de mort"* on it. The will that Relf had acted under bore no such marking.

Delacroix had come in to oppose, but these words, at such variance with his own interest, and so in keeping with the claims that Mrs. Gaines' witnesses had always advanced, produced a profound impression.

But Judge Lea refused to be swayed from the main issue. He wrote out as his judgment an opinion that marked him as a partisan of neither side. He held that the existence of the lost will had been proved; and the charge that it had been destroyed or revoked by Clark, as asserted by Delacroix and others, had been "satisfactorily rebutted." This was heavily pro-Gaines, but on the other hand the Judge was adamant in construing the literal demand of the Code, outlining how an olographic will must be proved. For such proof, two credible witnesses were required, persons who must swear that they recognize the testament as "entirely written, dated, and signed in the testator's handwriting, as having often seen him write during his lifetime."

If such witnesses were alive, Judge Lea held, it would be necessary for the court to examine into their sources for knowing and recognizing the handwriting of the testator whose will they sought to establish. Also there was the regulation calling for a *date;* no Gaines witness had given any definite evidence regarding a date. The Code was specific: Olographic wills must be *dated.*

Impartial as he apparently was, Lea laid down an effectual barrier against Mrs. Gaines' petition. Her witnesses were dead and could not be examined as to their knowledge of Daniel Clark's handwriting. They had failed to mention a particular date at the head of his last will. For these reasons, the Second District Court refused to probate.

Of course, Myra appealed. The Judge allowed a "devolutive appeal" to the Louisiana Supreme Court, and James

Gardette, her half brother, went the necessary bond. Then there came what in the language of our day would be called a "break" in her favor.

V

Louisiana was suddenly shocked to learn that the Chief Justice of the state, Thomas Slidell, had been assaulted at the polls and had received such injuries that he was forced to resign from the bench.[8] That threw open the highest judicial position in the state while the Gaines appeal case was pending. The Judge to be elected would pass on the appeal, and if no one else knew it, Myra Clark Gaines did. With a versatility equal to that of Daniel Clark himself she left the courts of law temporarily and began to do battle on a front where her opponents never dreamed she would appear. She went into politics.

Although hated by New Orleans generally and much disliked by the officials and the courts, she had found out through the years that she undoubtedly had a certain following in the city. It was rather inarticulate and it was small, but it was definite. Some few people of influence had let her know privately that they believed in her. She had personal friends or relatives who were loyal; others had, or thought they had, something to gain by her success; some disliked her enemies, while many, American-like, were with her simply because she was a brave woman fighting an uphill fight. At any rate, by this time Mrs. Gaines knew that there were some on whom she could count, and the political imbroglio gave her an opportunity to use them.

An intense campaign began to develop as the election

for Chief Justice came on. The Democratic party in the state had in John Slidell, brother of the former Justice, a political boss of the modern type. Slidell was in fact giving Louisiana its first taste of machine politics, to the undisguised alarm of the conservative element. He put forth as his candidate J. K. Elzee. The opposition—mostly Whig, with heavy support from the anti-Catholic Know-Nothings—nominated Edwin T. Merrick.

Judge Merrick [9] was a jurist of high rank who enjoyed public confidence through his ability and character. For some reason Myra had come to believe that he was favorable to her claims, and that it was to her interest to assist in electing him. So she threw herself into the campaign with all the force she possessed and, it is said, even made speeches in his behalf. It would not be just to infer that Merrick had an understanding with Mrs. Gaines or even that he was aware of her efforts in his behalf, but she was convinced that his victory was hers.

The campaign proved exceedingly bitter, with the *Courrier de la Louisiane* screaming at the Know-Nothings in French on one page and in English on the other. But Slidell's city machine had alarmed the state and Merrick was swept into office by a great majority.

VI

Besides the newly elected Chief Justice, the state bench at that time consisted of Judge Lea who had decided adversely to Mrs. Gaines in the lower court; Judge A. M. Buchanan, who had certainly been against her once when the old General had put his hand on his sword in court;

also Judges Voorhies and Spofford, men who presumably had never before sat on the case.

When the appeal came up, Judge Buchanan recused himself, giving as his reason the fact that he had decided matters involved previously; but Lea decided to sit and see his own judgment through. Merrick and the two other judges were to be the deciding factors.

It soon became apparent that Judge Lea was to be as much a part of the opposition as was the opposing counsel, Mr. Duncan. But when the fateful decision was handed down, Judge Lea appeared in the minority. E. T. Merrick for the court wrote an opinion that was destined to stand as the high peak of the case.

After reviewing Judge Lea's reasoning as he had expressed it in the court below, and doubtless before his compeers on the bench, Judge Merrick gave the principles which he felt compelled the court to allow the establishment of the lost will.

"The rules for the opening and proof of testaments . . . nowhere say that other cases may not arise to which the strict letter of these rules may be inapplicable, and that the Judge may not receive in extraordinary cases other equally satisfactory proof that the requirements of the law have been fulfilled. . . .

"The loss or destruction of the will of Daniel Clark in 1813, and the long period which has elapsed since his death justify a resort to secondary evidence."

One almost suspects that Merrick was applying the principles of equity to the interpretation of the Civil Code!

"It is therefore ordered, adjudged and decreed that the will of Daniel Clark, dated New Orleans, July 13, 1813 as set forth in the plaintiff's petition, be recognized as his last will and testament . . . and it is further ordered that Francois Desuau Delacroix be confirmed as testamentary executor of said last will and testament, and that letters testamentary issue to the said Delacroix, and that the cost of this proceeding be borne by the succession." [10]

In vain did Judge Lea dissent: "If the witnesses were alive it would be the duty of the court to enquire into the particular sources of the knowledge of Mr. Clark's handwriting."

But nothing could now stop the long-lost will. The aging Relf, staggered at the result, did manage to secure a rehearing as he had been inadvertently made a party to the record. The Court gave him a crust of comfort by allowing him the right to oppose the newly probated will "in any manner allowed by law as fully as he could have done had he not been made a party to these proceedings." But that was all.

Myra Clark Gaines had probated her father's will—a will that thousands believed had never been written at all—*forty-three years* after her father's death!

Justice Wayne Lays Down
the Law

O N A Monday morning early in January, 1857, G. B.
Duncan, Myra's old opponent, was standing in the Federal
court at New Orleans addressing Judge McCaleb.

"Five years ago," Mr. Duncan said, "I . . . ven-
tured to address your Honor a few words of congratulation
that . . . the Supreme Court had . . . finally, entirely and without reservation put an end to the [Gaines]
controversy.

"Well, sir, the case is *here*. The controversy is not
ended. . . . And I think I may safely say that the controversy never will be ended if the complainant can help
it." [1]

The case was certainly there. Standing flatly on the
newly probated will Myra had filed a bill against F. D.
Delacroix, averring that he ". . . soon after the death of
Daniel Clark . . . took possession and has ever since
held and disposed of for his own use, seventy-five slaves

. . . bequeathed complainant. . . . That more than 300 slaves have been born from the female slaves aforesaid, . . . that the aforesaid slaves now living and their increase are worth $300,000; that the hire of said slaves . . . amounts to $300,000; and that the interest due thereon amounts to $500,000. . . ." [2]

Old Delacroix was being sued a cool million and more for his part in the 1813 treachery.

It is noteworthy that the new bill was in the Federal court and was filed *in chancery*. It was to be that sort of suit!

A short time after this, Myra laid down another bill of the same nature in the same court, this time against the City of New Orleans. The corporation had held itself "interested" in the Blanc tract [3] in order to block her petition to probate. Now she took the corporation at its word and sued to recover the "rents, fruitage and titles" involved in the land in question.

As if this were not enough, while these cases were still pending, in the spring of 1857 Mrs. Gaines began a third suit, this time against Messrs. Lizardi, John Slidell, and Alfred Hennen and fifteen others as possessors of several lots in the square between Poydras and Perdido Streets. She meant to recover everything.

Judge McCaleb heard the cause, or causes, during that year. The well-worn depositions were presented once more, the old arguments revamped and rehashed. A second generation of witnesses had supplanted the first. Young Major Pierre G. T. Beauregard was put on the stand in place of his father, and the swarthy army officer testified to the good character of Mrs. Harper. The Major said that she was a good friend of his mother "and a lady of high talent and respectability in society."

There was again a sharp skirmish over the old ecclesiastical record, always a moot point. Elliott Robbins,[4] one of Myra's lawyers, said that Zulime, to the day of her death, steadfastly maintained that she had never been before an ecclesiastical tribunal. She had indeed brought suit to prove the nullity of her marriage with DesGrange, but vowed to the end that her supposed signature to the ecclesiastical record was a pure forgery, and that the time would come when it would be proved to be such. Perhaps this was the time, for, in order to establish the genuineness of Zulime's signature in the disputed record, her old dotal agreement, drawn up between the Carrières and DesGrange in 1794 was brought forth. The signature of Zulime as done in 1794 and the signature to the supposed ecclesiastical record of 1802 were undoubtedly the same, but an expert examination showed that the name on the 1794 paper had been freshened up *by a steel pen*. No such pens were made in 1794. It looked like fraud practiced while the litigation was progressing, and lent color to the charge that the whole supposed record of the trial of DesGrange had been fabricated.

Another fight occurred over the supposed signature of Daniel Clark to the partnership record of June 19, 1813, used by the opposition to show that Clark left overwhelming debts. Throughout the whole case, Relf and Chew always contended that Clark was not solvent at the time of his death, and that they had been put to great trouble to satisfy his creditors. As the inquiry progressed into the state of Clark's finances, one Saturday afternoon Mr. Mc-

Connell, an opposing lawyer, together with a son of Richard Relf, secured the books of the old Chew & Relf concern and took them away. They could not thereafter be found. Again the cry of trickery was raised.

The new Gaines case, it appeared, was very much like the old one.

II

A main question of interest in the new case was: How much did the former decision of the Supreme Court affect the present suits? Myra's opponents argued that the whole thing was *res adjudicata;* that the new suit was in no way different from the former one; and, as the highest court in the land had fixed her status as illegitimate, she could not "take" property by will. She was not and could not be heir-at-law of Daniel Clark.

But Myra had changed front entirely on that point since the will had been probated. She was not claiming now as heir-at-law, but as the *beneficiary of her father's will,* lately set up by the Supreme Court of Louisiana. Mr. Bonford, one of her counsel, told the court that it "made no difference who she was, her father gave this property to her by will in 1813." The same gentleman deprecated the attempt to drag in the matter of Mrs. Gaines' filiation, saying that this was an "excrescence" in the case. Eheu! It was not so for the first fifteen years!

One of her opponents pleaded the statute of limitations and argued that Mrs. Gaines should have put in her claim sooner—that she was guilty of "laches," that is, of "going to sleep" on her rights. But Judge Smiley, another of her counsel, returned the sufficient answer: "No man living can charge laches on the complainant. She can never be charged with sleeping on her rights."

The veteran Duncan in taking his stand against the woman whom he had fought for ten years, undertook to call a roll of those who had appeared in the case before but were now dead. "Death appears to have cut down the high and the low, and so insatiate has he been," said Mr. Duncan addressing Judge McCaleb, "that they actually conveyed to Washington City the allegation of your honor's death, and the then erratic President of the United States commissioned your successor."

But McCaleb was still on the bench and decided the case, April 17, 1858. He was adverse and so was his decision. He held that the present contention of the complainant was in no way different from the former and was *res adjudicata*. She was pretending to stand on the new ground of a will, but to McCaleb it was the same old case. Certainly it was the same woman with the same claim; the reader may feel that it was also the same Judge McCaleb.

It is unnecessary to say that she appealed again to the Supreme Court of the United States. No man living could charge her with laches.

III

The Court that got the case now rolling up for its adjudication had been passing through dark and stormy waters since 1851. While the Clark will contest was raging in New Orleans, the Supreme Court was wrestling with the constitutional status of a certain Negro slave taken from a slave state to a free. Was he property or was he a person? Taney with a majority had decided that Dred

Scott was property. A minority held that he was not. The decision made clear the utterly impossible situation that slavery had brought on.

The names of some of the Justices will be familiar. Wayne was there, older, grayer, thinner, the touch of aristocratic hauteur slightly deepened; Catron, likewise older, blockier; McLean too was rounding out a long term of service. The rather dour Grier still remained, and of course the Chief Justice, Taney. Peter V. Daniel, who with Wayne had supported the losing Gaines side nine years before, died during the summer recess just before the new appeal came up. The President had not yet filled his place. One of the new Justices, John A. Campbell, had been Myra's lawyer; Nathan Clifford of Maine was the other.

The Court had come up in the world, so to speak, since the days of 1851. At this very term the Justices inaugurated their "sitting in the new apartments." The Capitol building had been enlarged by the addition of two great wings,[5] and the Court now took over the old Senate chamber where it was to remain until 1936 when the nation at last gave its highest tribunal a magnificent building of its own.

Perin of New Orleans had done well in the lower court, so Myra felt, and gave promise of being serviceable in Washington. But after her own fashion she took no chances and set out to get the best lawyer obtainable. "No case can ever be too strong," was one of her maxims. So for argument before the Supreme Court she retained the Honorable Caleb Cushing.[6]

This versatile jurist had served in Congress, on inter-

national diplomatic missions, as a soldier in the Mexican
War, as a practicing attorney, as a judge, and now at sixty
years of age, was enjoying a reputation for encyclopedic
knowledge and was carrying on a tremendous practice before the Supreme Court, "the universal attorney for and
against the government." [7] One Washington correspond-
ent said of Cushing, "He would give an owl the blues to
listen to." But the Justices always heard him with profound attention, and as an advocate he was worthy to take
rank with the other great lawyers who had represented
Myra.

She herself was on hand in Washington to hear the appeal argued. During the previous winter she had engaged
rooms at the National Hotel, the famous hostelry which
until quite recently looked down in vacant grandeur
upon Pennsylvania Avenue. At that time it was a fashionable place and a great rendezvous for politicians. Myra
stayed there for some time with Rhoda and her little
grandchild.

Her need for money had now become acute. Apparently the princely sums which she once had at her disposal
had dwindled away. On the eve of the trial of her new appeal in Washington she was forced to borrow a thousand
and fourteen dollars to attend to some of her petty obligations. [8]

IV

The appeal now before the Supreme Court became
known in the record as *Gaines* v. *Hennen*.[9] It was the third
of the suits Myra had instituted in the lower court, and
Hennen, one of the defendants, personally appeared to

represent his own and the rights of the other codefendants. With him he had the redoubtable and somewhat irascible Louis Janin of New Orleans, an old opponent of Myra but one who had not hitherto been fighting her at such close quarters.

The record in this case went to a thousand printed pages, and to it were added the records of the previous hearings. Hennen and Janin relied on the 1851 decision; Cushing and Perin on the newly established will. Naturally, the whole case was tried over again, with Cushing's speech as the outstanding feature.

The Court took the case under advisement. It was pretty certain that Catron, Grier, and Taney would be adverse. It was equally certain that Wayne and Campbell would be favorable—strongly so. What Nelson and Clifford would do, no one knew; McLean had taken no part in the decision of 1851.

The victory went to Wayne.

V

It had been nine years since Justice Wayne had written what he thought to be the end of the long litigation by his dissenting opinion which closed with the lofty pronouncement on human conduct. Now the case was back again. He had always believed in the justice of Myra's claims because he believed in the essential facts on which those claims were based. It was over questions of fact, rather than principles, that courts as well as individuals differed in the Gaines case. Justice Wayne honestly believed Myra was right; Justice Catron honestly believed she was wrong.

Both men found law to support their convictions. The only
difference between them was that in 1851 Catron had
Justices Taney, Grier, Curtis, and McKinley with him,
while Wayne had only Justice Daniel. This time Wayne
emerged victorious carrying with him Justices McLean,
Nelson, Clifford, and, it appears, Campbell; Catron was
left with Taney and Grier in the minority. It was Wayne's
hour of triumph and also a vindication of his great dissent
of nine years before. The Court naturally let him write the
decision.

"The litigation which has grown out of the wills of
Daniel Clark . . . [has been] the subject of five appeals
to this Court.

"This is the sixth. It presents the controversy differently
from what it has been before. It also presents points for
decision which were not raised in . . . preceding
cases. . . .

"Now she [Mrs. Gaines] comes here with a support
which her cases have not had before . . . with a decision
of the Supreme Court of Louisiana, directing . . . that
the will of Daniel Clark . . . dated at New Orleans,
July 13, 1813 . . . should be recognized and executed
as such. . . ."

Then Justice Wayne opened again the whole case and
point by point sustained the long-time contention of the
"fair litigant." The action of the Louisiana Supreme Court
was commended, Wayne saying that "the doctrine of the
Common law is in accordance with the view taken by the
Supreme Court of Louisiana concerning lost deeds and
wills."

The *res adjudicata* argument based on the 1851 decision was overturned; and then the ecclesiastical record was examined with a thoroughness that it had scarcely received before. Wayne's copious learning in the Latin Code was shown to advantage, as he outlined the powers of the Spanish Inquisition and reviewed the royal ordinances of Charles V and Philip II bearing on the legality of such a proceeding as was alleged to have been held against Des-Grange.

For page after page the decision continued, taking up anew the evidence relied on by Myra's opponents, brushing it aside. Even the old collusive argument in the Patterson case was looked into, and the Court held that while this was "an indiscreet arrangement between General Gaines and Mr. Patterson, not to be tolerated in a court of justice, it was not one of intentional deception in contemplation of any undue advantage."

The Court concluded: "Our judgment is, that by the law of Louisiana, Mrs. Gaines is entitled to a legal filiation as the child of Daniel Clark and Marie Julia Carrière, begotten in lawful wedlock; that she was made by her father in his last will his universal legatee; that the Civil Code of Louisiana, and the decisions and judgments given upon the same by the Supreme Court of that State, entitled her to her father's succession, subject to the payment of legacies mentioned in the record. We shall direct a mandate to be issued accordingly, with a reversal of the decree of the court below, and directing such a decree to be made by that court in the premises as it ought to have done. Thus, after a litigation of thirty years, has this court adjudicated the principles applicable to her rights in her father's estate. They are now finally settled."

Then the Court made this pronouncement on the case as a whole: "When hereafter some distinguished American lawyer shall retire from his practice to write the history of his country's jurisprudence, this case will be registered by him as the most remarkable in the records of its courts." [10]

VI

Justice John Catron wrote a dissenting opinion exactly as Wayne had written one nine years before. The two Justices had scarcely changed ground at all, Wayne merely had more of the Court with him this time.

Catron's dissent restated the decision of the 1851 case, with the addition this time of a more practical reason: "If the decision [1851] be overthrown, ruin must be the consequence to the very many who have confided in its soundness. In a rapidly growing city like New Orleans much of the property supposed to be protected by our former decree must have changed hands. Large improvements must have been made in the nine years since that suit was decided. If the twenty odd defendants to this bill can be recovered against, so can the others."

Chief Justice Taney stood with Catron, but Justice Grier went beyond both and expressed his individual dissent in one of the shortest and most vitriolic pronouncements ever to come from a member of the Supreme Court.

"I wholly dissent from the opinion of the majority of the Court in this case, both as to the law and the facts. But I do not think it necessary to vindicate my opinion by again presenting to the public view a history of the scandalous gossip which has been buried under the dust of half a

century, and which a proper feeling of delicacy should
have suffered to remain so. I therefore dismiss the case, as
I hope, for the last time, with the single remark, that if it
be the law of Louisiana that a will can be established by the
dim recollections, imaginations, or inventions of anile gossips, after forty-five years, to disturb the titles and possessions of the bona fide purchasers, without notice of an
apparently indefeasible legal title, 'Haud equidem in-
video, miror magis.' "

Which being translated meant that Justice Grier was
amazed and disgusted. The son of a Presbyterian manse
in Pennsylvania had no patience with the moral laxity of
the voluptuous city of the South.

VII

The jubilant Myra now rose to her zenith. Always admired and popular in Washington she was able at last to
bask in the glow of victory. She could even ignore the fact
that Franklin Tenney, manager of the National Hotel, had
become so exasperated at her repeated refusal to pay her
hotel bill that he had seized five of her trunks just a short
while before this. She could live on hope apparently, but
the National Hotel had to have something more substantial. Now that she was armed with the Court's decree, who
could doubt that all her hopes were to be fulfilled and her
patrimony assured? She was a national heroine. The Beadle
Press, just releasing the first dime novels—which in the
early days were founded on fact—gave to the public,
Myra: The Child of Adoption. The story, written by a
friend of Myra, did not hesitate to give names, dates, and

places, though it was sold as a "thriller." The more decorous *Harper's Weekly* carried her story on its cover page as "The Great Gaines Case," and illustrated it with a picture of Myra herself. Everywhere she was receiving congratulations, and then————

Down at Charleston, South Carolina, her late witness, General Pierre Gustave Toutant Beauregard, gave an order [11] and at 4:30 A.M. April 12, 1861, a gun belonging to a seaside mortar battery threw a shell out toward Fort Sumter. The Civil War had begun.

In a surprisingly short time the newly organized Confederate States government passed a law directing that "any judgment rendered by a court of the United States, shall be null and void in any seceded State." [12]

Myra had won her case only to lose all the benefits of victory.

War Adjourns Court

MRS. GAINES went to Richmond to see what she could do with the Confederate States government,[1] but the Confederate States government had more pressing matters to attend to than the claims of one woman against citizens of the southern city of New Orleans. Richmond, now grown far beyond the limits of the little town where Aaron Burr had once been tried, was again teeming with life and bustle, but this time the soldier and not the lawyer was dominant. Feverish activity was everywhere. McClellan's vast horde down on the Chickahominy, or news from the Shenandoah Valley, or monotonous messages of disaster from the middle South as war drew its cordon tighter, blotted out all attention to lesser things. Even had the Confederacy possessed anything like an adequate judicial system, it is doubtful that such a judiciary would have acted against the will of so many in the sovereign state of Louisiana. The war was being fought, in part at least, over some of the very questions of conflicting control which the Gaines case had brought to the fore. As for New Orleans,

that city "abandoned herself, heart and soul, to the cause
of the Southern Confederacy," as Grace King expressed it.
The guns of the Washington Artillery, New Orleans'
pride, were then thundering away in Virginia, while many
a Creole "Zouave" or Louisiana "Rifle" had gone northward to take his station in the South's powerful gray wave.

Perhaps while in Richmond Mrs. Gaines went into one
of the departments to see her onetime lawyer, the late-
Justice Campbell, now assistant Secretary of War. Only
the Alabamian, of all the men on the Supreme bench, had
handed in his resignation when war came. He did not believe in secession and tried to prevent it, but when the
South called, John A. Campbell answered. He never again
sat on the tribunal where his great fame had been made,
though happily, as it turned out, he was long after destined
to practice before it, and to be honored by both its bench
and bar.

In Richmond, Campbell was given a secondary position
in the War Department, and there, a clerk among clerks,
the great Justice whose legal lore had impressed the nation,
was to be seen day after day attending to the minutiae of
department orders or the unlovely machinery of the draft.[2]
Henry S. Foote, who found Campbell bent over his desk
at this type of work "under the supervision of men who,
compared to him, were mere pygmies in intellect," said
that it reminded him of "Epaminondas sentenced to
sweep the streets of Thebes." But the hour belonged to
Mars, not Minerva.

Justice Wayne also was southern and so was John
Catron of Tennessee, but they both stayed on the Supreme
bench. Cynicism might suggest that they were two old

men clinging with the timidity of age to positions that guaranteed security amid a nation's chaos. Catron's philosophy of "taking people as they are, not as they ought to be," might be used against him here, but there was something else. Catron and Wayne were both Andrew Jackson men. The memory of an old presidential toast had come ringing down through the years: *"The Federal Union; it must and shall be preserved."* Curiously enough, no Jackson man, south or north, stood for secession. In Texas, Sam Houston, governor and until then idol of the state, sat on the porch of the Executive Mansion and with a sad and sardonic gleam in his eyes watched the legislature march by to take the state from him and add it to the Confederacy. Another Jackson man.

Myra made her way back north through the lines—"in spite of Mr. Secretary Stanton," commented the acid Janin later—but not without danger. In some way she was taken prisoner at the little hamlet of Darkesville, now in West Virginia. She afterward declared that she would have lost her life there had it not been for a chivalrous southern colonel named George W. Benson [3] of Marietta, Georgia. This gentleman secured her release and managed to have her conveyed safely to the North where she established a legal residence in Brooklyn. There presumably she remained for the duration of the war, the great suit having at last run into something that could stop it, at least for a time.

II

While the armies march and countermarch, and all litigation stands still, it may be a good time to look more closely into some of the unusual features of the Gaines case.

Lawsuits can often be settled by compromise, and the legal profession has again and again advised that parties to such a conflict of interests as this case represented should settle out of court. But how could the claims of Myra Clark Gaines be compromised? How may one make concessions on one's legitimacy? Either one is born in lawful wedlock, or one is not, and there's an end on it. One cannot trade off a mother's chastity for so many arpents of land, or for the "rentals and accrued interest" on three hundred slaves. Had Myra made any attempt to do so, she would have lost at once all defensible title to the land and slaves in question. On the other hand, Relf and Chew could not admit the legality of the Clark-Zulime marriage without endorsing all Myra's claims. Richard Relf could scarcely settle matters by admitting that he had destroyed Clark's last will. Furthermore, Myra by nature was no compromiser, as the reader has no doubt gathered. The two sides were utterly irreconcilable, and there was nothing to do but fight it out. That was done and the courts finally pronounced some things true and some things false, thus settling the case as far as the law could do; but to this day no one actually knows which claim was right.

Out of this impossibility of compromise arose the great bitterness that animated both sides. If one was right, the other was wrong. If Richard Relf had destroyed the last will of Daniel Clark and had squandered Myra's patrimony, then he was an unmitigated scoundrel and those allied with him were well-nigh as bad. But if Clark had never married Zulime, if Myra were illegitimate, then her aunts were perjurers, and the whole affair was a diabolical attempt to wreck the reputation and fortune of some of the foremost citizens of New Orleans. Property of vast extent was also involved, and the very roofs over the heads of countless families depended on the integrity of Relf or the dishonor of Zulime. No wonder Myra was hated, shot at, and mobbed. A man who, as a boy, knew her intimately, has declared that for a time she kept a cat in her New Orleans residence and fed it morsels of all food prepared for her table. Poison! And so a feline cup-taster.

The side arguments and half arguments heard during the case would themselves fill a large volume. Theories of all sorts were spun out. Some held that Clark had indeed made a last will declaring Myra legitimate but had too much sense to try to palm it off as such and destroyed it himself before the end; others thought he was the victim of a hallucination, imagining Myra legitimate because he came to wish her so with such fervor. But one Justice dismissed this by affirming that Clark would never have jeopardized the last will by declaring in it that one daughter (Myra) was legitimate and the other (Caroline) not, unless he had known this to be the truth.

The tale of Lubin, the Negro, was also subjected to scorn. Did anyone imagine that Daniel Clark, even though dying, could have thought that a black slave would be allowed to walk away from his house after the owner's death bearing on his back a locked trunk? The idea was preposterous, and, argued one attorney, Daniel Clark gave no such order. Certainly Lubin was *not* allowed to walk away with anything.

So it went. The debate ranged over small matters as well as great. Each theory in a sense made a self-consistent case; but between the two sides there was a great gulf fixed. By 1865 seventeen Justices of the Supreme Court had passed on the case and were almost equally divided as to matters of fact. Where did reality lie?

III

Included in the case and adding something more of enigma to it was the character of Richard Relf. To the day of his death Relf furnished the opposing shadow. He was the arch-villain of the whole case to Myra and was published to the world as such by every advocate employed on the Gaines side. Through all the long years, Relf said very little after the Whitney libel suit, though he was always to be found as the nucleus of every coalition against Myra. Colorless in type, he, too, was a mystery. Was he, as his lawyer Duncan pictured him, a quiet, reserved man of the clerical type, working industriously day in and day out in his small office, going and coming methodically, a trusted, respectable banker and friend whose life had been ruined by the pitiless publicity and relentless attack of Myra? Or was he the spider who had diabolically spun his web over the Clark fortune and had secretly torn up the last will of his dead benefactor and so possessed his property? The partisans on either side had their answers ready. Relf was an unselfish gentleman, an abused, unsung hero; Relf was a detestable villain. There was no halfway judgment on him either.

A curious incident happened in 1857 just after Mrs. Gaines had probated the 1813 will. Rhoda's husband, a young doctor, Robert Strother, took it into his head to go

to see Richard Relf. Ostensibly he went to ask if Daniel
Clark had ever had any Illinois land, but Dr. Strother admitted later that he had great curiosity to see this Relf of
whom he had heard so much.

Strother seems to have been a free and easy sort and
made the visit without saying anything to Myra about it.
Relf received him courteously, said that Daniel Clark never
had owned any lands in Illinois, and Strother arose to take
his leave. Before doing so, on the spur of the moment,
Strother in an offhand way blurted out that "forget and
forgive" was *his* motto, and asked Relf why he and Mrs.
Gaines didn't "bury the hatchet."

"You will be an old man before long," the doctor added
in an attempt to be jocular.

"I am already old," said Richard Relf.

Relf later began to ponder the strange visit of Dr.
Strother and what he might mean by "bury the hatchet."
He suspected that Strother had been sent by Myra. She,
knowing nothing of the visit, was greatly astonished to receive a letter from Relf about two months after this:

May 13, 1857.

Dear Madam: In a brief interview I a short time ago had
with the doctor, your son-in-law (whose name though
then announced, I do not now recollect, otherwise this
note would be addressed to him,) he intimated that it
would be gratifying to you that I should call upon you in
order, as he expressed himself, that we might bury the
hatchet, a message, I confess, so unexpected, as not only
to surprise but confuse me so much at the moment, as to
prevent my entering into any explanation with him, which

I have since regretted; and now, presuming that the intimation given by the doctor was authorized by you, I beg leave to assure you that I have never entertained any other than the kindest feelings toward you personally. I have not forgotten my fondlings with you in your childhood, Mr. Clark's affection to you, nor my early intimacy with your mother; but higher considerations, the obligations of a sacred trust committed to me by one whose memory you should revere, and justice to third parties, compelled me, however reluctantly, to thwart what I conscientiously believed to be your unfounded pretensions.

I am very respectfully,
Richard Relf [4]

Myra would not answer by letter, but having heard her son-in-law's story, authorized him to say to Mr. Relf in person that on her part she "freely forgave him for all the wrongs and persecutions he had inflicted upon her."

"I delivered that message to Mr. Relf," reported Strother later, "and assured him that the suggestion of burying the hatchet proceeded from me."

Richard Relf died shortly afterward.

IV

The war dragged through its four long years, leaving the South ruined. Louisiana suffered horribly. Farragut had taken New Orleans, his fleet sailing disdainfully by old Forts Jackson and St. Philip where General Gaines long before had his headquarters. The defenseless city capitulated to the fleet, and the Stars and Stripes were run up

above the Custom House. Then came General Benjamin
Butler and military rule with its sordid aftermath, the
"grand, gloomy and peculiar" Custom House standing
above Canal Street, a hostile fort in the heart of the city.[5]

At the close of the war Myra resumed operations
exactly where she had left them. Her great victory of early
1861 had been fruitless of anything but glory, and monetary returns were absolutely nonexistent. She had made all
sorts of promises, given notes right and left, borrowed
where she could, and so kept going, but the "vexatious delays," as her friends euphoniously called them, continued
to block progress.

It may be recalled that she had started *three* suits in the
Federal court in 1857. One was against Lizardi, Hennen,
and others, one against the City, and one against Delacroix.[6] The Supreme Court had decided the first named in
her favor in 1861, and it was felt that the decision would
give her the others, the subject matter being the same. But
the war stopped everything. Meanwhile, Myra, for good
measure, started *another* bill in chancery against P. H.
Monnseaux and one hundred and ninety defendants.
Then in December, 1865, the lower court decided against
her in *Gaines* v. *New Orleans* and *Gaines* v. *Delacroix*.
Delacroix was now dead and so was Relf, but a younger
Delacroix had taken his father's place, and the city itself
was very much alive. Of course Myra appealed each adverse decision but it took two years more for the cases to be
heard in Washington.

No matter how hard pressed financially she became,
Myra never had any trouble securing lawyers who would
take her case. The fame of it was tempting to some, and so

were the princely fees which were to come out of the estate
to be recovered. However, although lawyers were satisfied
with promises and fame, storekeepers and hotel proprietors were not. Bills began to come at her with increasing
insistence, and two or three suits against her for small
amounts made rather unlovely appearances at this time.
A man named Cadwallader Doddridge from West Virginia alleged that she had employed him as her lawyer in
1859 and had promised him "a large and magnificent fee"
contingent on her success in the Hennen suit. Myra
claimed that she had never retained this Doddridge for her
lawyer, but had promised him a two per cent commission
if he could "effect a sale of her property in New York."
Doddridge sued and his suit ran for years in the District of
Columbia Court.[7] While waiting for the Supreme Court
to hear her appeal in 1867, another suit was entered against
her by the endorser of a note for $1,000 borrowed back in
1860. The great Cushing himself had to take a hand and
file a defense for her but finally she confessed judgment
and got a stay of execution.

Not to be outdone at this petty warfare, she came back
at Franklin Tenney of the National Hotel in a suit to recover the money represented by the trunks he had taken in
1860;[8] one especially, "a valuable Russian trunk bought
by the General for ninety dollars," she insisted should be
returned. She affirmed that Mr. Tenney had promised that
when she paid her hotel bill the trunks would be given
back. She settled with him in February, 1867, but upon
her demand for the trunks, Mr. Tenney sent back only
one, "containing an old soldier's coat, clotted with blood
. . . the odor being disagreeable"—not hers at all. Not

knowing how to get what she wanted in any other way, she sued Mr. Tenney. This midget suit finally ended as a drawn battle.

In such desultory warfare two years went by, but at the December term, 1867, "the now well worn case," was once more before the Supreme Court.

The Court Reaffirms

THE case was old but the court that heard it in the winter of 1867 was almost new. Taney was dead and in the seat of the Chief Justice was the commanding Salmon P. Chase, a jurist who had political talents as well as judicial. Some alleged that Abraham Lincoln put Chase on the Supreme bench in order to block his presidential aspirations. He had been brought up by an uncle, the same Philander Chase who had volunteered to be one of Myra's witnesses. But as it turned out, the Chief Justice did not hear Myra's cause, having a more spectacular role to play. He was at this very time called to preside over the Senate of the United States in the impeachment proceedings against President Andrew Johnson.

John McLean had died and Noah H. Swayne, another Ohioan, had been named to his place. Samuel Miller, destined to "write more opinions than any judge living or dead," had been on the bench since 1862.

Lincoln had placed a personal friend on the bench when he named the rugged David Davis [1] of Illinois to that position. So close were Davis and the President, that after Lincoln's death, Justice Davis became the personal administrator of his estate. Davis was a born politician and had the unjudicial habit of expressing his views on public questions with a vigor that created echoes far beyond the cloistered precincts of the Court.

An additional Justice was authorized by a special enactment in 1863, and so Lincoln was given another place to fill. This time the honor fell to Stephen J. Field, of the remarkable family of that name. The new Justice looked like a patriarch, with great flowing beard and gigantic, well-poised head, but there was no sign of senility in the direct eyes or the strong mouth. He made a picturesque and powerful addition to the Court. His brother, Cyrus W. Field, was at that time engaged in laying the Atlantic cable.

These were the new Justices about to take their places in the growing roll of those who had passed on the Gaines case. Nelson and Clifford were yet in active service on the bench, and so was Myra's old enemy, Grier, doubtless looking more dour than ever as the case which he had dismissed in 1861—he hoped "for the last time"—faced him again.

But two Justices whose figures had become very familiar to court attendants through the past years were no longer to oppose each other over the claims of Myra. Catron and Wayne had both gone.

Just as the Court opened in 1867 with the Gaines case before it, Solicitor General Black asked the presiding Justice to order a suitable memoir [2] prepared for a former member of the Court, the late James Moore Wayne.

"Those of us who have played our part in the case will pass away. The case will live. . . ."

As the cause now came to trial the City of New Orleans was represented again by the truculent Louis Janin, with Messrs. Miles Taylor and McConnell in support. Myra retained Caleb Cushing. Both sides relied on former decisions, Cushing on the 1860 action of the Court and also on the old Patterson case, Taylor and McConnell on the 1851 decision. The Court's judgment was given by Justice Davis. Some of the arguments advanced by the Court will throw light on phases of the case hitherto little emphasized and may assist the reader to arrive at a final conclusion regarding the two great questions of the long contest.[3] The Court's decision affirmed:

"The legitimacy of Mrs. Gaines is the turning-point of this controversy: for, since the probate of the will of 1813, if legitimate, she cannot be deprived of the estate of her father by any of the defences interposed in this suit. . . . This court decided, in the Hennen case, that by the law of Louisiana she was entitled to a legal filiation as the child of Daniel Clark and Marie Julie (Zulime) Carrière, begotten in lawful wedlock. Was that a mistaken judgment?

"To this question we will first direct our attention. We shall not attempt to give the history of the litigation which, it is to be hoped, will be closed by this decision. It is enough to say it has been pursued by the complainant through a third of a century, with a vigor and energy hardly ever surpassed, in defiance of obstacles which would have deterred persons of ordinary mind and character, and has enlisted, on both sides, at different periods, the ablest talent of the American Bar.

II

"This case seems to have been defended on the idea that every presumption was against the legitimacy of Mrs. Gaines. But, as she was declared legitimate by her father in his last will and testament, common justice, not to speak of legal rules, would require that such a declaration should be overborne by the strongest proof; and yet detached portions of evidence, scattered through the record here and there, are invoked to destroy the dying declarations of an intelligent man, that a beloved child was capable of inheriting his property.

"The inquiry naturally arises, what motive had he [Clark] to declare his child legitimate if he knew the facts were otherwise? He was a man of superior intelligence, and long residence in Louisiana, and necessarily knew by the laws of the state he could secure to his child enough of his large property to make her rich, if she were illegitimate. Is it conceivable that such a man would risk a declaration of legitimacy, which he knew to be false, and thus jeopard the estate, which he insisted with so much confidence he had secured to his child, and in the security of which he said 'he would die contented'?

"It is argued that the conduct and letters of Clark, for years before this are inconsistent with the idea of Myra's legitimacy. Conceding this is so, and yet it in nowise dis. proves the good faith and sincerity of Clark when he made his will. The conduct of Clark is susceptible of easy explanation. He had contracted an unfortunate marriage, and, in many respects, a disreputable one, having married a person with whom he had previously lived improperly, who, without a divorce, had married again. Possessed of commanding influence, and high position, and mingling in social intercourse with the best society of the country, it was natural, while in strong health and the full tide of prosperity, he should be desirous of concealing such a marriage; but when sickness overtook him, and he necessarily reviewed his past life, it was just as natural he should wish to repair the consequences of his folly (to use no harsher term) by a deliberate acknowledgment that the child born of that marriage was legitimate, and could, therefore, inherit his estate.

"The difficulty of acknowledging the marriage to Zulime was greatly increased by her subsequent marriage to Gardette. Clark could not acknowledge it to the world without injuring her, which no right-minded man under the circumstances would wish to do. It is easy to see the struggle in the mind of Clark on this subject. He had sustained improper relations with a woman of uncommon personal attractions, to whom he was passionately attached. This woman he afterwards married, and lived with in secret for several years. Estrangement took place, and he separated from her. She had repaired to Philadelphia to procure evidence of her marriage; but being unable to get it, and advised of its invalidity, had married another man with whom she was quietly living. Two children were the result of the intercourse between them—one born before and the other after marriage—the latter the legitimate heir of the father, if he married the mother, believing in good faith she was capable of contracting marriage. To acknowledge a marriage with such surroundings was to lose social caste, and put in peril a woman whom he once loved and still professed to respect. Not to acknowledge it was to bastardize a child for whom he had great affection, and to see a large part of his estate go to others, who had no claims on his bounty. There were thus presented to his mind conflicting motives. Duty to himself and society, and affection for his child, prompted him to proclaim his marriage, while pride, the fear of social degradation, and the natural desire not to inflict additional injury upon Zulime, impelled him to a contrary course. That he yielded to the influence of unworthy motives, and lived for years a life of deception, only proves that his baser nature during that time got control, and that he acted as other men in similar circumstances have acted before him. But, before he died, the better nature of this man of lofty pride and sensitive honor was aroused and gained the ascendency. He atoned in some measure for the errors of his past life; for he not only made a public acknowledgment in the last solemn act of his life, that his child was legitimate, but a short time previous to his death frequently repeated the declaration to Mrs. Harper, who had nursed the child in infancy, and to Boisfontaine, who managed his plantations, and was with him when he died.

III

"But the will itself, in another clause, furnished corroborating evidence of Mrs. Gaines' legitimacy. A legacy of five thousand dollars is left Caroline DesGrange, with a suitable annuity until her majority. The person thus designated was the natural child of Clark by Zulime, and yet he avoids calling her his child, gives her the name of the ostensible husband of her mother at the time of her birth, and recognizes Myra as his legitimate and only daughter. Many reasons may have influenced Clark to pursue this course. Delicacy to the mother may have induced him to reveal no more than was necessary to accomplish his purpose; or an unwillingness, by his will, to affix a brand of reproach on this child, who was lawfully entitled to bear the name of DesGrange, may have been the motive; or a wish that Myra, the object of his greater affections and superior bounty, might never know the wickedness of his life, may have prompted his course. It is not necessary to inquire whether these considerations, singly or together, constituted the reasons for the peculiar wording of the legacy. It is enough to know from the legacy that Clark had both children in mind when he drew his will. If so, and he knew both were illegitimate, why discriminate so largely in favor of one against the other? No answer can be given to this question on the assumption he knew the birth of both to be dishonorable; but it is easily answered, if one was legitimate and the other not.

"The attempt to impeach the validity of this will shows the importance attached to it by the defence in determining the issues we are now considering. But the will cannot be attacked here. When a will is duly probated by a State court of competent jurisdiction, that probate is conclusive of the validity and contents of the will in this court.

"But why, if the will is invalid, has the probate of it rested for twelve years unrecalled, when express liberty was given by the Supreme Court of Louisiana for any one interested to contest it in a direct action with complainant? If, with this clear indication of the proper course to be pursued, the probate of the will still remains unrevoked, the reasonable conclusion is, the will itself could not be successfully attacked. Be this as it may, while unrevoked it is the law of this case, and so this court held in *Gaines* v. *Hennen*.

IV

"We will proceed now to consider the question of actual marriage. Madame Sophie Despau swears to the solemnization of a marriage between Clark and Zulime, by a Catholic priest, in Philadelphia, in 1802 or 1803. If this witness is to be believed there is an end of the case, for no amount of negative testimony that Clark could not have made the marriage will weigh down the testimony of an unimpeached witness, who was present and witnessed the ceremony. But why does she not tell the truth? Is it because she was the sister of Zulime? Who so likely to be present at a private marriage, as a near relative of one of the parties? Clark knew he was contracting a marriage which would lessen his standing in society, and might not want any very dear friend or relative present. Not so with Zulime. She was marrying a man of rank and position, with whom she had lived in unlawful intimacy, and what so natural than that she should take with her to Philadelphia, as a witness to her happiness, the same sister who had witnessed her previous disgrace when Caroline was born? Is she not to be believed because she speaks of Caroline as one of the children born of the marriage of her sister with DesGrange, when she must have known she was the child of Clark? It is doubtless true she knew Clark to be the real father of the child; but she certainly did not falsify in stating Caroline was born of the DesGrange marriage. This was true, and yet Clark had seduced the wife and was the father of the child. But is she to be condemned and her evidence discarded because she does not disclose the frailties of her sister, and instead of answering plainly that Caroline was the child of Clark, speaks of her as born of the marriage with DesGrange? DesGrange was, in the eye of the law, the father, though Clark was, in fact, the father; and although Madame Despau knew the real parentage of Caroline, we cannot say she did not believe she was answering properly the cross-interrogatories propounded to her. At any rate, we cannot say her testimony in this regard casts suspicion on the evidence given to establish the marriage. We concede something to the infirmity of human nature. This aged witness, testifying forty-six years after events which must have indelibly fixed themselves on her memory, and when concealment of anything, no matter how unpleasant, would do harm rather than good, still shows pride of family, and studiously avoids the condemnation of her unfortunate sister, for she can speak of her sufferings, but not of her frailties. All this may prove weakness of character, but does not tend to prove she told a falsehood when she testified to the marriage of Clark and Zulime.

V

"But it is argued with earnestness and ability there was no marriage, because those who knew Clark intimately swear to their belief that one of his proud nature would never marry a person with whom he had previously lived unlawfully. Opinions of witnesses on such a point can have no weight in determining the issue we are trying. Men of equal position and equal pride with Clark have married those with whom they were living unlawfully, and why should not Clark do the same thing? If he seduced Zulime and could lawfully marry her, it was his duty to do it; and can we say he was too proud to marry her, and thereby repair the wrongs she suffered at his hands? To say so would be to reflect upon his memory more than is necessary.

"In denial of the marriage it is said, if Clark had not been free to do so, he would never have written a letter, stating if he could secure the affections of Miss Caton he would offer himself to her. This letter was written after his estrangement from Zulime and separation from her, and before her intermarriage with Gardette. It cannot be denied the writing of it was a base and inexcusable act, and in itself affords an additional proof, if any were necessary, how easy the descent, when a man, with a fixed purpose, is leading a life of deceit. Clark, for years, had been imposing himself on the world in a character different from his real one, and when his affections were weaned from Zulime he attempted to do what, if he had succeeded in doing, would have blackened his memory forever. But fortunately, before he died, his line of conduct was changed. Affection for his child and uncertain health, doubtless subdued him, and induced him to disclose what, as an honorable and honest man, he should never have wished to conceal. In resolving the issue of marriage or no marriage, the effect of this letter is unimportant when opposed to the direct testimony that there was a marriage, on which we have offered sufficient comments. Without pursuing the subject further, it is our conclusion from the whole record, as a matter of fact, that the father and mother of complainant were married.

"Courts, in the administration of justice, have rarely had to deal with a case of greater hardship, or more interesting character and history, than the one we are now considering. . . .

"To the discredit of the friends of Daniel Clark, this child grew to womanhood in utter ignorance of her rights and parentage, and did not ascertain them until 1834 (then not fully); since which time she has been endeavoring to obtain her rightful inheritance. Owing to the lapse of time, it was difficult to reach the truth, and, necessarily for many years, she groped her way in darkness; but finally she was able to show the great fraud perpetrated against her; for, in the judgment of the Supreme Court of Louisiana, she established the validity of that very will, which, forty-three years before, her father had executed in her favor. This action of that court settled what was before doubtful—her civil status—and removed the difficulty she had formerly encountered in pursuit of her rights. The questions of law and fact applicable to those rights were determined in the case of *Gaines v. Hennen*. After argument by able counsel, and on mature consideration, we have reaffirmed that decision. Can we not indulge the hope that the rights of Myra Clark Gaines in the estate of her father, Daniel Clark, will *now* be recognized?"

The Famous Litigant

IN SPITE of all the difficulties and disappointments of her life, the years were sitting lightly upon Myra. *Putnam's Magazine,* singing her praises after the decision just given, said: "Mrs. Gaines, now over sixty, does not look a day over forty." [1]

The little woman with her quick, birdlike movements and her inimitable way of moving hands and shoulders when she talked, was invariably the center of her immediate circle. "The most interesting conversationalist I ever knew," one gentleman observed to the writer. She threw herself heart and soul into her words and when talking of her "rights" took on an air of intensity and excitement that was doubly compelling. In her insistence to be heard she would press close to her auditor, and a woman who knew her has said that she has seen her seize the buttons of a gentleman's coat, literally holding him to her words. She knew how to wheedle, cajole, or threaten to gain her ends, and haunted her lawyers' offices that she might key them up to the proper pitch of enthusiasm.

She could change her plans in a moment to front some new crisis, but her lifelong purpose was never altered. A superficial observer might dismiss her as erratic, fickle, and likely to be enthusiastic at one moment and disheartened the next, but her whole career was a denial of such a valuation. She always returned blow for blow in her long legal contest, and was a fighter born. No sooner had her opponents published one statement than she was out with another. She knew the value of "holding her public," as the modern age would term it, and so met thrust with counterthrust.

She had the amazing power of dismissing or overlooking facts that were staggering to her more logical lawyers. But perhaps in this she was not so much illogical as superlogical. She had learned by the rules of the legal game that facts may not always be facts; facts are what courts declare them to be. If perchance a court ruled that black was white, white it became for anyone whose whole life was lived in court. Logic? Perhaps, for a lifelong litigant.

She was always blessed with good health and her faultless complexion and chirrupy laughter assisted in creating the impression that she was much younger than she really was. She continued to wear her hair in ringlets about her face after the fashion of her youth, though in her later years observant women suggested unpleasantly that the pendant ringlets were no longer natural. Her curiously colored hair and youthful ways caused talk among the more decorous matrons of her generation, but what was talk to Myra Clark Gaines?

In spite of financial hardship and increasing debt, she continued to hold a favorite place among the elite of Washington. Society there, while simple in antebellum days,

was at least exclusive until the time of the Grant administration. It was a fashionable set "able to find amusement
without houses or carriages, or jewels or toilettes, or pave-
ments or shops." [2] Mrs. Ellett wrote *Court Circles of the
Republic* about this time to let the nation know who was
who in Washington. Myra was given a prime place in this
volume, and considerable acclaim for "achieving a victory
that has evoked the admiration and sympathy of the entire country." The volume carried a steel engraving of Mrs.
Gaines.

At the last presidential reception but one of Andrew
Johnson's stormy term, Mrs. Ellett notes that "Mrs.
Gaines, just arrived from New Orleans was radiant, as
ever." She wore "a pearl colored satin trimmed with black
lace, with a light dress bonnet decorated with a large
aigrette of costly diamonds."

"She must have been very successful in her ejectment
suits," observed a woman looking her over appraisingly.

"Oh," replied another, "every now and then they send
her a million to keep her quiet."

II

Washington was amused over an incident that occurred
at this time between Myra and Dr. Mary Walker,[3] a
famous character of the capital who was "as familiar as the
monument itself." The doctor, who had served as a nurse
in the war, had adopted man's clothing and usually wore a
black beaver hat, long double-breasted coat, black trousers,
and patent leather pumps. George R. Brown says the doctor "was as much a man as the Almighty ever intended

she should be." Mrs. Ellett caustically set her down as "an advocate of woman's rights who was exhibiting herself at this time . . . as an illustration of the superior health-fulness of masculine attire."

It chanced that Myra was coming out of the Patent Office one day when she saw Dr. Walker approaching. Myra looked her over disapprovingly and, as she came up, with little ado said: "Please discard those pantaloons."

But at last Woman had met Woman.

"Why should I do so?" the doctor rejoined.

"Because it shocks the moral sentiment of the whole people," Myra said. "You have no right to do this. The world is not made alone for you or me. We are only part and parcel of the whole. You place my sex in a false posi-tion, in a light to be ridiculed and treated with contempt by the other sex. Had I assumed your garb, I should have failed to obtain the sympathy of the virtuous and good throughout the country, in this great struggle for my rights. If your object is imitation, then do not, I pray, imitate that which God has not made half so perfect as woman; that is—man."

But the lectured had been looking at the lecturer.

"Why do *you* dress in this gay style of lace and flow-ers?"

"If told that my dress was repugnant to the public taste," returned Myra, "I would instantly change it. I ad-mit that it looks more youthful than my years would war-rant; but, feeling young, I dress according to those feelings. When I feel old, I will dress according to my age."

"Who are you, Madam?"

"I am Mrs. Gaines."

"Oh! I am very happy to know you. I was not prepared to see so young a looking woman. I expected to see a lady at least twenty years older than you appear to be. What is the secret of your looking so much younger than you really are?"

"This is the secret, Madam: I feel kindly towards every human being. There should not be a sorrowing heart within my knowledge if I could prevent it. I look upon life thus: That we are placed here by our Heavenly Father to assist each other and do every possible good in our power. Money is merely a loan to effect that object. Though I have had one of the severest battles of life for nearly thirty-seven years, persecuted and wronged out of my estate since childhood, yet notwithstanding all this, I entertain no feelings of revenge or bitterness towards any one, and the world today looks to me as bright and beautiful as though I had never passed through such terrible scenes of grief and sorrow; and in all these trials I have never for a moment ceased to entertain an everlasting, undying faith in my God, upon the principle that so long as I was true to myself He would be true to me. My life has been devoted to duty. A fashionable woman I never was. God has blessed me with a remarkable constitution, and these probably are the reasons, Madam, why they say I look so many years younger than I really am. Now permit me to renew my request that you change that unseemly garb. What can be the object of your wearing this dress, Madam?"

"My health."

"Your health! That cannot be, for I—continually exposed to all weathers—enjoy the best of health, and look

younger today than you do. Pardon me for saying that I
fear your only motive proceeds from a vulgar love of no-
toriety, to which none of our sex should ever descend." [4]

But there was another account of this meeting given out
by Dr. Walker in which she did not come out so decidedly
second. Myra referred to this in a letter to Mrs. McNeill
Potter and wrote: "Her version of it, which you enclosed
me, is like herself, extremely vulgar." [5]

III

Myra was to learn during the sixties, if she had not
known it before, that winning a suit and getting something tangible out of it were different propositions. She had
the judgment of the highest court ordering the lower court
in Louisiana to enter a decree in her favor, and a Master in
Chancery had been duly appointed to ascertain the amount
of rents and accrued interest due her since 1834. But "vexatious delays" again occurred. Louisiana was in the first
throes of reconstruction, the district judge was "interested"
against her, and no judge from the Supreme Court was
present. Not until May, 1871, were the judgments entered upon the mandates in New Orleans.

The city itself had ceased to be greatly concerned over
the Gaines case, having matters of much greater import
engaging its whole attention. The passing of Richard Relf
and Delacroix had put an impersonal aspect on the whole
affair, and most of the bitterness and acrimony of the earlier
years died with them. The day of the mob had long gone
and the succeeding generation apparently did not resent so
keenly her "pretensions." Furthermore, the war had

changed the very face of the earth for the South, and at this time Louisiana was in chaos, with a carpetbag government and military rule giving the state its first taste of reconstruction.[6] All commerce was crippled and the railroad was now assuming a power that threatened to strangle forever the city's once great river trade. The "iron horse," crossing streams on stringer bridges, was creating new cities to the north and west, opening the western states, rushing trade to the big ports on the Great Lakes or the Atlantic, not to New Orleans. The steamboat was correspondingly dropping back as a carrier of commerce, and the city near the river's mouth saw "hard times and worse a'comin'."

The political situation was indescribable. "With the whole machinery of government framed for the one purpose of keeping them in power . . . and the white population disfranchised into civil impotence, with the United States army always garrisoning their polling places, counting their votes, and doing duty for them—and with a returning board of their own to certify their elections, it is impossible to conceive of a more perfect millenium for the aspiring Republican politicians of that day—and they recognized it."

Amid such turmoil, small wonder that New Orleans people had no time to worry over a judgment given for or against Mrs. Gaines whom many had never seen. Let her worry over her own affair!

That she was worried, especially with regard to the Federal judge to be named, is evident; she wrote President Grant: "It is very important to me as well as to a great portion of the community of New Orleans, that a disinterested judge should be appointed. Permit me to suggest the name of Judge J. Smith Whitaker, a zealous Republican and a supporter of your administration. This gentleman is acknowledged by the bar of New Orleans as a man combining rare legal ability, integrity of character and all the qualities of a refined gentleman." [7]

In view of future developments in Louisiana, it may be regretted that Grant did not take her advice and appoint Whitaker, who, though a Republican, was an Orleanian who enjoyed the respect of his disfranchised fellow citizens. A Federal judge of his stamp might have averted some of the more heinous offenses of the next few years. Had Whitaker rather than Durell been named, perhaps there would have been no fighting on Canal Street and no monument there today to the fallen White Leaguers.

IV

Justice Davis had closed the Supreme Court's decision in 1867 with a hope "that the rights of Myra Clark Gaines will *now* be recognized," and had underlined the *now* with a sort of judicial bang. The Court wanted it understood that when a case was settled, it should stay settled. But was it settled? No one seemed to think so, not even Myra herself, who found it necessary to force matters at every juncture in order to get any action at all. The closing months of the bitter sixties saw her throwing forward her lines along all fronts, especially in New Orleans, where she laid down another suit, this time against Joseph Fuentes [8] and seventy-four persons who were holding a valuable tract of Clark land. This henceforth became known as the Fuentes property. Meanwhile in Washington she went after Mr. Tenney for her long-confiscated trunks, and also won the petty suit brought against her by Cadwallader Doddridge who had claimed for ten years that she owed him for services as her lawyer. The District of Columbia court did not think so. Exit Mr. Doddridge. Enter, however, one Oliver Barrett, to whose boardinghouse on 4½ Street she had taken her family and effects after the National Hotel had turned her out. Mr. Barrett also wanted back rent, and averred further that Mrs. Barrett had once loaned Mrs. Gaines twenty dollars. So *Barrett* v. *Gaines* began in the District of Columbia Court of Claims, another petty suit [9] that Myra managed to satisfy after a number of years. But regardless of debts or creditors, she and her daughter Rhoda, now married again, after a divorce from Robert Strother, to a man named James Y. Christmas, went to one of the huge, unwieldy, Grant receptions:

"Mrs. Gaines wore black and gold lama with gold frieze and embroidery. Mrs. Christmas, the daughter of Mrs. Gaines, in white alpaca with blue satin train, and gold jewelry. The daughter of Governor Ward of New Jersey, in pale silk with point lace panier . . . etc." [10]

On the same day in which she began suit against *Fuentes et al.,* in New Orleans, a powerful countermove was made against her. Fuentes himself with many of his allies, as well as the Corporation of New Orleans, filed suit in the Second District Court of the City for the *purpose of revoking the probate of the 1813 will.* [11] The reminder dropped by the Supreme Court that "any one who wished to contest this will might do so," had not been lost on the Orleanians. They now intended to have the state court look again into the matter of the Clark will which had been so amazingly set up in 1856.

Myra moved at once to have the case transferred to the Circuit Court of the United States, on the ground that she was a citizen of New York while the petitioners were citizens of Louisiana. But removal to the Federal court was the last thing her opponents wished to happen. The state court sustained their objection.[12]

It required little wisdom to see what the New Orleans tribunal meant to do, but Myra was scornful. She wrote Mrs. McNeill Potter that her opponents seemed to have lost sight of the Code of Louisiana, which allowed only *five* years in which to make such a move against a probated will. Thirteen years had now passed since the will of 1813 had been set up. Myra added:

"The only effect of said suits has produced a warm sympathy throughout the community, and I may say, the press also."

Times had indeed changed when Myra Clark Gaines was relying on the Code of Louisiana and the statute of limitations!

V

On December 4, 1871, the District Court—as everyone knew it would—revoked the probate of the 1813 will, thus leaving Myra with no foundation for the gigantic suits in which she was engaged. She appealed of course to the Supreme Court of Louisiana, but such were conditions in the state that two years dragged by before her appeal could be heard by the Republican court that the carpetbag government of Louisiana had established.

During this time there was constant strife over the rulings and estimates of the Master in Chancery, who was going steadily ahead, as the Federal court had ordered, estimating the rents and interest on the property that Myra had been given. The City fought back with fervor whenever its own holdings were menaced. One piece of land where New Orleans had placed some pumping machinery proved a veritable battlefield. The conflict with the City over the worth of the pumping-station property came to a definite head when the United States court rendered a verdict to sustain the report of the Master in Chancery. The City appealed and another chapter of the Gaines case was on its way to Washington for trial. But this time the former roles were reversed. The perpetual complainant now became the defendant, while the City was the appellant, asking the Court to overrule the order of the Master in Chancery who had put a value of $125,267.77 on the pumping-machine property.

Myra was fortunate after the war in retaining from time to time former Justice John A. Campbell. Campbell, however, was too busy with other great cases to take up this one in Washington, and Myra had to be content with Messrs. J. Q. A. Fellowes and James Emott for the defense of her interests against the City's appeal. New Orleans relied on its stalwarts, Messrs. Miles Taylor and James McConnell.

Again the great Court had changed its personnel. President Grant had put in new Justices: Ward Hunt of New York, William Strong of Pennsylvania, Morrison R. Waite of Ohio, and Joseph P. Bradley of New Jersey. Clifford, Swayne, Miller, Davis, and Field remained, but Salmon P.

Chase, the Chief Justice, died before this case was heard. Waite took his place. Grier had at last gone, forced off the bench by action of his fellow Justices who felt that his extrajudicial alliances and conduct had been prejudicial to the Court.

Justice Hunt wrote the decision following the hearings on the New Orleans appeal. It was a sweeping affirmation of the Gaines rights. But scarcely had this decision been given in Washington when the Supreme Court of Louisiana cut the ground from beneath her feet. The probate of the will of 1813 was revoked.

VI

The State Supreme Court at that time was frankly a section of the party machinery then controlling Louisiana.[13] At the head of the court was John Theodore Ludeling, neither scalawag nor carpetbagger, but one destined to personify for future Louisianians many of the evils of reconstruction. The son of a Prussian officer under Blücher, he had been born in New Orleans and as a lifelong Republican had earned the respect of the dominant party in antebellum days; but at the head of the Supreme Court during the Grant administration, Ludeling "left a bad taste in the mouth of the white people of the state," Henry Plauché Dart observed tartly. Ludeling, who wrote the decision revoking the probate of the will, clearly showed that he had been reading the scathing dissent of Justice Grier, as he concluded by affirming: "It is not the law of Louisiana, that a will can be established by the dim recollections, imaginations, or inventions of anile gossips."

That ended it. The great victory of 1856 was done away by the court of 1873.

This decision would have been hailed with enthusiasm years before, but now there was a palpable lack of public interest. People had ceased to care about lesser ills in the face of chaotic conditions about them. Ludeling and his court were part and parcel of the carpetbag government then ruling the state, and the disfranchised citizenry found little pleasure in contemplating any of its doings. Change had altered so many of their institutions that the conservative Orleanians may have felt a sort of nostalgic friendliness even toward the once unpopular Gaines case. That, at least, was a permanent landmark. Furthermore, it could be remembered that Mrs. Gaines had come to New Orleans and fought the whole city to a standstill, singlehanded, long before damyankee bayonets were ever dreamed of. That a court whose whole power rested on those bayonets had decided against her was nothing greatly to her discredit.

The revocation of the probate, however, left matters in an anomalous situation. On the one side was a Master in Chancery estimating rents up in the hundreds of thousands of dollars due Myra by order of the United States Supreme Court. On the other was the Supreme Court of Louisiana which had just taken away the foundation for her rights to the "rentals and fruits" of her father's property. Myra, of course, realized that her entire hope lay with the national government. The revocation of the will would have ruined her, had it come before the decisions of the Supreme Court in '61 or '67. But the will, standing at the time of those decisions, had acted as a steppingstone upon which she rested long enough to move to what she hoped was an unshakable position. She simply sued out a "writ of error" as the lawyers term it and appealed to Washington to reverse Louisiana's carpetbag court.

A few months after this, April 8, 1874, far across the ocean the childless, withered old Duchess of Leeds died at St. Leonard's-by-the-Sea. In youth she had been the beautiful Louisa Caton of Baltimore.

The sands were running.

VII

For two or three years following the revocation of the probate of the 1813 will, while Myra was waiting for Washington to act on her writ of error, she boarded at the home of the Reverend John W. Harmon on Camp Street in New Orleans.[14] He had for some years edited a publication known as the *Southern Organ* and in this had warmly espoused Myra's cause, especially during the campaign to elect Merrick Chief Justice. Through the years he had remained her steadfast ally and was glad now to open his house to her. One winter Rhoda Christmas and her family came to stay with Myra in this home also. It is not on record that the board was paid any too well during this time, and there is reason to suspect that the more worldly-wise Mrs. Harmon mentioned this fact frequently in the privacy of the family circle; but her husband, always hopeful, always dynamically exuberant, brushed all this aside. Mrs. Gaines was going to win and she would pay.

One of the Harmons, then a boy, says that the house became a veritable mecca for lawyers. He remembered particularly one visit made to Mrs. Gaines by M. F. Bonzano, a citizen of standing in the city. Mr. Bonzano and Myra were sitting in the modest parlor of the Camp Street home talking over some phase of her case. As the conversation progressed, she grew excited and sprang to her feet. The gentlemanly Bonzano arose just as quickly. Seeing this, her manners came to the rescue and she said: "Sit down, Mr. Bonzano."

Mr. Bonzano bowed: "Sit down, Mrs. Gaines."

She did so and then he resumed his seat. Again the conversation grew rapid and again she sprang to her feet, the courteous Bonzano once more arising just as she did.

"Sit down, Mr. Bonzano."

"Sit down, Mrs. Gaines."

Again and again the scene was repeated.

The family noted one fact that caused continual private speculation. She was never seen, in the house or out of it, without her hat. This was a curious little bonnet of silk with the curls flowing from under it. She wore it at the table, in her room, everywhere.[15] No one ever saw her without it. One of the sons declared that he was summoned to her door time and again to run some errand for her, but always the hat-and-curls ensemble was duly in place. The Harmons finally concluded that the curls were attached to the hat and came off when—or if—it did. They never knew.

"It Is About Time"

ITHAS been impossible to do more than trace the main
trunk line of the Gaines case in this volume; the subsidiary
cases and collateral issues make a labyrinth into which no
reader would care to penetrate far. Included among the
collateral cases were suits that lawyers who had served Mrs.
Gaines brought against her in the impossible effort to collect before she did. One feels, however, that the lawyers
who took her case realized full well what they were doing
when they entered her service. However, some of these
suits became exceedingly annoying. Janin, her bitter foe,
said Myra never paid any of her lawyers and "always
abused them." But then Mr. Janin was not unbiased.

Myra enjoyed roseate dreams of what she would do
with her money when she got it. That she should finally
secure the fortune was never doubted for an instant. She
promised in a letter to the mayor of New Orleans that she
would build an institution for widows and orphans for the
city. "My sole object . . . is to do good," she wrote to a
friend.

Sometime after the Supreme Court had sustained the rulings of the Master in Chancery, Mrs. Gaines met a great number of the people whose property was affected by the decision. For the first time many of them saw the ogress who had been frightening them from infancy. They found her a little lady with self-assured air and pleasant face, who instantly put them all at ease by saying that she did not want to dispossess anyone and would not; she knew their homes were precious to them and was sure that they had no intention of defrauding her or anyone else. For her part, Myra added, she had no desire to hurt anyone but simply wanted a fair rental and return on the property which had been so long denied her.[1]

This magnanimous speech made a tremendous impression on the city and was told over the nation. Owing everyone herself, she forgave those who owed her and stood by her bargain ever afterward, even to her own financial hurt. Daniel Clark was again on the deck of the *Comet* risking life and fortune to save the shipwrecked sailors, hull down on the horizon. He and his daughter both had their faults, but smallness of soul was not among them.

The people in New Orleans had by this time come to consider Myra something of a dealer in magic. That she had been able to gain decision after decision through court after court, when, as their parents assured them, she had no case at all, gave her the reputation of being a witch. To counteract this, Louis Janin in 1874 brought out his *Explanation of the Fraudulent Character of the Claims of Mrs. Myra Clark Gaines*. Janin bewailed the fact that he was the "only surviving contemporary witness" of "all phases" of the case, as the older lawyers who knew the hollowness of her claims had all gone. Janin blamed the "weak Judge Lawrence who did not understand that the United States should have the power of chancery in Louisiana," for giving her a start. "The immediate cause of Mrs. Gaines' temporary success," he added, "was a bungling decision regarding an olographic will by the probate court of New Orleans."

One absolutely ridiculous story was told by Janin in illustration of the dread the populace had now come to entertain for Mrs. Gaines. It seems that a certain Mr. Christ wanted to buy a corner lot somewhere in the city but before doing so insisted that the owners should guarantee him that Myra Clark Gaines would never claim it. They assured him that she could not possibly do this, as the lot in question lay well outside the area of Clark land and had never been thought of in connection with the Clark estate. But Mr. Christ demurred; no one knew what Mrs. Gaines might claim. They then brought him a map of the city and pointed out the sections involved in the Gaines litigation, making it clear that the lot he wished was beyond all possible limits. Still Mr. Christ was not satisfied, and Janin says that before he would buy he made the owners go to Myra and get her to sign a guarantee that she would never make any attempt to get this particular lot. Janin, who entirely missed the humor of it, asserted indignantly that Mrs. Gaines charged five hundred dollars for signing such a deed—which does not sound like her.

II

In October, 1875, the Supreme Court in Washington got Myra's appeal on the writ of error, and reversed the

Supreme Court of Louisiana,[2] but not without a powerful dissent from Justices Bradley and Swayne and Chief Justice Waite. This hearing was far more critical for Myra's fortunes than was dreamed at the time, and, had she lost, her lifetime of struggle might have gone for nothing. The three dissenting Justices held, in brief, that proceedings to revoke a will were not matters subject to Federal review. But with her she had Justices Clifford, Miller, Davis, Field, Strong, and Hunt. The bearded Field wrote the fateful decision. But this, while a victory for Myra, really meant no more than that she was still able to stand on the 1813 will. It was the reversal of a revocation and confirmed the probate of 1856. She was allowed to go on "claiming" as she had always done. She would have done so anyhow.

Louisiana by the end of the seventies had reached a condition of more stable political equilibrium. Meanwhile Ludeling and his court had been turned out by force and a Democratic court installed, but the count of Louisiana's electoral vote for President in the Hayes-Tilden contest provoked new bitterness. The state's vote was finally given to Hayes and assisted materially in securing his election, but, playing politics for what it was worth, the losing side was strong enough to secure a promise from the coming administration that the troops would be withdrawn from the state. This promise was fulfilled after the inauguration of Hayes, and carpetbag rule collapsed at once. New Orleans began slowly to build again. Its long battle with the river and disease, with natural forces as well as with poor government, had bred a resourcefulness in its leaders that was to bear fruit in future. Captain Eads built the jetties to give a deep-water channel out through the mud lumps at the river's mouth. The pumping machinery set upon Myra's land foreshadowed the gigantic pumps and magnificent system which the city of today employs to drain and ditch the area that had long been burdened with stagnant water and seepage from the river. The "New South" became conscious of itself.

III

In Washington Myra now found herself distinctly passée. Mrs. Ellett was dead and the social dynasty that had reigned with her had likewise passed. A new group had poured through the expansive portals of the capital and "snobbery had swished upon the scene." People now looked curiously at little Mrs. Gaines with her corkscrew curls, and some of the new arrivals began to speak of her as the "New Orleans Claimant." She would scarcely have liked this title; she had come to enjoy the unique distinction that her solitary role had given her.

A young stranger was once introduced to her on Pennsylvania Avenue and she saw by his face that he had not caught the full significance of her name. "Don't you know who I am?" she asked, peering up at him. "I am Myra Clark Gaines." She pointed to the gray dome of the Capitol. "I have suits all the way from that building to the Gulf." [3]

In spite of age her children and grandchildren came to depend on her more and more. So did General Gaines' son, Edward, and his wife. Rhoda Christmas died in 1879, leaving three little children for whom she made her mother promise to care. Myra promised, though she was borrowing money up to the hilt. Then her son, William Whitney with his family came to be with her. She told her troubles to a friend:

"I very much fear I shall never recover my spirits from the death of my beloved daughter, the greatest affliction of my life. I struggle to live and do my duty. My affairs have not progressed as rapidly as I hoped. I defeated near three years ago upward of four hundred families. I had not the heart to deprive them of their homes, or collect a dollar rent as their circumstances were very much reduced. They, however, last spring . . . subrogated all their rights to me, rents, revenues, use of property . . . to the city of New Orleans. . . . I then filed a bill *versus* the city and am now contending for the amount due me. I shall not obtain a final judgment against the city until next winter. In the meanwhile I am compelled to borrow money at a high interest of 2½ per cent a month to sustain myself, son and his family, including my son-in-law and his family. I have a bill before Congress for about 80,000 acres but I fear Congress will adjourn previous to its passage." [4]

This was in 1880. In addition to pursuing the lengthy processes of litigation, she had joined the innumerable company of those then besieging Washington in the attempt to get Congress to pass bills to satisfy real or fancied claims. Her particular interest lay in some of the old Morales land, possibly along the Gulf Coast, as Daniel Clark had obtained title to several vast tracts when Spain ruled. But Congress proved as tardy as the courts, although after the time-honored manner of such claimants she was encouraged when a senator promised to "do what he could," or when Judge Bright, chairman of the House

Committee of Land Claims, said he would "report favorably very soon the bill to transfer . . . [her] claims to the Court of Claims."

Meanwhile a new Federal judge, E. C. Billings, had succeeded the hated Durell in New Orleans. The new appointee suddenly electrified Myra by deciding "important points" in her favor.

"I must say I was not prepared for it. It was most fortunate for me I came before a judge who entertained no prejudice against me, a sentiment that has prolonged my difficulties and troubles many years." [5]

But "important points" were not money, and hoping to bring matters to a head she started another suit to compel the City to respond for all the "rents, fruits, revenues and profits" on the whole one hundred and thirty-five arpents in the Blanc Tract.

It had now become increasingly evident that the Gaines case was going to come up against New Orleans itself. Private defendants had altogether ceased to respond or make any effort to meet Myra's claims, all now relying on the City to protect them. Her suits, or "suit" as everyone termed it, had become a civic problem like drainage or flood control. The ordinary householder refused to be concerned over it. The City gave him his title deeds; let the City see that these were clear.

But the City was slow in moving. Even Myra began to grow impatient. On the very day a critical trial of the case was set for a hearing, she wrote: "I think it is about time the city who has assisted my opponents for so many years, should be made to remember that there is an end to all earthly things. . . . No doubt their calculation has been to wear me out, consequently at my death the suit would be abandoned. But lo and behold, hundreds of my principal enemies have passed away, and I in constitution do not feel older than when I was thirty years of age. I have indeed great cause to be thankful to my heavenly Father." [6]

At this time there were reports current that Mrs. Gaines had been offered a compromise by the City but this she quickly denied. She had in fact promised two old gentlemen friends of General Gaines who had been lending her money that she would not compromise without their consent. "I can not honorably violate the sacred promise I have given these two good friends, who have simply taken my note and honor to repay the large amount they have loaned me."

IV

During this time she was boarding in Washington with her son, William Whitney, and his family, and her son-in-law, Christmas, and his three children, in what Washington called the Catacazy House at 1336 I Street. The place had originally been built for Justice Campbell, but after the war the Russian minister, Catacazy, and his statuesque, golden-haired wife made it their home. The Catacazys had now gone, and the house was a high type of boarding place conducted by the Misses Harrover. There the Gaines connection all lived until one black day in June, 1881, when James Christmas shot and killed William Whitney. [7]

Washington papers in screaming headlines announced "Fratricidal Affair," and recounted parts of Myra's story in connection with the shooting and subsequent arrest. It appears that the two men had been in business together but had never got along well. William Whitney was reported to have been subject to epilepsy and had several times made threats against his brother-in-law. He felt that Christmas was trying to supplant him in his mother's affections. Myra's own attitude was much speculated upon. But six months later she could write: "I have not seen him [Christmas] nor held any communication with him since that unfortunate tragedy. I have throughout the whole and terrible affair acted with great prudence. Should Mr. C. be acquitted, which is the general impression, upon the ground that he shot my son in self-defence, he will immediately leave this city; which it is my wish also that he does so." [8]

It turned out as she had intimated, and Christmas was exonerated. Later on she said confidentially that he "had to do it." Her deposition helped Christmas materially. She had lived her whole life amid court scenes, but the criminal docket, with hard-faced Washington policemen standing about, was different. Nevertheless, in her resilient way she threw off the effect of the tragedy and took care of the fatherless little Whitneys, in addition to the three motherless Christmas children.

V

As E. C. Billings had proved to be a judge "without prejudice," Mrs. Gaines was very hopeful that he would be renominated by "General Garfield," after that gentleman's inauguration. Billings also was quite anxious for that event, and we find Myra reporting his presence in Washington, "with his excellent wife." [9] Myra went every day to the Senate to learn who would be named to the Eastern District of Louisiana. She had long since come to appreciate the truism that chancery practice depends tremendously on the chancellor. It turned out as she wished, and Billings was reappointed.

Indomitable as she was, Myra was beginning to realize that time was now against her, just as it had been on her side twenty years before when she was outliving so many of her opponents. But that she should not live long enough to finish her great suit she would never admit for an instant. A friend in Washington urged her to make a will and was so tactless as to suggest that she might die with her vast fortune unprovided for.

"I am not going to die," was the short rejoinder.

Later on she wrote in a calmer mood: "I shall continue to pray and now finally believe I shall live until I arrive at the age of one hundred and fifty. Dr. Parr, an Englishman, lived to be one hundred and fifty-two. My only and sole object in wishing to live this long is to do good. The very thought that I will have the power makes me happy." [10]

Like her father, she was the victim of schemers and sycophants and was caught many times by those who had special interests to advance. She invested in patents that were utterly worthless and once put money into an invention which was to use water in place of coal for propelling trains, "a very cheap way of running cars," she naïvely explained to her daughter-in-law.[11] To one friend she wrote regretting that she could not go into "this great scheme in China," [12] whatever that may have been.

She realized her weakness along this line but explained

MYRA CLARK GAINES CASE

it by saying, "I unfortunately inherited that trait, cre-
dulity, from both my father and my mother." [13]

Finally her friends had to step in. "Now as to your
proposition, to enter into this great speculation," she responded to one importunate plea, ". . . I am compelled
to decline it, having made a solemn promise to those parties
who have been loaning me money without security that
hereafter I will not go into any speculation however tempting." But she could not resist adding, "However I believe
that you will be enabled to succeed before I shall."

She continued to take an interest in public affairs. Myra
had always been opposed to woman's rights—that is, the
collective movement that began to be called by that name
—and when a Louisiana convention was called for the purpose of framing a new constitution for the state. Mrs.
E. T. Merrick, there to speak for woman's suffrage, was
surprised to see Myra who had come to oppose it. "Mrs.
Gaines, the famous litigant, with a few other notables,
occupied the center of the room, and youth and beauty retired into a corner," Mrs. Merrick caustically reported
later. [14]

VI

The great contest had now narrowed down, or widened
out, to *Gaines* v. *New Orleans*. The City had taken the
place, certainly in Myra's mind, of all single individuals
opposed to her. She lost a private suit in 1881, when the
Supreme Court, for once, decided against her, holding that
those who had purchased the old Cannes Brulées property
years and years ago could not be charged with buying in
bad faith. [15] To offset this, however, she had reason to be-

lieve that the Circuit Court in New Orleans would decide
for her in the case against the City, and early in 1882 was
greatly disappointed to learn that the decision might not
come for several months more—"that is, a *final* judgment," [16] she wrote hopefully.

"But I am not impatient," she explained, "when you
consider fifty years! a few months more appear a trifle." [17]

Some time later she admitted: "For nearly a week I have
not had one cent. Have borrowed ten from a lady in the
house." But on that same day she instructed her lawyer
to refuse all compromise and "strike out on bended
knee." Her curls may have been pinned on but her courage was not.

As it turned out, it was not until May, 1883, that the
Circuit Court acted. Then Judge Edward C. Billings, born
in Vermont four years after she had first begun to sue in
New Orleans, handed down the decision she had been trying to get for fifty years. As easily as though he were imposing a five-dollar fine, the Federal judge ordered "that
the complainant, Myra Clark Gaines, do have and recover
judgment against the defendant, the City of New Orleans,
in the sum of one million, nine hundred and twenty-five
thousand, six hundred and sixty-seven and eighty-three
one-hundredths dollars, with interest. . . ." [18]

Judge Billings had done his part handsomely.

VII

Would the City appeal? It was the great question. New
Orleans authorities realized that an appeal was expensive
and also that the Supreme Court had become increasingly

insistent that Mrs. Gaines be allowed to collect her rents and revenues.

"The impression continues that the city will not appeal," Myra wrote hopefully. "But I cannot obtain any money until the taxes are paid." [19]

Decision after decision had been given her, but no money. Even the two elderly friends of the General had at last stopped advancing her loans.

The mayor of New Orleans, possibly with the idea of developing support for a proposed appeal, issued a circular calling on property holders to unite and sign the necessary bond of $50,000. Myra later noted with satisfaction that the property holders did not respond.

But there were thirteen die-hards, several members of the city council and lawyers opposed to her—"not worth a dollar," Myra said of them—who agreed to sign the appeal bond. It meant the old round of sickening delay.

"If my counsel had only justified them," Myra wrote almost tearfully again and again. She had not been on the field herself, and her lawyers had failed to "justify," i.e., challenge the financial status of the bond guarantors. Napoleon's marshals were not Napoleon.

Compromise again was mentioned but Myra would have none of it. Alfred Goldthwaite of Alabama, the nephew of Judge Campbell, was acting for her, as was W. H. Wilder, an attorney, of New Orleans who had increasingly assumed control of her affairs. She wrote Goldthwaite that all the lawyers felt that the Supreme Court would sustain Judge Billings' decision. "It is therefore a settled determination on my part neither to accept or offer a compromise." [20] She hoped that Goldthwaite "would

argue before the Supreme Court, the importance of grant-
ing me an increased amount on the bond." To achieve this
result she asked Goldthwaite to urge his uncle, Judge
Campbell, to argue for the increased bond: "I would most
sincerely regret should Judge Campbell decline arguing
said points, as he is unequalled, and would have a very
great influence with the Court."

As it turned out, Campbell did go over from Baltimore,
where he was then residing, and argued for the increased
bond before the Supreme Court, using Goldthwaite's
brief.

"I was in hopes that Judge Campbell would have written one himself, as it would have had more weight with
the Court," Myra informed a friend, "but it is useless to
regret this." [21]

She knew her lawyers. Campbell was the only one of
the big four, Walter Jones, Reverdy Johnson, Caleb Cushing, and himself, who lived to stand by her until the end.

When the Supreme Court did not grant the increased
bond, Myra took it philosophically. "Upon a moment's
reflection I found myself uttering grateful thanks to my
Heavenly Father that said decision was not *upon the merits
of the case*." [22] That battle at last was over.

She wrote her lawyer, Wilder, after the Christmas holi-
days of 1883: "Never have I been in greater want. Six of
the children spent eleven days, being holiday, with me and
compelled me to go into debt. The fact is, I am in debt
everywhere." [23]

A little later in the year: "I deeply regret to tell you that
the whole of the property I am in possession of is under
seizure. Five of them are some of my old lawyers, Messrs.

Randolph, Moise, Bonford and Smiley. These gentlemen are dead but their heirs have sued." [24]

But in her penury, with a little Zulime, Rhoda, and Myra, a small James and William of the third generation looking to her for sustenance, she proved adamant to a suggestion that she foreclose upon the individual householders in New Orleans. She wrote her lawyer: "I trust when you speak of Mr. Gurley's disposing of the Bayou property St. John's, and also the Maitou and Blanc properties, he does not include any of that portion of the Blanc tract that those parties occupy that I *defeated* in 1877. I *cannot* and *will not* consent to those defendants being turned out of *their homes*." [25]

Just a "quaint slight figure, with . . . sharp features pinched by anxiety, in whose light blue eyes gleamed the fire of an unquenchable hope." [26]

As Good As New

*I*T WAS early in January, 1885. New Orleans had staged its "Cotton Exposition" as a signal that hard times were over. The railroad had slowly throttled the great steamboat trade, but to be a railroad center was a distinction also. The practical value of the port was unquestioned. The city had discovered its past, and was becoming conscious of its "charm"; the possibilities of Mardi Gras were dawning on the commercial mind. Soon some smart Yankee was to come along and teach the psychological and advertising value of calling the region about Jackson Square the *Vieux Carré.*[1]

To be sure, the drainage problem had not then been solved, and cellars under houses and graves under ground were equally unknown. The city's water system was in its infancy; every home of size had a huge wooden cistern where water from the roof was stored; there were still open ditches with stagnant pools along many side streets awaiting the systematic and scientific attack that would remove these problems and make New Orleans as healthful as any

other large community. Nevertheless, in 1885, the days
of Gayoso, Clark, and Claiborne seemed to a Louisianian
as far removed as those of Bienville himself.

Horsedrawn cars now trailed along several of the main
thoroughfares of the city. One of these was popularly
known as "the snake line," and, had a visitor taken a car
on a certain morning early in the new year, he could have
been carried within a block or so of the residence of L. L.
Davis at 150 Thalia Street. There a strangely assorted company had been quickly assembled to act as witnesses to a
will. The testator was Mrs. Myra Clark Gaines, now quite
ill.

She had not wanted to make a will, and in fact up to
that day had flatly rejected the suggestion—a matter that
was giving concern to her son-in-law, James Y. Christmas,
as well as her agent and attorney, William H. Wilder.
Christmas had come down from Washington with Mrs.
Gaines, and, while it is said that she never quite trusted
him, he was the father of Rhoda's children and the nearest
male relative, and therefore she needs must lean on this
man in spite of the shadow that his pistol had put between
them. Both Christmas and Wilder were exceedingly
anxious that the vast properties which it was now clear she
would receive should be properly provided for by testament. Strange that after a lifetime of difficulty over a will,
she should be so loath to make one of her own.

The two men knew that Dr. William H. Holcombe
was to make a professional call on Mrs. Gaines that day
and were counting heavily on the doctor's persuasive
powers to aid them in getting her to execute a testament.
Dr. Holcombe [2] was one of that older generation of phy-

sicians who combined culture with common sense, classical learning with astute worldly wisdom. He was looked upon with great respect by New Orleans, and justly, as he took the lead in many civic matters. He had been treating Myra now for a few days for bronchial trouble and a deep cold.

Christmas and Wilder had already enlisted the interest of Dr. Holcombe concerning the proposed will, and he had tactfully made an attempt to get Myra to act, saying that "old people sometimes collapse and die with lung trouble very rapidly."

Myra saw through his words and said at once that she was not going to die and there was no need to make a will. At the doctor's insistence, however, she promised to think it over.

"I told her she was a very sick woman and things of that importance should be attended to," the doctor reported.

"I am not going to die, sir," [3] she said.

But as she grew weaker she did send for Wilder and finally said, "I wish to make my will. . . ."

II

She lay in bed in a small upstairs room [4] accessible only through another room, that occupied by her son-in-law. Wilder brought a notary, John F. Butts, to assist him in drawing up the will, but when Butts arrived Myra refused to allow him to enter her room. The little bonnet with the curls was at last off, and she preferred for the notary to sit outside her door.

Wilder then began to draw up the will, writing down the various items and calling out each one to Myra for confirmation. But progress was slow. Butts finally called in and told Wilder he would be all day writing a will at that rate, and that he would do the writing if Wilder would dictate. This procedure was adopted, and the notary turned an old washstand in Mr. Christmas' room into a writing desk—"a very inconvenient one to write a will on," [5] he remarked later. So with Wilder asking Myra's wishes and relaying her commands to Mr. Butts, who could of course hear everything, the will was drawn up.

It followed her oft-expressed wishes and left several bequests to those who had helped her. She remembered General Gaines' son, then blind and dependent, with $25,000. Her grandchildren were amply provided for, and she insisted that the will should declare each one legitimate. That clause in her father's will had proved a tower of strength to her. She remembered with a $10,000 bequest Colonel Benson, who had saved her life in the War, and the Reverend J. W. Harmon with whom she had stayed for a while in New Orleans with a like amount, saying that he had been a "true friend to me in my adversities."

As soon as the will was finished, there was a hurried call for witnesses. A Dr. Harrison came up; Mr. Davis, the owner of the house, was there; they sent for the clerk at the drugstore on the corner of Magazine and Thalia streets who had promised to come over when all was ready. Then Dr. Holcombe was announced.

Mrs. Gaines was propped up on pillows and they read her the will. Now, however, she showed little interest and no further inclination to help them. They asked her about signing it. She said she could not. She was fighting her last battle and doing it in her own way.

Holcombe saw her dart a look of resentment at Christmas. "There was a general impression in my mind," the doctor said later, "that this woman was very reluctant to do that thing . . . she couldn't believe she was going to die, and they were forcing something on her which she didn't like and like an old petulant woman she was angry at it." [6]

But to her statement that she could not sign, the doctor said: "Oh, yes, you can. We will all help you."

They gave her a book and on this he placed the will and put a pen in her hand. Then cramping her fingers between his, Dr. Holcombe guided or pushed the pen and so a mark was made. Asked if she acknowledged this as her will she nodded briefly, or so they said. It was all a bit too suggestive of giving up the fight, and she did not intend that death itself should make her do that.

III

She died on January 9, 1885. It was her wish that she should be buried beside her father with whose life her own had been so strangely interwound. This was done, but when, within the precincts of the crumbling, vaulted cemetery of St. Louis, the tomb of Daniel Clark was opened, the surprising discovery was made that there was nothing whatever within it. No fragment of bone or button or wood remained—nothing. Was it the last mystery? [7]

It had been just ninety-nine years since Daniel Clark had first landed in the old Spanish town of New Orleans, but of that day little remained that he would have recog-

nized. Only the changing, changeless face of the great
river would have appeared the same—the river that had
seen La Salle and Bienville and Gayoso and Burr and
Gaines and Farragut and thousands of others pass in procession across its inscrutable face, the great river that like
life itself rolls irreversibly on.

IV

Then came anticlimax. A few days after the death of
Mrs. Gaines, a woman named Marie Perkins Evans
brought out a will which she claimed Myra had written
and had given her shortly before she died. Mrs. Evans and
Myra had been friends of a sort at one time, but the purported will was clearly fictitious and the popular judgment
was that Mrs. Evans was trying to become "Myra Clark
Gaines the Second." The Evans will, however, was set up
against the heavily witnessed testament that Myra had
signed when Dr. Holcombe guided her hand. While a
patent fraud, it was so cleverly defended that it required
years to dispose of it. The intricacies of the Evans will case
came to be fearfully involved, but the matter was finally
ended, when the Surrogate of King's County, New York,
decided in favor of the regular will.[8]

Meanwhile the Gaines case itself with its attendant
planetary suits moved on haltingly. "When she died," a
newspaper man wrote satirically, "her case was as good as
new." But this was more clever than correct. When she
died the case was unchanged but the soul had gone out of
it. Christmas, Wilder, and Goldthwaite carried it on for
the Gaines heirs and it was heard three more times before

the Supreme Court. Then Justice Bradley in 1891 [9] wrote a decision that, while partial denial of some of the technical claims, forced the City of New Orleans to pay the sum of $576,707.92 to the Gaines estate. Myra's generosity to private titleholders and various agreements she had made saved the City from paying the full amount Judge Billings had ordered.

This ended the litigation. It had run from 1836 and had been before the Supreme Court for about sixty years. Thirty Justices had sat on it in one or another of its aspects, not to mention the numerous judges and officers of the state or Federal courts before whom it appeared. The last time the record of the case was carried to Washington from New Orleans two trunks were required to contain it and the Supreme Court frankly admitted its inability to read the record as presented.[10] One authority states that from first to last thirty lawyers "if not more" were in Mrs. Gaines' service, of whom seventeen died during employment. The same authority estimated that the costs of the suits alone amounted to $250,000 and that she actually paid her lawyers $600,000 as fees.[11] The cost of the suit in the Federal court in New Orleans at one of its hearings in the eighties was $34,000. It is no wonder that the poor lady had to borrow postage stamps in Washington and "was in debt everywhere."

It has been mentioned that the Reverend John W. Harmon—the author's grandfather—was a beneficiary of the will of Myra Clark Gaines.[12] At first he was delighted at being able to convince his family that his long-continued championship of Mrs. Gaines' good intentions was not mistaken. The family was duly impressed at the news of the legacy, and then the months slowly began to pass as the Evans will tangle was superposed on the almost inextricable Gaines litigation. Mrs. Harmon had always flatly refused to concede that anything would ever come of "Mrs. Gaines' money." Nothing had come of it except fine words for the past thirty years, and as year after year went by the "legacy" became a family joke and eventually was forgotten altogether.

Then one day in the early nineties Dr. Harmon was summoned by telegram to come to New Orleans—the Gaines estate was to be settled. He went, and $10,000 in greenbacks was counted out to him—quite a fortune for a retired minister. According to the story which has been passed down in the family, he stuffed the money into his little traveling satchel, got on the train, threw the satchel in the rack over his head, and calmly went to sleep under it! Like General Gaines, there was nothing on his conscience either.

Arrived safely at his home in Mississippi he marched magnificently into the room where his skeptical wife sat and threw the satchel into her lap. "There!" he boomed triumphantly; "I always said we'd get it."

V

"The case shows," wrote Justice Wayne in 1851, "the hollowness of friendships formed in the greediness for gain. . . . A kindred between virtue and lasting respectability. . . . Irregular yieldings to passion . . . bring ruin upon children. . . ."

It shows all that, but it shows something else: That

there is a spirit in man—or shall we say, woman—that can set itself against overwhelming odds and triumph in spite of all difficulties. Like the stone lion at Waterloo or the crosses on Tarawa, the great volumes of Supreme Court records now containing this case are monuments to human courage.

Indeed, Myra Clark Gaines' own indomitable spirit is the weightiest argument for the validity of her claims. That a woman with such scant basis for truth as her opponents alleged could have contended as she did for well-nigh sixty years is unthinkable. Nor was she self-deceived or hypnotized by hope. It is impossible to follow her through her life and watch her long battle against hopeless odds without coming to the conclusion that this woman was a passionate believer in her own cause. No fraudulent claimant could have found the inner courage to take the buffetings of fate as did Myra Clark Gaines, and as she knew intimately her much-abused aunts, as well as her enigmatic mother, it is to be presumed that she obtained from them the absolute truth. That she continued to fight bravely and hopefully on with the full information they gave her is itself evidence of transcendent importance.

"The case will live," observed Justice Wayne. So it has after a fashion, for "the profession still looks to it for what has been ruled upon its merits." It yet lives in the minds of some who remember the little woman dressed in black with black mitts upon her hands, who "puttered about carrying a large black bag containing papers connected with her many suits." [18] It lives in the records of the Supreme Court now reposing in the handsome marble building where the great Court will henceforth make its home.

But these are records and recollections only. The case, after all, was Myra Clark Gaines herself, gone with all her hopes and claims, her averments and prayers, to stand before the One Judge whose decisions are always in Equity, whose judgments know no reversals.

Notes

Book One

DANIEL CLARK

1. Daniel Clark, *Proofs of the Corruption of Gen. James Wilkinson, and of his connexion with Aaron Burr* . . . (Philadelphia, 1809), 105, Note 45.
2. J. D. D. Bellechasse in *Gaines* v. *Lizardi*, Supreme Court Record of 6 Wallace, Part II, 234.
3. Clark, *Proofs of the Corruption of Gen. James Wilkinson*, 105.
4. Grace King, *New Orleans, The Place and the People* (New York, 1904), 104–129.
5. Clark, *Proofs of the Corruption of Gen. James Wilkinson*, 9; also, Note 45.
6. Clark, *Proofs of the Corruption of Gen. James Wilkinson*, 9; also Thomas Marshall Green, *The Spanish Conspiracy* (Cincinnati, 1891), 120; also General James Wilkinson, *Memoirs of My Own Times* (Philadelphia, 1816), II, 108.
7. Charles Étienne Arthur Gayarré, *History of Louisiana* (New Orleans, 1903), III, 211.
8. Clark, *Proofs of the Corruption of Gen. James Wilkinson*, 9; also Note A.
9. King, *New Orleans, The Place and the People*, 129.
10. Sam Henry Wandell and Meade Minnigerode, *Aaron Burr* (New York, 1927), I, 25. Also "Papers bearing on James Wilkinson's Relations with Spain, 1787–1789," *American Historical Review*, IX (1903–1904), 748; I. J. Cox, "General Wilkinson and his later intrigues with the Spaniards," *American Historical Review*, XIX (1913–1914), 794.
11. Edward Channing, *A History of the United States* (New York, 1905–1925), IV, 311.
12. "Documents: Despatches from the United States Consulate in New Orleans, 1801–1803," *American Historical Review*, XXXII (1927), 801–824.
13. Daniel Clark to Daniel W. Coxe, January 13, 1798, *ibid.*
14. Gayarré, *History of Louisiana*, III, 397.
15. Daniel Clark, dispatch in Archives of State Department, Foreign Relations.
16. William Empeson Hulings to the Secretary of State of the United States, February 20, 1801, Archives of State Department, Foreign Relations.
17. "Documents: Despatches from the United States Consulate in New Orleans, 1801–1803," *loc. cit.*
18. Clark, *Proofs of the Corruption of Gen. James Wilkinson*, 61; also Clark's statement to Congress, *ibid.*, Note 45.

19. *Ibid.*, 113; also Note 51.
20. *Ibid.*, 79.
21. *Ibid.*, 77.
22. Daniel Clark to Timothy Pickering, Archives of State Department, Foreign Relations.

ZULIME

1. New Orleans *Times-Democrat*, January 10, 1885.
2. Zenon Cavellier describing DesGrange in deposition, May 30, 1849, *Gaines v. Lizardi*, 6 Wallace, Part II; also Jean Canon's testimony, *ibid.*, 375.
3. New Orleans *Times-Democrat*, January 10, 1885.
4. By the Treaty of San Ildefonso, October 1, 1800.
5. Madame Sophie Despau, testimony, 6 Wallace, 573–723, Part II.
6. Clark, *Proofs of the Corruption of Gen. James Wilkinson*, 142.
7. *Ibid.*, 169 (Jefferson's message).
8. Edward Channing, *A History of the United States*, IV, 307.
9. Beckles Willson, *America's Ambassadors to France* (London, 1928), 83.
10. Daniel Clark to James Madison, April 9, 1802, Archives of State Department, Foreign Relations.
11. *Id.* to Chew and Relf, June 27, 1802, in 6 Wallace, 573–723, Part II.
12. *Id.* to Daniel Coxe, *ibid.*
13. Madame Rose Caillavet's deposition, *ibid.*
14. Daniel Clark to Richard Relf and Beverly Chew, *ibid.*, 687.
15. *Ibid.* Same letter gives view of London.
16. James Kendall Hosmer, *The History of the Louisiana Purchase* (New York, 1902), 123.
17. Robert Livingston to James Madison, November 11, 1802, Archives of State Department, Foreign Relations.
18. Daniel Clark to *id.*, December 23, 1802, Archives of State Department, Foreign Relations; also Gayarré, *History of Louisiana*, III, 471.

THE FLAG AT THE CABILDO

1. *Id.* to *id.*, March 8, 1803, Archives of State Department, Foreign Relations.
2. *Ibid.*; also Channing, *A History of the United States*, IV, 326.
3. Wilkinson, *Memoirs of My Own Times*, II, 249.
4. Clark to Daniel Coxe, January 31, 1807, 6 Wallace, 573–723, Part II, 428.
5. *Id.* to Madison, New Orleans, March 8, 1803, Archives of State Department, Foreign Relations.
6. Henry Adams, *History of the United States of America during the Second Administration of Thomas Jefferson* (New York, 1890), I, 225.
7. Hosmer, *The History of the Louisiana Purchase*, 67.
8. Clark to Madison, April 27, 1803, Archives of State Department, Foreign Relations.
9. *Ibid.*
10. *Id.* to *id.*, October 20, 1803, Archives of State Department, Foreign Relations.
11. *Ibid.*
12. "Documents: Despatches from the United States Consulate in New Orleans, 1801–1803," *American Historical Review*, XXXIII (1927), letter of Woodson Wren to James K. Polk, Natchez, Miss., 356n.

NOTES

13. Gayarré, *History of Louisiana*, III, 607.
14. *Ibid.*, 610.
15. Clark to Madison, December 3, 1803, Archives of State Department, Foreign Relations.
16. Gayarré, *History of Louisiana*, III, 605; also Clark to Madison, November 29, 1803, Archives of State Department, Foreign Relations.
17. Gayarré, *History of Louisiana*, III, 613.
18. Letter of Woodson Wren to James K. Polk, *loc. cit.*
19. Gayarré, *History of Louisiana*, III, 615, 620; also King, *New Orleans, The Place and the People, in loc.*
20. Thomas Jefferson to Daniel Clark, July 17, 1803, in 6 Wallace, 573–723, Part II, 610.
21. Colonel J. D. D. Bellechasse, testimony, *ibid.*, Part I, 164.

MYRA

1. Clark's wealth, influence, habits and manner of living at this time described by witnesses, testimony and records found in the Gaines case reports, especially the 6 Wallace record.
2. Clark to Daniel Coxe, February 18, 1804, Supreme Court Record of *Gaines* v. *Relf*, 12 Howard, 639.
3. Hosmer, *The History of the Louisiana Purchase*, 173.
4. Gayarré, *History of Louisiana*, IV, 17, 19; also Dunbar Rowland (ed.), *Official Letter Books of W. C. C. Claiborne, 1801–1816* (Jackson, Miss., 1917), I, 67 (Claiborne to Madison).
5. Gayarré, *History of Louisiana*, IV, 19.
6. *Ibid.*, 20.
7. *Ibid.*, 68.
8. Rowland (ed.), *Official Letter Books of W. C. C. Claiborne*, III, 305.
9. Gayarré, *History of Louisiana*, IV, 38.
10. Aimée Baron Boisfontaine, testimony, 6 Wallace, 573–723, Part II (last half), 941.

AARON BURR ARRIVES

1. Gayarré, *History of Louisiana*, IV, 80.
2. James Parton, *The Life and Times of Aaron Burr* (8th ed.; New York, 1858), 44.
3. Clark, *Proofs of the Corruption of Gen. James Wilkinson*, 94.
4. Parton, *The Life and Times of Aaron Burr*, 46.
5. *Ibid.*, 48.
6. Wilkinson, *Memoirs of My Own Times*, II, appendix 22.
7. Clark, *Proofs of the Corruption of Gen. James Wilkinson*, 94, 107.
8. Matthew L. Davis, *Memoirs of Aaron Burr* (New York, 1837), 382.
9. Clark, *Proofs of the Corruption of Gen. James Wilkinson*, 93.
10. The alimony record in *Gaines* v. *Relf*, United States Supreme Court Record of 12 Howard; reproduced in many other hearings of the Gaines case.
11. Adams, *History of the United States of America*, I, 230. Merry's dispatch to Lord Mulgrave, November 25, 1805, MS. in British archives, per Adams.
12. John Wesley Monet, *History of the Discovery and Settlement of the Valley of the Mississippi* (New York, 1846), I, 451.

13. Clark, *Proofs of the Corruption of Gen. James Wilkinson*, 102.
14. Rowland (ed.), *Official Letter Books of W. C. C. Claiborne*, III, 325.

GENTLEMAN FROM ORLEANS

1. Clark, *Proofs of the Corruption of Gen. James Wilkinson*, 97, 98.
2. J. D. D. Bellechasse, testimony, 6 Wallace, 573–723, Part I, 160.
3. *The National Encyclopedia of American Biography* (New York, 1892), article, Samuel White; also Rossiter Johnson (ed.), *The Twentieth Century Biographical Dictionary of Notable Americans* (Boston, 1904–1910), article, Samuel White.
4. Wilkinson, *Memoirs of My Own Times*, II, 7.
5. John E. Semmes, *John H. B. Latrobe and His Times* (Baltimore, 1917), 215, 216.
6. George C. Keidel, "Catonsville Biographies," *Maryland Historical Magazine*, XVII (1922), 74; also the Baltimore *Sun*, March 14, 1915.
7. Harrison Rhodes, "Annapolis and Annapolitans," *Harper's Magazine*, CXXXVIII (1919), 641.
8. Ann S. Stephens, *Myra: The Child of Adoption, A Romance of Real Life* (New York, 1860), 31–33.

THE DUEL

1. Clark, *Proofs of the Corruption of Gen. James Wilkinson*, 82; also Note 54, pp. 116–124.
2. Daniel Clark to Daniel W. Coxe, June 12, 1807, in record *Gaines* v. *Lizardi*, 6 Wallace, Part II, 457.
3. Clark, *Proofs of the Corruption of Gen. James Wilkinson*. (Contains many indirect references to summons to Richmond. Appears to have been urgent request of Burr and friends rather than a subpoena.)
4. Charles Biddle, *Autobiography of Charles Biddle* (Philadelphia, 1883), 321; also Daniel Clark to Daniel W. Coxe from Charleston, September 27, 1807, in 6 Wallace, 573–723, Part II.
5. Nicholson MS., in Library of Congress, September 1, 1808.
6. Wilkinson, *Memoirs of My Own Times*, II, 7, 8.
7. Clark, *Proofs of the Corruption of Gen. James Wilkinson*, 82.
8. Biddle, *Autobiography*, 321.
9. Clark, *Proofs of the Corruption of Gen. James Wilkinson*, 123.
10. Gales and Seaton, *Annals of the Congress of the United States* (Washington, 10th Congress, 1st session), December 31, 1807.
11. Clark, *Proofs of the Corruption of Gen. James Wilkinson*, Note 84.

END OF ROMANCE

1. Stephens, *Myra: The Child of Adoption*, 45; also H. M. Jenkins, "Romance of Mrs. Myra Clark Gaines," *Putnam's Monthly Magazine*, XII (1868), 207.
2. Daniel W. Coxe, testimony, 6 Wallace, 573–723, Part II.
3. *Ibid.*, for Gardette-Zulime marriage record.
4. Daniel Clark to Daniel W. Coxe, 6 Wallace, 573–723, Part II, 695.
5. *Ibid.*
6. Wilkinson. *Memoirs of My Own Times*, II, 8.

7. Gales and Seaton, *Annals of the Congress of the United States*, April 25, 1808.

DEFEATED

1. Rowland (ed.), *Official Letter Books of W. C. C. Claiborne*, IV, 169.
2. Wilkinson, *Memoirs of My Own Times*, II, 49.
3. *Proceedings of the Court of Inquiry in the case of General James Wilkinson* (July 4, 1808), Archives of the War Department, Washington; also Clark, *Proofs of the Corruption of Gen. James Wilkinson*, 53, and Note 26.
4. Robert Goodloe Harper to Daniel Clark, September 12, 1808, in 6 Wallace, 573–723, Part II.
5. Samuel White to *id.*, May 20, 1808, *ibid.*
6. Rowland (ed.), *Official Letter Books of W. C. C. Claiborne*, IV, 251.
7. *Ibid.*, 316.
8. *Ibid.*, 272.
9. Bishop Philander Chase, testimony, 6 Wallace, 573–723, Part II.
10. Samuel White to Daniel Clark, May 30, 1809, *ibid.*
11. Étienne Mazureau, letter, *ibid.*

THE WILL

1. Dissolution of partnership, *ibid.*
2. Old Probate Record, 56, reprinted in 6 Wallace, 573–723, Part I.
3. *Ibid.*, 20.
4. Caroline Chew Stanard and Julia Brockle Wood, testimony, 6 Wallace, 573–723, Part II.
5. Stephens, *Myra: The Child of Adoption*, 57–59.
6. Samuel B. Davis, testimony, 6 Wallace, 573–723, Part II.

DEATH ON THE BAYOU ROAD

(The actions and moves of Daniel Clark in this chapter are followed by putting together the testimony of various persons whose depositions are found in the record of the case.)

1. Francis B. Heitman, *Historical Register and Dictionary of the United States Army* . . . (Washington, 1903), Samuel B. Davis.

MIST ON THE RIVER

1. Monsieur Gallien Preval, Notary, testimony, 6 Wallace, 573–723.
2. J. D. D. Bellechasse, testimony, *ibid.*
3. *Ibid.*
4. Francois D. Delacroix, petition, in old Probate Record, 6 Wallace, 573–723, Part I.
5. *Ibid.*, for will of 1811.
6. *Ibid.*, for Bellechasse's further account.
7. A. M. W. Stirling, "A Transatlantic Invasion," *The Nineteenth Century*, LXVI (1909), 1058.
8. Old Probate Record, 56, reprinted in 6 Wallace, 573–723, Part I.
9. Samuel B. Davis, testimony, *ibid.*, Part II.
10. Clark's epitaph in Latin in *Gaines* v. *New Orleans*, 6 Wallace, 15.

Book Two

DELAMORE PLACE

1. "Historic Homes of Wilmington," the Wilmington (Delaware) *Every Evening*, April 18, 1914; "Delamore Place Passing," the Wilmington *Delmarvia Star*, May 22, 1921; Elisabeth Montgomery, *Reminiscences of Wilmington* (2d ed.; Wilmington, 1872), 72; also Stephens, *Myra: The Child of Adoption*, 85.
2. Heitman, *Historical Register*, I, 360, Samuel B. Davis; *Historical and Biographical Encyclopedia of Delaware* (Wilmington, 1882), 321, with steel engraving of Colonel Samuel B. Davis; Wilmington *Journal and Statesman*, June 8, 1855; Wilmington *Delaware Gazette*, September 8, 1854.
3. William B. Marine, "Bombardment of Lewes by the British," *Papers of the Historical Society of Delaware*, XXXIII (1901), 4, 7, 9; J. T. Scharf, *History of Delaware* (Philadelphia, 1888), I, 288; Pennock Pusey, "History of Lewes, Delaware," *Papers of the Historical Society of Delaware*, XXXVIII (1902).
4. *Delaware General Assembly, Journal of the House of Representatives for 1839*, 166, 291, 351.
5. Stephens, *Myra: The Child of Adoption*, gives an account of Myra's childhood, schooling, and flight; Jenkins, "Romance of Mrs. Myra Clark Gaines," *loc. cit.*, 207, confirms at many points.
6. Philadelphia *Gazette and Daily Advertiser*, September 17, 1832.
7. William Foote Seward (editor-in-chief), *Binghamton and Broome County* (New York, 1924), I, 50.

MYRA ON THE LEVEE

1. J. D. D. Bellechasse, testimony, 6 Wallace, 573–723, Part II.
2. The details of the visit and conversation of Myra and Bellechasse are not in the written record. This account was given the author by Reverend N. B. Harmon and is substantially as he heard Mrs. Gaines tell it.
3. Edwin L. Jewell, *Jewell's Crescent City Illustrated . . . with a map and general strangers' guide* (New Orleans, 1873), *in loc.* Also A. Oakey Hall, *The Manhattaner in New Orleans, or Phases of "Crescent City" Life* (New Orleans, 1851).
4. Beverly Chew's commission from President Monroe, 6 Wallace, 573–723.
5. Caroline Barnes, testimony, *ibid.*
6. Refer to the "natural child admission" in chapter "Evidence Against Myra."

THE LINES ARE DRAWN

1. William Wallace Whitney, letter in the New York *Evening Star*, November 11, 1835; reprinted in 6 Wallace.
2. Richard Relf, letter to the editor, New York *Evening Star*, December 19, 1835; reprinted in 6 Wallace.
3. Will of Mrs. Mary Clark, 6 Wallace.
4. Marquis James, *The Raven: A Biography of Sam Houston* (Indianapolis, 1929), 259.
5. *Ibid.*, 263.

Yellow Jack Serves a Summons

1. Thomas J. Semmes, *The Civil Code as Transplanted in Louisiana* (New Orleans, 1882); William B. Hatcher, *Edward Livingston, Jeffersonian Republican and Jacksonian Democrat* (University, Louisiana, 1940), 245–269.
2. *Ex parte Whitney,* 13 Peters (1839), 404.
3. *Ibid.*
4. Reverend Theodore Clapp, *Autobiographical Sketches and Recollections during a Thirty-five years' Residence in New Orleans* (Boston, 1857), 203, for yellow fever of 1837.
5. Stephens, *Myra: The Child of Adoption, in loc.*

The Supreme Court

1. Glenn Brown, *History of the United States Capitol, 1792–1900* (Washington, 1902), I, 28.
2. Charles Warren, *The Supreme Court in United States History* (Boston, 1922), for the Court at this time.
3. Hampton Lawrence Carson, *The History of the Supreme Court of the United States; with biographies of all the chief and associate justices . . . with portraits of the 58 judges . . .* (Philadelphia, 1902), for description of the personnel of the Court.
4. Elisabeth F. Ellett, *The Court Circles of the Republic, or the Beauties and Celebrities of the Nation* (Hartford, 1869), 330; Alexander A. Lawrence, *James Moore Wayne, Southern Unionist* (Chapel Hill, N. C., 1943), for definitive biography.
5. Joseph Packard, "General Walter Jones," *The Virginia Law Register,* VIII (1901), 233; the Boston *Post,* January 30, 1839; Warren, *The Supreme Court in United States History,* II, 247, 343.
6. *Ex parte Whitney,* 13 Peters, 404.

The General

1. *Barnes* v. *Gaines,* Louisiana Annual Reports, 5 Robinson (1843), 134.
2. Heitman, *Historical Register,* Edmund Pendleton Gaines; Barritt and Lossing, *Pictorial Fieldbook of the War of 1812* (New York, 1868), 835; James W. Silver, *Edmund Pendleton Gaines and Frontier Problems, 1801–1849* (Nashville, 1935); John S. Jenkins, *The Generals of the Last War With Great Britain* (Buffalo, 1849), chapter on General Gaines; *Proceedings of the Military Court of Inquiry in the case of Major General Scott and Major General Gaines* (Washington, 1837), Files of the War Department; also Allen Johnson and Dumas Malone (eds.), *Dictionary of American Biography* (New York, 1928–1937), Edmund Pendleton Gaines.
3. *Gaines* v. *Lizardi,* 6 Wallace, in record.
4. *Barnes* v. *Gaines,* Louisiana Annual Reports, 5 Robinson (1843), 134.
5. Ellett, *The Court Circles of the Republic,* 574.
6. William Wirt Howe, memoir on "François-Xavier Martin," prefacing François-Xavier Martin, *The History of Louisiana from the Earliest Period, To which is appended Annals of Louisiana, with a Memoir of the Author by Judge W. W. Howe* (New Orleans, 1882).

THE EXCITING FORTIES

1. Ann H. Wharton, *Social Life in the Early Republic* (Philadelphia, 1902), 287.
2. Eliza Ripley, *Social Life in Old New Orleans* (New York, 1912), 170.
3. Ellett, *The Court Circles of the Republic*, 563. Also personal description of Mrs. Gaines given author by the Rev. N. B. Harmon of Vicksburg, Mississippi, emphasizing vivacity and gestures.
4. Ellet, *The Court Circles of the Republic*, 332.
5. Justin H. Smith, *The War With Mexico* (New York, 1919), I, 197.
6. Ellett, *The Court Circles of the Republic*, 279.
7. *Gaines* v. *Relf*, 15 Peters, 9.
8. John Livingston (ed.), *Biographical Sketches of Eminent American Lawyers*, article, Richard Smith Coxe (New York, 1852), Part 4, 692.
9. *Gaines* v. *Relf*, 15 Peters, 9.
10. *Barnes* v. *Gaines*, Louisiana Annual Reports, 5 Robinson (1843), 134.
11. *Gaines* v. *Relf*, 12 Howard (1851), lists Francis Scott Key among Gaines counsel.
12. B. C. Stiner, *Life of Reverdy Johnson* (Baltimore, 1914); also much material in biographical dictionaries.
13. New York *Herald*, January 16, 1844.
14. *Gaines* v. *Chew*, 2 Howard (1844), 619.
15. Smith, *The War With Mexico*, I, 476; Allan Nevins (ed.), *Polk: The Diary of a President, 1845–1849* (New York, 1929), January 5, 1846; also New Orleans *Picayune*, June 7, 1849; also Johnson and Malone (eds.), *Dictionary of American Biography* in its article on Edmund Pendleton Gaines.
16. *Record of the Court of Inquiry in the case of Major General Edmund Pendleton Gaines*, Fortress Monroe, 1846; also letter from the Adjutant-General of the United States Army to the Honorable John W. Gaines, April 26, 1909, explaining the Court of Inquiry of 1846 in the case of General Gaines. Files of the War Department, Washington.
17. Nevins (ed.), *Polk: The Diary of a President, 1845–1849*, 139. (*Diary* date, August 15, 1846.)
18. *Ibid.*, *Diary*, January 25, 1847.

Book Three

MYRA'S WITNESSES

1. The testimony of the various witnesses whose accounts are published in this chapter will be found in the record of the Gaines case repeated many times. The author takes the Supreme Court Record of 6 Wallace (*Gaines* v. *Lizardi*, 6 Wallace, 573–723, Part II) as the most convenient and best display of testimony, documents, etc., relating to the case. He has abridged to some extent the testimony as it is reproduced here and disregarded the interrogatory and cross-interrogatory form of question and answer in order to make a running account. The depositions are, however, the exact words of the witnesses.

EVIDENCE AGAINST MYRA

1. *Ibid.*
2. Charles Étienne Arthur Gayarré, "New Orleans Bench and Bar in 1823," *Harper's New Monthly Magazine*, LXXVII (1888), 889, for Mazureau.

THE PATTERSON APPEAL

1. *Patterson* v. *Gaines*, Supreme Court Reports, 6 Howard, 550.
2. Lawrence, *James Moore Wayne, Southern Unionist*, for description; also Livingston (ed.), *Biographical Sketches of Eminent American Lawyers*, James Moore Wayne; Ellett, *The Court Circles of the Republic*, 330, for a woman's view of Justice Wayne.
3. *Virginia Historical Register and Literary Advertiser*, I (1848), 43.

SWORD AT REST

1. Charles Patterson, testimony, regarding collusion, in *Gaines* v. *Relf*, 12 Howard, 472.
2. This incident regarding the carriage told the author by his father, the Rev. N. B. Harmon, who had it from Mrs. Gaines.
3. Claude Moore Fuess, *Daniel Webster* (Boston, 1930), II, 312.
4. Caroline Chew (Mrs. John) Stanard, testimony, 6 Wallace, 573–723, Part II.
5. Bishop Philander Chase, testimony, *ibid.*
6. New Orleans *Picayune*, June 7, 10, 1849; New Orleans *Weekly Delta*, June 11, 1849.
7. New Orleans *Picayune*, June 10, 1849, Dr. Clapp's eulogy.

THE ECCLESIASTICAL RECORD

1. The "ecclesiastical record," the "alimony record," the "mutilated record," and the "Latin certificate," all textually reproduced in this chapter, are found in 6 Wallace, 573–723, Part II.
2. *Gaines* v. *City of New Orleans*, a small reprint booklet of portions of this case (fully reported in 6 Wallace) has the speech of Mr. Elliott Robbins regarding Zulime and ecclesiastical court, 12.

COLONEL PRESTON FOR THE DEFENSE

1. Alexander Walker, *The Great Gaines Case. United States Circuit Court, a Full report of the great Gaines case in the suit of Myra Gaines, vs. Chew, Relf and others . . . reported by Alexander Walker*, taken from the *Daily Delta* (New Orleans, 1850). Speech of Colonel Isaac Preston (abridged). Also Campbell's in next chapter.

JOHN A. CAMPBELL FOR MRS. GAINES

1. Carson, *The History of the Supreme Court of the United States.* II, 350; also Henry G. Connor, *John Archibald Campbell, Associate Justice of the United States Supreme Court, 1853–1861* (Boston, New York, 1920), 11–13.

JUDGMENT

1. *Gaines* v. *Relf*, 12 Howard (1851), 472.
2. Carson, *The History of the Supreme Court of the United States*, I, 298; *The National Cyclopedia of American Biography* (New York, 1892), X, 147, for John Catron; also Johnson and Malone (eds.), *Dictionary of American Biography*, John Catron.
3. *Gaines* v. *Relf*, 12 Howard (1851).

Book Four

THE LOST WILL

1. Jewell, *Jewell's Crescent City Illustrated*, for this period; also Hall, *The Manhattaner in New Orleans*.
2. *Supreme Court* [sometimes *"Surrogates Court"*] *King's County* [New York]. —*General Term. Second Judicial Department, In the matter of the Probate of the last Will and Testament of Myra Clark Gaines, Deceased. Julietta Perkins and Marie P. Evans, Appellants. Record of Appeal* (Washington, 1896), I, 412. (Hereafter cited as *Evans Will Record*.) This litigation is outlined in New York Supreme Court Reports 74 Hun, 95; 83 Hun, 225; and 84 Hun, 520.
3. Carson, *The History of the Supreme Court*, II, 352; Connor, *John Archibald Campbell*, 17; also 20 Wallace, ix.
4. *The Present Position of Mrs. Gaines Claim, to the Estate of Her Father, Daniel Clark*, no author (Washington, N.D., circa 1852).
5. Wilmington *Delmarvia Star*, May 22, 1921, "The Passing of Delamore Place"; Wilmington *Delaware Gazette*, September 8, 1854.
6. *Succession of Clark*, 13 Louisiana Annual, 138; New Orleans *Louisiana Courier*, December 18, 1855.
7. New Orleans *Times-Democrat*, January 10, 1885.
8. Henry Plauché Dart, "The History of the Supreme Court of Louisiana," *Louisiana Historical Quarterly*, IV (1921), 14; John S. Kendall, *History of New Orleans* (Chicago & New York, 1922), I, 206.
9. Johnson and Malone (eds.), *Dictionary of American Biography*, Edwin T. Merrick; *The National Cyclopedia of American Biography*, X, 147; Caroline E. Merrick, *Old Times in Dixie Land, a Southern Matron's Memories* (New York, 1901), 13, 14.
10. *Succession of Clark*, 13 Louisiana Annual Reports (1855), 138; New Orleans *Louisiana Courier*, December 19, 1855.

JUSTICE WAYNE LAYS DOWN THE LAW

1. *Myra Clark Gaines* v. *New Orleans, Delacroix et al.* (Washington, 1858), booklet reprinting portions of case.
2. New Orleans *Picayune*, April 11, 1856.
3. Probate record in 6 Wallace, 573–723, Part I.
4. *Gaines* v. *City of New Orleans*, booklet reprinting portions of case, citing New Orleans *Weekly Delta*, December 15, 1857, for Mr. Robbins' speech.

5. Glenn Brown, *History of the United States Capitol*, II, 115.
6. Claude Moore Fuess, *The Life of Caleb Cushing* (New York, 1923), II, 294.
7. George Alfred Townsend, *Washington, Outside and Inside* (Hartford & Chicago, 1874), 109.
8. *William D. Colt* v. *Myra Clark Gaines*, at Law, District of Columbia Court (1867).
9. *Gaines* v. *Hennen*, 24 Howard (1860), 555.
10. *Ibid.*, 615.
11. Alfred Roman, *Military Operations of General Beauregard* (New York, 1884), I, 42.
12. Louis Janin, *Explanation of the Fraudulent Character of the Claims of Mrs. Myra Clark Gaines, to the City of New Orleans with copies to be had at the office of Colonel J. B. Walton, auctioneer, 162 Common St.* (Washington, 1874), 10.

WAR ADJOURNS COURT

1. *Ibid.*
2. Carson, *History of the Supreme Court*, II, 352.
3. *Evans Will Record*, III, 2 (Colonel Benson).
4. Richard Relf to Myra Clark Gaines, May 13, 1857, in 6 Wallace, 573–723, Part II.
5. Ella Lonn, *Reconstruction in Louisiana After 1868* (New York, 1918), *in loc.*; King, *New Orleans, The Place and the People*, 300.
6. *Gaines* v. *Lizardi, Gaines* v. *City of New Orleans, Gaines* v. *Delacroix*, 6 Wallace, 573–723, Parts I, II, III, IV.
7. *Doddridge* v. *Gaines*, 5691 at Law (1868), District of Columbia Court.
8. *Gaines* v. *Tenney*, 5706 at Law (1869), District of Columbia Court.

THE COURT REAFFIRMS

1. Carson, *History of the Supreme Court*, Justice David Davis; also, Johnson and Malone (eds.), *Dictionary of American Biography*.
2. Introduction to volume of reports of 6 Wallace.
3. 6 Wallace report for the Court's decision, in full.

THE FAMOUS LITIGANT

1. Jenkins, "Romance of Mrs. Myra Clark Gaines," *loc. cit.*, 201.
2. Claud G. Bowers, *The Tragic Era* (Cambridge, 1929), 249–260.
3. George R. Brown, *Washington, A Not Too Serious History* (Baltimore, 1930), 443.
4. *Ibid.*, 444; Ellett, *The Court Circles of the Republic*, 575.
5. Mrs. Gaines to Mrs. McNeill Potter, July 14, 1869, *Evans Will Record*, III, 211. (This letter, Mrs. Gaines to Mrs. Potter, referred to in the records of this particular case as "printed record," p. 443.)
6. Lonn, *Reconstruction in Louisiana After 1868, in loc.*; also King, *New Orleans, The Place and the People*, 300.
7. Mrs. Gaines to President Grant, *Evans Will Record*, III, 283. (Referred to as "Exhibit Xc.")
8. *Fuentes* v. *Gaines*, 25 Louisiana Annual, 85.

9. *Barrett* v. *Gaines*, 4711 at Law (1868–1880), District of Columbia Court.
10. Ellett, *The Court Circles of the Republic*, 563.
11. *Fuentes et al.* v. *Gaines*, 25 Louisiana Annual, 85.
12. *New Orleans* v. *Gaines*, 15 Wallace (or 82 U.S.) (1872), 624.
13. Dart, "The History of the Supreme Court of Louisiana," *loc. cit.*, 14; *National Cyclopedia of American Biography*, XIII, 592 (Ludeling).
14. The Rev. N. B. Harmon of Vicksburg, Mississippi, statement to author.
15. *Ibid.*

"IT IS ABOUT TIME"

1. James Grant Wilson and John Fiske (eds.), *Appleton's Cyclopedia of American Biography* (rev. ed.; New York, 1900), article, Myra Clark Gaines; also letter of Mrs. Gaines, January 31, 1882, *Evans Will Record*, III, 298 (marked "exhibit X.9").
2. *Gaines* v. *Fuentes et al.*, 92 U.S. (1875), 10.
3. F. R. Arthur, testimony, *Evans Will Record*, II, 70.
4. Mrs. Gaines to Mrs. Perkins, May 18, 1880, *Evans Will Record*, III, 146. (Referred to as "document A-8.")
5. *Id.* to "My dear Sir," April 6, 1878, *Evans Will Record*, III, 280. (Referred to as "Exhibit T.")
6. *Id.* to John W. Harmon, December 3, 1880, original letter.
7. *The United States* v. *James Y. Christmas*, 13955, District of Columbia Court, June 25, 1881. Case called February 27, 1882.
8. Mrs. Gaines to "My dear Sir," January 2, 1882, *Evans Will Record*, III, 293. (Referred to as "Exhibit X 7.")
9. *Id.* to "My dear Sir," February 28, 1881, *Evans Will Record*, III, 292. (Referred to as "Exhibit A 10.")
10. *Id.* to John W. Harmon, letter in possession of author.
11. Hattie L. Whitney, testimony, *Evans Will Record*, I, 453.
12. Mrs. Gaines to Mrs. Perkins, January 17, 1882, *Evans Will Record*, III, 147. (Referred to as "Document A 9.")
13. *Id.* to Mrs. Emilie F. Mazaret, April 6, 1882, *Evans Will Record*, III, 4. (Referred to as "Serial no 2.—Exhibit A.")
14. Merrick, *Old Times in Dixie Land*, 127.
15. *Davis* v. *Gaines*, 104 U.S. (1881), 386.
16. Mrs. Gaines to Mrs. Perkins, January 17, 1882, *Evans Will Record*, III, 147. (Referred to as "Document A 9.")
17. *Id.* to Colonel R. C. Hutchinson, January 4, 1882, *Evans Will Record*, III, 276. (Referred to as "Serial no. 83.—Exhibit R.C.H. no 12.")
18. *Myra Clark Gaines* v. *City of New Orleans*, 8825, *Circuit Court of the United States for the Eastern District of Louisiana, in equity, May 5, 1883*. Copy in *Evans Will Record*, III, 261.
19. Mrs. Gaines to Hutchinson, December 19, 1882, *Evans Will Record*, III, 273. (Referred to as "Serial no 82.—Exhibit R.C.H. no 11.")
20. *Id.* to Albert Goldthwaite, September 27, 1883, *ibid.*, 311. (Referred to as "Exhibit H.")
21. *Id.* to "My Dear Sir," January 8, 1884, *ibid.*, 329. (Referred to as "Exhibit IV.")
22. *Id.* to William H. Wilder, January 22, 1884, *ibid.*, 231. (Referred to as "Serial no. 45.")

23. *Id.* to *id.*, January 3, 1884, *ibid.*, 230. (Referred to as "Serial no. 44.")
24. *Id.* to Mrs. Marie P. Evans, May 15, 1884, *ibid.*, 125. (Referred to as "Serial no. 24.")
25. *Id.* to William H. Wilder, August 26, 1884, *ibid.*, 243. (Referred to as "Serial no. 57.")
26. Brown, *Washington, A Not Too Serious History*, 444.

As Good as New

1. Kenneth L. Roberts, "The Charm City," *The Saturday Evening Post*, CXCIX (1927), 20–21.
2. W. H. Holcombe, M.D., *Encyclopedia of Louisiana*.
3. William H. Holcombe, testimony, *Evans Will Record*, I, 67.
4. John F. Butts, testimony, *ibid.*, 54.
5. *Ibid.*
6. William H. Holcombe, testimony, *ibid.*, 67, 214; also William H. Wilder, testimony, *ibid.*, 569.
7. Washington *Evening Star*, January 12, 1885.
8. *Evans Will Record*, and New York State Supreme Court Reports, 74 Hun, 95; 83 Hun, 225; 84 Hun, 520.
9. *New Orleans* v. *Gaines Administrator*, 131 U.S. (1888), 191; *New Orleans* v. *Gaines Administrator; Gaines Administrator* v. *New Orleans*, 138 U.S. (1891), 595.
10. J. Carroll Payne, "A Celebrated Case—The Myra Clark Gaines Litigation," Georgia Bar Association, 28th session, Report 135, reprinted as pamphlet in Howard Memorial Library, New Orleans.
11. *Ibid.*; Perry Scott Rader, "The Romance of American Courts. Gaines vs. New Orleans," *Louisiana Historical Quarterly*, XXVII (1944), 314, questions any definite estimates.
12. Nuncupative Will of Myra Clark Gaines, *Evans Will Record*, III, 2.
13. Payne, "A Celebrated Case," *loc. cit.*, for last description of Mrs. Gaines and for final idea.

Bibliography and Critical Notes

This book, written on the basis of what the Supreme Court finally declared to be the facts in the case, takes the records and reports of that Court as its principal source. These reports outline the case as a whole and furnish through their accompanying records and briefs a wealth of information bearing upon all phases of the respective lives of Daniel Clark and Myra Clark Gaines. Scores of letters, to and from the principal characters involved, are preserved among the Court records, as well as sworn testimony from numbers of persons touching upon the public and private lives of the parties involved.

The United States Reports (Supreme Court) consulted and used were: *Ex parte Whitney*, 13 Peters (1839), 404; *Gaines v. Relf*, 15 Peters (1841), 9; *Gaines v. Chew*, 2 Howard (1844), 619; *Patterson v. Gaines*, 6 Howard (1848), 550; *Gaines v. Relf*, 12 Howard (1851), 472; *Gaines v. Hennen*, 24 Howard (1860), 555; *Gaines v. Lizardi et al., Gaines v. City of New Orleans et al., Gaines v. Delacroix et al.*, 6 Wallace (1867), 573–723; *New Orleans v. Gaines*, 15 Wallace or 82 U.S. (1872), 624; *Gaines v. Fuentes*, 92 U.S. (1875), 10; *Smith et al. v. Gaines*, 93 U.S. (1876), 341; *Davis v. Gaines*, 104 U.S. (1881), 386; *New Orleans v. Gaines Administrator*, 131 U.S. (1888), 191; *New Orleans v. Gaines Administrator, Gaines Administrator v. New Orleans*, 138 U.S. (1891), 595.

Of these the 6 Wallace record cited above was found to contain the most convenient and best organized collection of material on the whole case. The volume marked "Part II" of the 6 Wallace record, 573–723, contains in its 2,200 printed pages the great bulk of testimony, letters and averments making up the case. This volume is referred to in the author's reference notes as "6 Wallace." It is to be regretted that the indexing of this volume is often ambiguous and misleading.

The Louisiana State Supreme Court records are valuable as covering other appearances of the Gaines case. These furnish a supplementary mass of testimony and findings. These records are: *Barnes* v. *Gaines,* 5 Robinson (1843), 314; *Succession of Clark,* 11 Louisiana Annual (1856), 124; *Heirs of Mary Clark* v. *Gaines,* 13 Louisiana Annual (1858), 138; *Delacroix* v. *Gaines, ibid.,* 177; *Van Wych* v. *Gaines, ibid.,* 235; *Fuentes et al.* v. *Gaines,* 25 Louisiana Annual (1873), 85; *Foulhouze* v. *Gaines,* 26 Louisiana Annual (1874), 84; *White* v. *Gaines,* 29 Louisiana Annual (1877), 769; and to these should be added an appearance of the case in the United States Circuit Court in New Orleans, *Fuentes* v. *Gaines,* 1 Wood (1871), 112.

In addition to these official reports, a volume published under the title Alexander Walker, *The Great Gaines Case,* was drawn upon for certain material. Its full title is, *The Great Gaines Case. United States Circuit Court, a Full report of the great Gaines case in the suit of Myra Gaines, vs. Chew, Relf and others . . . reported by Alexander Walker* (New Orleans, 1850).

For biographical material further covering the life of Daniel Clark, recourse was had to Daniel Clark, *Proofs of the Corruption of Gen. James Wilkinson, and of his connexion with Aaron Burr, with a full refutation of his slanderous accusations in relation to the character of the principal witness against him . . .* (Philadelphia, 1809). This contains numerous autobiographical references and is of primary value.

Clark's diplomatic dispatches when he was consul at New Orleans prior to the cession of Louisiana are preserved in the Archives of the State Department at Washington under the classification, Foreign Relations, 1798–1803. The more significant of these dispatches were published as "Documents: Despatches from the United States Consulate in New Orleans, 1801–1803," *The American Historical Review*, XXXII (1927).

Works which outline Clark's part in the Louisiana events of his day are: François-Xavier Martin, *The History of Louisiana from the Earliest Period* (New Orleans, 1882); Charles Étienne Arthur Gayarré, *History of Louisiana*, 4 vols. (New Orleans, 1903). The author found Gayarré most readable and apt as a reference work. For Clark's place in the national scene and for Louisiana's prime position in international affairs, recourse was had to: Edward Channing, *A History of the United States*, 6 vols. (New York, 1905–1925); Henry Adams, *History of the United States* (during the administration of Jefferson and Madison), 9 vols. (New York, 1889–1891). For Clark's part in the Wilkinson-Burr imbroglio the author consulted: Thomas Marshall Green, *The Spanish Conspiracy* (Cincinnati, 1891); Royal O. Shreve, *The Finished Scoundrel; General James Wilkinson, sometime Commander-in-Chief of the Army of the United States who made intrigue a trade and Treason a Profession* (Indianapolis, 1933); General James Wilkinson, *Memoirs of My Own Times*, 3 vols. (Philadelphia, 1816); Sam Henry Wandell and Meade Minnigerode, *Aaron Burr*, 2 vols. (New York, 1927); I. J. Cox, "General Wilkinson and his later intrigues with the Spaniards," *The American Historical Review*, XIX (1913–1914).

Of great help to understanding this whole era in Louisiana is Dunbar Rowland (ed.), *The Official Letter Books of W. C. C. Claiborne, 1801–1816*, 6 vols. (Jackson, Miss., 1917). Gales and Seaton, *Annals of the Congress of the United States* (Washington, 10th Congress), has been consulted for Clark's speeches and position in Congress. The article on Daniel Clark by I. J. Cox in the Allen Johnson and Dumas Malone (eds.), *Dictionary of American Biography*, 20 vols. and index (New York, 1928–1937), is terse, clear, and authoritative.

For the life of Myra Clark Gaines, the Federal and Louisiana State records previously cited provide the bulk of biographic material. Mrs. Gaines' own letters, some seventy-five or more, were

published after her death in the records of the Evans' will litiga-
tion: *Supreme Court, King's County.—General Term. Second
Judicial Department. In the matter of the Probate of the last
Will and Testament of Myra Clark Gaines, Deceased. Julietta
Perkins and Marie P. Evans, Appellants. Record of Appeal,*
4 vols. (Washington, D.C., 1896). The reports of this litigation
—in contradistinction to the record of appeal just cited—are 74
Hun, 95; 83 Hun, 225; and 84 Hun, 520, New York State
Supreme Court Reports. The volumes containing the record of
appeal also carry much testimony from various persons concerning Mrs. Gaines' activities and habits in her later years. All the
letters reproduced were written after 1870. There are few, if any,
letters of Mrs. Gaines bearing an earlier date except the two or
three published as part of the Gaines case itself.

The author found a book of important resource in Mrs. Elisabeth F. Ellett, *The Court Circles of the Republic, or the Beauties
and Celebrities of the Nation* (Hartford, 1869). This volume,
besides its many laudatory references and interesting anecdotes
concerning Mrs. Gaines, carried a steel engraving depicting her
appearance in middle life.

A special source referred to by the author in certain instances
is Mrs. Ann S. Stephens, *Myra: The Child of Adoption, a
Romance of Real Life. Beadle's Dime Novels, No 3.* . . .
Printed by Irwin P. Beadle & Company (New York, 1860).
This book is of course historically suspect from its name and
nature, but supporting its account are these facts: The author is
said to have been a friend of Mrs. Gaines and the book declares
itself to be a "romance of real life"—which it is. The correct
names of the principal characters are used throughout, except that
Relf is "Ross." ("Mr. Clark," "De Grainges," "Zulima," "Mr.
D" for Davis, and "Myra.") It was published when Myra was
at the zenith of her fame and an author would scarcely have taken
liberties with her life's intimate records in so public a way had
the allegations and incidents not been true. Furthermore, all the
information given in *Myra: The Child of Adoption* which can
be checked by unimpeachable sources is found to be correct.

The author, therefore, after putting in this caveat, has drawn upon Mrs. Stephens' account for the following: The details of Zulime's visit to Baltimore, the account of Myra's meeting with William Whitney and her flight from Delamore Place, Clark's last meeting with Zulime, Relf's suppression of the Clark-Zulime correspondence, William Whitney's illness and death. Other sources hint at or outline these situations, but in order to give content to the record at the above-mentioned points, Mrs. Stephens' account has been called upon.

Certain magazine articles which featured Mrs. Gaines' story have been of considerable value. These are: Benjamin C. Howard, "The Gaines Case. Reports of Cases argued and adjudged by the Supreme Court of the United States at the December term, 1851," *The Southern Quarterly Review,* XXV (1854); H. M. Jenkins, "The Romance of Mrs. Myra Clark Gaines," *Putnam's Monthly Magazine,* XII (1868); John S. Kendall, "The Strange Case of Myra Clark Gaines," *Louisiana Historical Quarterly,* XX (1937). Setting forth the case from a lawyer's point of view, have appeared: J. Carroll Payne, "A Celebrated Case—The Myra Clark Gaines Litigation," *28th Session of the Georgia Bar Association, Report no. 135;* A. D. Young, "A Romance of the Courts," *The Green Bag,* XVIII (1904); Perry Scott Rader, LL.D., "The Romance of American Courts. Gaines vs. New Orleans . . . ," *Louisiana Historical Quarterly,* XXVII (1944). This last reviews the case in its entirety in an able, analytical way, and as a trained jurist, Mr. Rader, who was the reporter of the Supreme Court of Missouri from 1897 to 1933, points out the niceties and refinements of the various arguments and decisions at each move in the case. He makes a curious mistake historically in asserting that General Gaines mysteriously disappeared in 1849 when on a steamboat excursion on Lake Ponchartrain and that his body was never found.

For data covering the lives of the various secondary characters who play subsidiary or minor roles in the record the author has resorted to all available biographical material. The military record of Colonel Samuel B. Davis is outlined in Francis B. Heitman, *Historical Register and Dictionary of the United States Army* . . . , 2 vols. (Washington, 1903), while Delaware newspapers and encyclopedias cited in the reference notes carry much information. General Gaines' life is covered in Heitman's register just cited, while War Department files give much information concerning his military career. Recourse was had also to: James W. Silver, *Edmund Pendleton Gaines and Frontier Problems, 1801–1849* (Nashville, 1935); John S. Jenkins, *The Generals of the Last War With Great Britain* (Buffalo, 1849); Barritt & Lossing, *Pictorial Fieldbook of the War of 1812* (New York, 1868). The enormous records of the Gaines case contain many references to, and actions of, "The General."

For the appearance and characteristics of the various justices of the Supreme Court who acted on the case, the author has used especially Hampton Lawrence Carson, *The History of the Supreme Court of the United States; with biographies of all the chief and associate justices* . . . *with portraits of the 58 judges* . . . , 2 vols. (Philadelphia, 1902); and Charles Warren, *The Supreme Court in United States History* (Boston, 1922). Each justice of course is adequately described and evaluated in the *Dictionary of American Biography* hitherto cited, and there is considerable other biographic material available upon each one.

For the development of New Orleans and the social customs and habits of life in that city during the time of this history, the following have been consulted: John S. Kendall, *History of New Orleans*, 3 vols. (Chicago, 1922); George W. Cable, *The Creoles of Louisiana* (New York, 1910); Grace King, *New Orleans, The Place and the People* (New York, 1904); Eliza Ripley, *Social Life in Old New Orleans* (New York, 1912); A. Oakey Hall, *The Manhattaner in New Orleans, or Phases of "Crescent City" Life* (New Orleans, 1851); Edwin L. Jewell, *Jewell's Crescent City Illustrated* . . . *with a map and general strangers' guide* (New Orleans, 1873); and Henry C. Castellanos, *New Orleans As It Was* (New Orleans, 1895).

Besides the *Dictionary of American Biography*, two comprehensive "cyclopedias" were referred to for biographic information concerning the prominent characters of this book These were James Grant Wilson and John Fiske (eds.), *Appleton's Cyclopedia of American Biography,* 12 vols. (rev. ed.; New York, 1900); and James T. White & Company (publishers), *National Cyclopedia of American Biography,* 30 vols. and index (New York, 1893). The article on Myra Clark Gaines in this last is very inaccurate and misleading.

In addition to written sources as outlined previously and as referred to in a more minute way in the reference notes, the author has used certain items of information furnished him personally by his father, the Reverend Nolan B. Harmon, of Vicksburg, Mississippi, and by his aunt, the late Clara Harmon Cope of Oxford, Georgia. Mrs. Gaines lived in their home for a time during her later years. The author's father remembers with great vividness many incidents connected with Mrs. Gaines and has often recounted details of her story as he was given these by her.

Index